Palgrave Hate Studies

Series Editors
Neil Chakraborti
School of Criminology
University of Leicester
Leicester, UK

Barbara Perry
Faculty of Social Science and Humanities
University of Ontario
Oshawa, ON, Canada

This series builds on recent developments in the broad and interdisciplinary field of hate studies. Palgrave Hate Studies aims to bring together in one series the very best scholars who are conducting hate studies research around the world. Reflecting the range and depth of research and scholarship in this burgeoning area, the series welcomes contributions from established hate studies researchers who have helped to shape the field, as well as new scholars who are building on this tradition and breaking new ground within and outside the existing canon of hate studies research.

Lucille Micheletto

Assessing Hate Crime Laws

A Multidisciplinary Perspective

palgrave
macmillan

Lucille Micheletto
Ghent University
Ghent, Belgium

ISSN 2947-6364 ISSN 2947-6372 (electronic)
Palgrave Hate Studies
ISBN 978-3-031-19019-3 ISBN 978-3-031-19020-9 (eBook)
https://doi.org/10.1007/978-3-031-19020-9

This Palgrave Macmillan imprint is published by the registered company Springer Nature Switzerland AG.
The registered company address is: Gewerbestrasse 11, 6330 Cham, Switzerland

To my families, babies, and friends

Acknowledgments

Conducting a PhD project, and then transforming it into a monograph has been a long journey, challenging and enriching at the same time. Of course, like all big projects it would have not been possible without the support of a great number of persons.

I wish to express my gratitude to my promoter, Gert Vermeulen, and to the members of the Guidance Committee, Nina Peršak and Michele Papa, for having supported me throughout the research process and encouraged me to publish my study as a book. Moreover, I would like to thank the members of the Defence Exam Committee, Petra Bárd, Tom Vander Beken, Sofie Depauw and Stéphanie De Coensel, for having examined my work in detail and provided me with precious insights. I also want to thank the reviewers who have assessed the book proposal as well as the first version of the manuscript. I have truly appreciated your comments and suggestions and I have taken most of them on board.

A special thanks goes to my spouse Irene, to my family, and to all the friends that have supported and accompanied me all these years, despite the geographical distance that separate us.

Praise for *Assessing Hate Crime Laws*

"This important and timely book—particularly in view of the noted rise of hate crime in societies of the Global North, further spurred by the COVID-19 pandemic and the societal reactions thereto—is an essential reading for anyone interested in the regulation of prejudice-based crime. Providing an excellent assessment and analysis of hate crime law in Italy as well as internationally, it presents an original and invaluable contribution to the existing legal scholarship in the highly topical field of hate crime."

—Nina Peršak, Scientific Director, *Institute for Criminal-Law Ethics and Criminology, Ljubljana, Slovenia*

"Lucille Micheletto's contribution to the legitimacy debate on hate crime laws is impressive: theoretically novel and empirically underpinned. Both the four-tier framework to analyse hate crime laws and the integrated legitimacy test, bridging Anglo-American and continental European criminalisation approaches, are doctrinally sound and appealing. Her choice to also draw on empirical data to conduct an applied legitimacy assessment is convincing and refreshing."

—Gert Vermeulen, Senior Full Professor of Criminal Law, *Ghent University, Ghent, Belgium*

Contents

Abbreviations

CJEU	Court of Justice of the European Union
CRPD	Convention of the Rights of Persons with Disabilities
ECHR	European Convention on Human Rights
ECtHR	European Court of Human Rights
EU	European Union
FRA	European Union Agency for Fundamental Rights
ICERD	International Convention on the Elimination of all forms of Racial Discrimination
ILT	Integrated Legitimacy Test
ISTAT	Italian National Institute of Statistics (*Istituto Nazionale di Statistica*)
LGBTI	Lesbian, gay, bisexual, transgender, intersex. In this research it is used as an umbrella term that encompasses all those persons that do not recognise themselves, or are not perceived, as cisgender or heterosexual. Thus, it also includes those persons that identify themselves non-binary, gender-fluid or queer
ODHIR	Office for Democratic Institutions and Human Rights
OSCAD	Observatory for Security against Discriminatory Acts (*Osservatorio per la sicurezza contro gli atti discriminatori*)
OSCE	Organization for Security and Co-operation in Europe
TFEU	Treaty on the Functioning of the European Union
UN	United Nations

List of Tables

1

Introduction

1 Aims and Scope of the Book

This book provides an innovative approach to analyse hate crime law from a multidisciplinary and holistic viewpoint. Building on existing literature on hate studies and criminalisation theory, it takes it forward by developing a multi-level framework which helps to understand the different dimensions of criminal laws addressing hate crime.[1]

Chapter 2 (*A Framework to Analyse Hate Crime Law*) summarises the most important aspects of hate crimes, and distinguishes them from other similar phenomena such as hate speech, discrimination and terrorism. Drawing on hate crime studies, four main components of hate crimes are then identified and linked to four salient elements of hate crime law. Concrete examples of hate crime provisions are also provided.

[1] This monograph is based upon a PhD project that was conducted at the University of Ghent (Belgium) and defended in January 2021. The original PhD thesis has been adapted and updated for the purposes of the present book. In December 2021 a chapter of the thesis was published as an article in the European Journal of Crime, Criminal Law and Criminal Justice (Brill), with the title "Towards an Integrated (and Possibly Pan-European?) *Prima Facie* Legitimacy Test: Merging the *Rechtsgut* Theory, the *Offensività* Principle, and the Harm Principle" (Micheletto, 2021). In consideration of the narrow focus of the present monograph, and to avoid duplication, the cited article will be only briefly summarised at the beginning of Chap. 3.

L. Micheletto, *Assessing Hate Crime Laws*, Palgrave Hate Studies,
https://doi.org/10.1007/978-3-031-19020-9_1

This exercise aims to achieve two complementary outcomes: first, it develops a tool to descriptively analyse and classify different hate crime provisions that at the same time can normatively guide legislators in drafting hate crime law; and second, the hate crime law models so identified will constitute, along with Italian hate crime law, the object of a further analysis in Chaps. 3 and 4.

Chapter 3 (*Analysis of Abstract Models of Hate Crime Law*) examines the legitimacy of abstract models of hate crime legislation. It begins by illustrating the philosophical premises of the concept of legitimacy that this study has decided to adopt. Then, it provides an overview of the origins and features of the Integrated Legitimacy Test (ILT). The ILT is then applied to the hate crime law framework developed in Chap. 2 in two stages. The first stage analyses hate crimes (and hate crime law) overall considered. The second stage assesses the legitimacy of their more specific features. The chapter's aim is to show that hate crimes hurt more and are more wrongful than parallel offences committed *without bias*; it also analyses how this extra harm and wrongfulness can be reflected in hate crime law, and examines whether different drafting approaches do, or do not, legitimately criminalise the bias component of hate crimes.

Chapter 4 (*Analysis of Italian Hate Crime Law*) provides an exemplar of the practical application of the ILT to a specific legislation. Here, Italian hate crime legislation is examined under both the four-tier framework and the ILT. This combined analysis allows us to better understand the rationale and (potential) scope of Italian hate crime provisions as well as to assess their legitimacy from an evidence-based viewpoint. Italian hate crime law constitutes an interesting case study for the application of the ILT to a concrete legislation. So far, all the legislative proposals to extend hate crime law to sex, gender, sexual orientation, gender identity and disability have been dismissed by Parliament. The discussions on the legislative reform mostly overlooked empirical data and analytical argumentation, and focused instead on populist and sometimes blatantly homo-transphobic, misogynist and ableist arguments. However, the arguments raised against hate crime law (especially with regard to certain "unpopular" grounds such as sexual orientation, sex/gender and gender identity/expression) are similar across many OSCE states and also at the European Union level. Thus, this book proposes an articulated and evidence-based approach to analyse hate crime law that can feed the current debate with substantive arguments, both in Italy and in those jurisdictions based on liberal-democratic premises.

2 The Concept(s) of Hate Crime and Hate Crime Law

Across the Organization for Security and Co-operation in Europe (OSCE) region's jurisdictions and in different fields of study, explanations as to what counts, or should count, for a crime to be considered as a hate crime vary notably. The *traditional* understanding of these types of offences frame them as violent crimes committed by hate-fuelled individuals, which often belong to a right-wing extremist group, against a member of an ethnic, religious or racial minority. Moreover, sometimes it is not clear whether a hate incident can be framed as a bias crime, hate speech, a discriminatory conduct or an act of terrorism. The widespread allusion to the emotion *hate* to refer to bias offences also complicates things. These crimes are not always about hate, and not all offences where offenders feel and express hate towards their victims can be properly labelled as hate crimes. Hate crime researchers have tried to elaborate a proper taxonomy and have come up with a number of definitions of bias offence. In particular, authors agree that the word *hate* is a misnomer (Brudholm, 2015, p. 85; Wickes et al., 2016, p. 239), or more precisely, an umbrella term that includes a wide range of emotions linked to *prejudice* more in general (Hall, 2013; Wickes et al., 2016).[2]

One of the key elements of the definition legislators and researchers do not seem to agree upon is which kind of victims groups should be included in the concept of bias crimes—and thus, in the corresponding law addressing the phenomenon. Many legislations cover only a small number of grounds—usually race, ethnic origins and religion; others also include sexual orientation, disability, and sometimes gender, gender

[2] Despite the limits and ambiguities of the expression *hate crimes*, this expression is widely used by civil society organisations, human rights bodies, authorities and scholars. Therefore, this study will use it along with similar expressions such as bias offences, bias-motivated crimes, and so on.

identity and/or expression, and other personal characteristics. What do these group memberships or personal features have, or should have in common to be included in the concept of hate crime? More in general, is it possible to formulate some kind of criteria to determine what the concept of hate crime should, or should not include?

Concerns surrounding the different ways the concept of hate crime can be framed are not merely theoretical; the way these types of offences are understood by research, the general public and politicians has a huge impact on the proper legal response this phenomenon receives. Hate crimes are first and foremost criminal conducts (e.g. arson, assaults, murder, threats, and so on) characterised by a further element, offenders' specific choice of their targets based on the latter's group membership (e.g. being Jewish) or personal features (e.g. a disability). Legal systems' common response to this phenomenon is thus the enactment of criminal law measures. These can, in turn, concern rules of criminal procedure—e.g. specific rules on evidence or foreseeing a special protection for victims of hate crimes—and/or *substantive* criminal law. Across the OSCE region, the typical legal response to hate crimes is the provision of a penalty enhancement when a conduct that already constitutes a criminal offence is committed in connection with a biased mental attitude of the offenders towards their victims. The rationale behind these measures is that, in application of the principle of proportionality, bias crime offenders should be punished *more* because hate crimes are somehow *worse* than parallel crimes.

The very first step of this study is to identify and define the object that it intends to examine. What do the expressions *hate crimes* and *hate crime law* mean in the context of the present work? Hate crime researchers have advanced different definitions of offences committed out of bias. The OSCE's Office for Democratic Institutions and Human Rights (ODHIR), for example, has proposed a working definition of hate crimes. It suggests that hate crimes have two elements: they must already constitute a criminal offence, and they must involve the deliberate targeting of someone because of their membership to a certain group against which the perpetrator feels some form of bias (ODHIR, 2009, p. 13). Albeit "general, minimal and inclusive" (Brax & Munthe, 2013, p. 18), this definition has some limitations. As it has been observed, it does not identify which base offences can be committed out of bias, nor does it explain how bias is linked to their commission or what kind of mental attitude can count as bias (Brax & Munthe, 2013, p. 18). On their part, Brax and Munthe suggest a more elaborate definition of bias offence. In their view, a hate crime consists of

> an (1) independently criminal act (such as assault, theft, murder, rape, harassment, and so on) where (2) some sort of negatively biased, disparaging and/or discriminatory attitude on part of the offender towards a social group to which the offender links the victim, is (3) in some qualified way connected to, plays a role in or explains the occurrence of the crime. (Brax & Munthe, 2013, p. 5)

Generally speaking, hate crime policies can be implemented in different fields of law and can also include preventive measures—such as educational policies—as well as restorative justice measures. Following Brax and Munthe's definition of hate crimes, this study will examine a specific kind of hate crime policy: those criminal law provisions that (1) foresee a penalty enhancement for those conducts which (2) already constitute an offence and (3) are somehow linked to the offenders' prejudice towards their victims (4) because of the latter's belonging to a certain social group. Therefore, with the expression hate (or bias) crime law, the present works will refer only to these types of legal provisions.

3 The International Standards on Hate Crime Law

From a human rights perspective, hate crimes are usually framed as a form of discrimination perpetrated through the commission of a criminal act (ODHIR, 2009, p. 19). Under International Human Rights Law, the principles of equality and non-discrimination mainstream the whole human rights structure. Moreover, in the wake of the adoption of the

Universal Declaration of Human Rights,[3] which places a particular emphasis on equality in dignity and rights, a number of treaties have been adopted to put these principles into practice, at least with regard to certain discrimination grounds. The International Covenant on Civil and Political Rights (ICCPR) imposes an obligation upon contracting states to ensure the rights thereby guaranteed, including the right to life (art. 6) and security of the person (art. 9), "without distinction of any kind, such as race, color, sex, language, religion, political or other opinion, national or social origin, property, birth or other status."[4] The International Convention on the Elimination of All Forms of Racial Discrimination (ICERD) expressly requires to criminalise "all acts of violence or incitement to such acts against any race or group of persons of another colour or ethnic origin".[5] Moreover, the prohibition of systematic racial discrimination is now understood as a norm of customary international law, thus being binding on all states at the international level (Hathaway, 2005, p. 36). More recently, art. 16 of the Convention on the Rights of Persons with Disabilities (CRPD), to which also the European Union (EU) is a party, has placed strong obligations on States Parties to adopt legislative and policy measures aimed at ensuring "that instances of exploitation, violence and abuse against persons with disabilities are identified, investigated and, where appropriate, prosecuted."[6] As to religion, the United Nations Declaration on the Elimination of All Forms of Intolerance and of Discrimination Based on Religion or Belief requires states to "prevent and eliminate discrimination on the grounds of religion" and to "take all appropriate measures to combat intolerance on the grounds of religion…"[7]

The ODIHR has taken a number of initiatives to counter hate crimes in OSCE participating states in cooperation with government

[3] Universal Declaration of Human Rights, adopted by the United Nations (UN) General Assembly on 10 December 1948.

[4] Art. 2 of the International Covenant on Civil and Political Rights (ICCPR), adopted by the UN General Assembly on 16 December 1966.

[5] Art. 4 of the International Convention on the Elimination of All Forms of Racial Discrimination (ICERD), adopted by the UN General Assembly on 21 December 1965.

[6] Art.16(5) of the Convention on the Rights of Persons with Disabilities (CRPD), adopted by the UN General Assembly on 13 December 2006.

[7] Art. 4 of the UN Declaration on the Elimination of All Forms of Intolerance and of Discrimination Based on Religion or Belief, proclaimed by the UN General Assembly on 25 November 1981.

institutions, criminal justice systems, civil society actors and other international organisations. They include monitoring mechanisms, data collection and assistance in drafting legislation, as well as specific training programs for law enforcement authorities, prosecutors, civil society organisations and educators.[8] Furthermore, in 2004 OSCE participating States committed themselves to "consider enacting or strengthening, where appropriate, legislation that prohibits discrimination based on, or incitement to hate crimes."[9] The ODHIR's 2009 practical guide on hate crime laws was drafted to guide States in fulfilling that commitment (ODHIR, 2009, p. 7).

The Council of Europe (CoE) has also been working extensively on hate crimes. In several soft-law documents, member States have been called to foresee an increased sentence when base offences are committed out of bias.[10] Moreover, the Council is currently working on a recommendation specifically addressing hate crimes. The preparatory works are still at an early stage, but a preliminary working document published by the CoE indicates that the Council intends to address hate crimes from a holistic viewpoint. For example, this document recognises "the need to develop a robust but flexible framework for protected characteristics which reflects the multiplicity and intersectionality of hate crime and the harm it causes, aware of the need to take the local context and relevant socio-political factors into account." The Recommendation will include "[w]orking definitions (including the concept of hate crime, bias motives, and relevant thresholds for criminality) and key terms (including hate, motive, bias, comprehensive, victims, special characteristics)" as well as different penalty enhancement models.[11] However, the preliminary draft

[8] See a summary of the ODIHR's activities at https://hatecrime.osce.org/odihr-tools, accessed 25 July 2022.

[9] OSCE, Permanent Council Decision No. 621, *Tolerance and the Fight Against Racism, Xenophobia and Discrimination*, 29 July 2004.

[10] For example, ECRI, *General Policy Recommendation N°7 (revised) on national legislation to combat racism and racial discrimination*, adopted on 13 December 2002 and revised on 7 December 2017; Parliamentary Assembly of the Council of Europe, *Resolution no. 2417, Combating rising hate against LGBTI people in Europe*, adopted on 25 January 2022.

[11] CoE's Committee of Experts on Hate Crime, *Preliminary outline of the draft Recommendation on combating Hate Crime*, 21 February 2022, https://rm.coe.int/item-06-pc-adi-ch-2022-3rev-preliminary-outline-of-the-draft-recommend/1680a686bb, accessed 25 July 2022.

does not mention which groups are intended to be covered. The Background document prepared by the CoE's Committee of Experts on Hate Crime refers to race, language, religion, ethnicity, nationality, sexual orientation, gender, gender identity, gender expression and disability, but it does not exclude other grounds that may be relevant in specific jurisdictions.[12]

On its part, the European Court of Human Rights (ECtHR) has adjudicated a wide number of cases concerning hate crimes. The Strasbourg Court has developed a jurisprudence based on the non-discrimination provision (art. 14) of the European Convention on Human Rights (ECHR) read in conjunction with other substantive articles of the Convention (see Mačkić, 2018; Harris et al., 2018).[13] So far, the ECtHR has examined hate crime complaints based on the victim's race or ethnic origins, religious affiliation, political opinion, gender, sexual orientation and disability. The ECtHR has taken a consolidated, but somehow cautious approach to hate crimes. Since the 2005 *Nachova and Others*, and 2007 *Angelova and Iliev* judgments against Bulgaria, the Court has ruled that States must ensure that bias motivation behind the crime is identified, recognised and investigated as such.[14] According to the Strasbourg Court, States are obliged to render visible—or, in the Court's terms, to "unmask"—bias motives leading to criminal offences "and to establish whether or not … hatred or prejudice may have played a role in the events."[15] A failure to do so would result in a violation of art. 14 in combination with other substantive provisions of the Convention, such as art. 2 (right to life), art. 3 (prohibition of torture and inhuman or degrading treatment), art. 6 (right to a fair trial), art. 8 (respect for private and family life and home), and art. 9 (freedom of religion). Thus, what stems from the consolidated case-law of the ECtHR is the obligation, on the

[12] CoE's Committee of Experts on Hate Crime, *Background document*, 27 January 2022, https://rm.coe.int/pc-adi-ch-2022-4-en-background-document/1680a67ed3 (accessed 25 July 2022).

[13] For a complete and up-to date reference of all the ECtHR's judgments on discriminatory violence, see the case-law Guide on Article 14 and Article 1 of Protocol No. 12 prepared by the Court Registry, at https://echr.coe.int/Documents/Guide_Art_14_Art_1_Protocol_12_ENG.pdf (accessed 25 July 2022).

[14] ECtHR, *Nachova and Others v. Bulgaria* [GC], nos. 43577/98 and 43579/98, 6 July 2005; *Angelova and Iliev v. Bulgaria*, no. 55523/00, 26 July 2007.

[15] See ECtHR, *Nachova and Others v. Bulgaria, cit.*, § 160.

part of the Member States, to investigate the bias component of crimes and establish whether it has been an important element of the offence. However, the Court has never explicitly ruled that States have a positive obligation to consider bias or hate as an aggravating factor in sentencing.

In a very recent case concerning the homophobic murder of a young man in Bulgaria, the Court has taken for the first time a clearer position in this regard. In this case, Bulgarian courts had established that the motive behind the attack had been the offenders' hostility towards homosexual persons. However, since Bulgarian law does not foresee any penalty enhancement for homophobic-aggravated crimes, the sentences imposed to the perpetrators were eventually very lenient. The ECtHR has considered that the lack of proportion between the sentences imposed and the seriousness of the offence "was chiefly due to the fact that Bulgarian criminal law had not properly equipped those courts to [consider homophobic motivation as an aggravating factor] rather than to the manner in which they dealt with the case."[16] The Court has therefore concluded that Bulgaria had violated art. 14 read in conjunction with art. 2, since "the State's response to the attack against the applicant's son did not in sufficient measure discharge its duty to ensure that deadly attacks motivated by hostility towards victims' actual or presumed sexual orientation do not remain without an appropriate response."[17]

Although this judgment is not final and might be overturned by the Grand Chamber or contradicted by a future judgment, it is relevant for three main reasons. First, it has been adopted unanimously by the Court, and has been accompanied by a concurring opinion of judges Eicke (UK) and Vehabović (Bosnia and Herzegovina). Second, the Court has decided to apply art. 46 of the Convention on the binding force and execution of judgments. It has considered that the human rights violations found in that case were "of a systemic character, in the sense that it resulted from the content of the relevant Bulgarian criminal law, as interpreted and applied by the Bulgarian courts" (§ 78). Therefore, it has required Bulgaria to "ensure that violent attacks (in particular, those resulting in the victim's death) motivated by hostility towards the victim's actual or presumed

[16] ECtHR, *Stoyanova v. Bulgaria*, no. 56070/18, 14 June 2022, § 73.

[17] ECtHR, *Stoyanova v. Bulgaria, cit.*, § 74.

sexual orientation are in some way treated as aggravated in criminal-law terms" (§ 79). Third, the Court's stance aligns with the position taken by the CoE Parliamentary Assembly as regards hate crimes against LGBTI people. In a recent resolution, the Assembly has called on member States to "amend criminal legislation as necessary to ensure that its provisions with respect to hate crimes clearly cover all offences committed against a person or group of persons based on their sex, sexual orientation, gender identity, gender expression and sex characteristics, include proportionate and dissuasive sanctions, protect victims' rights and make provision for them to receive compensation" and "make motivations based on sex, sexual orientation, gender identity, gender expression and sex characteristics an aggravating circumstance for all ordinary offences."[18]

Since the Council Joint Action of 15 July 1996 concerning racism and xenophobia,[19] the European Union has undertaken a number of legal and policy initiatives to combat hate crimes in the region. The most relevant so far is the 2008 Framework Decision.[20] Its art. 4 requires Member States to consider racist or xenophobic motivations as aggravating circumstances or, alternatively, to empower courts to take such motivations into consideration when determining the penalties to be applied. The Framework Decision covers a very limited number of personal characteristics (race, colour, descent, national and ethnic origins, and religion). It excludes from its scope other features that are nonetheless covered by the EU equality and non-discrimination law (i.e. sexual orientation, gender identity, disability, gender and age). However, these and other grounds are taken into consideration by the 2012 Victims' Rights Directive, which request Member States to offer specific protection to "victims who have suffered a crime committed with a bias or discriminatory motive which could, in particular, be related to their personal characteristics" (art. 22§3) such as "race, colour, ethnic or social origin, genetic features,

[18] Parliamentary Assembly of the Council of Europe, *Resolution no. 2417, Combating rising hate against LGBTI people in Europe*, adopted on 25 January 2022, Points 14.1 and 14.2.

[19] Joint action of 15 July 1996 adopted by the Council on the basis of Article K.3 of the Treaty on European Union, concerning action to combat racism and xenophobia (96/443/JHA), O.J. L 185, 24 July 1996, 5–7.

[20] Council Framework Decision 2008/913/JHA of 28 November 2008 on combating certain forms and expressions of racism and xenophobia by means of criminal law, O.J. L 328 of 6 December 2008.

language, religion or belief, political or any other opinion, membership of a national minority, property, birth, disability, age, gender, gender expression, gender identity, sexual orientation, residence status or health" (whereas no. 9).[21] Nonetheless, even when properly and fully implemented by States, these rules are of a procedural nature and do not imply any change of substantive criminal law in terms of penalty enhancement.

The EU's stagnant position on these issues seems, however, to be changing. In December 2021, the European Commission presented an ambitious initiative that aims to modify the Treaty on the Functioning of the European Union (TFEU) to extend the list of "EU crimes" to hate speech and hate crime.[22] The Council of the European Union backed the Commission's initiative in March 2022.[23] If approved, this amendment will constitute the legal basis for the enactment of EU criminal legislation in the field of hate crimes and hate speech. According to art. 83(2) TFEU, "the approximation of criminal laws and regulations of the Member States" in this area can be pursued through the enactment of directives. These establish minimum standards "with regard to the definition of criminal offences and sanctions" and need to be implemented by Member States. The Commission's Communication to the European Parliament and the Council does not specify which strands will be covered. However, this document refers to a wide range of documents produced over the years by the EU, the CoE, and the UN addressing race, ethnic origins, religion, language, sexual orientation, gender identity and expression, sex and gender, disability, and age.[24] The inclusion of (at least) these grounds is thus to be expected. From a legal and systematic point of view, it would be logical and "legally sound" to actually include all the strands already

[21] Directive 2012/29/EU of the European Parliament and of the Council of 25 October 2012 establishing minimum standards on the rights, support and protection of victims of crime, and replacing Council Framework Decision 2001/220/JHA, O.J. L 315, 14 November 2012.

[22] See the Commission's press release at https://ec.europa.eu/commission/presscorner/detail/en/ip_21_6561 (accessed 25 July 2022).

[23] See the press release of the Justice and Home Affairs Council, 3-4 March 2022, at https://www.consilium.europa.eu/en/meetings/jha/2022/03/03-04/ (accessed 25 July 2022).

[24] European Commission, *Communication from the Commission to the European Parliament and the Council. A more inclusive and protective Europe: extending the list of EU crimes to hate speech and hate crime*, 9 December 2021, https://ec.europa.eu/info/sites/default/files/1_1_178542_comm_eu_crimes_en.pdf (accessed 25 July 2022).

enclosed in art. 21 of the EU Charter of Fundamental Rights (Peršak, 2022, pp. 97–98).[25]

4 Hate Crime and Hate Crime Law in Italy

In Italy, data collection of hate crimes is still underdeveloped in comparison with other countries such as the United States, the United Kingdom, Canada or Sweden. However, the data provided so far to the ODIHR by Italian authorities[26] and civil society organisations[27] is useful to have a first idea of the phenomenon.

According to the official information provided to the ODHIR, the number of hate crimes reported either to the police or to civil society organisations has been quite stable between 2017 and 2020 (around 1100 per year), whilst it had been significantly lower in the previous years (736 in 2016, 555 in 2015, 596 in 2014, 413 in 2013, and 71 in 2012).[28] The reported incidents involved a wide range of targeted groups (ethnic groups, such as migrants and people of Roma origins, religious groups such as Muslims, Jews and Christians, and other social groups such as LGBTI people, women and persons with disability). Most hate incidents involved a racist bias (around 77%), while anti-LGBTI and disability hate incidents constitute 6% and 17%, respectively. These numbers, however, only partially reflect the extent of the phenomenon. One of the main problems is that most victims are reluctant to report hate crimes to

[25] Art. 21 covers sex, race, colour, ethnic or social origin, genetic features, language, religion or belief, political or any other opinion, membership of a national minority, property, birth, disability, age or sexual orientation, as well as nationality.

[26] For more information about how data on hate crimes is officially collected in Italy, see the OSCE's website: https://hatecrime.osce.org/italy (accessed 25 July 2022) and Perry (2019).

[27] Along with the official data collection, a number of Italian NGOs gather data on hate crimes and incidents committed against specific social groups. As to LGBTI people, see for example the report prepared by Centro Risorse LGBTI (2020); other NGOs monitor instead racist and religious motivated crimes, such as Lunaria (https://www.lunaria.org/il-razzismo-nel-2018-on-line-il-nostro-nuovo-focus/), Associazione 21 luglio (https://www.21luglio.org/), Osservatorio anti-semitismo (https://www.osservatorioantisemitismo.it/); see also the webpage of Vox-Osservatorio Italiano sui Diritti, available at http://www.voxdiritti.it/ (all accessed 25 July 2022).

[28] These data are made public on ODHIR's webpage https://hatecrime.osce.org/italy (accessed 25 July 2022).

the police. The wide dark figure of hate crimes underreporting, in fact, is a well-known problem (Pezzella et al., 2019), especially with regard to those personal characteristics that are not covered by hate crime law (Godzisz & Viggiani, 2018, pp. 182–183). For example, a study carried out on the perceived victimisation of LGBTI people in Italy shows that only 6.7% of the respondents that have been victims of a hate incident have reported it to the police (Centro Risorse LGBTI, 2020). On the other hand, unless the elements of the offence—including the bias motive—are properly assessed and proved in a fair trial, the reported data merely refers to the victims' *perception* that a given crime has been committed on the basis of a biased motive. Moreover, an increase in hate crime reporting can be related to an improvement in the data collection system, or can reflect more trust in police on the part of victims. Nonetheless, these figures taken together with the numerous hate crime incidents reported by the press suggest that the phenomenon of hate crimes in Italy is an issue that should be taken seriously by authorities and lawmakers.

Italy's colonial and fascist past, as well as its long-term misogynist and patriarchal culture, can partially explain how racism, sexism, homophobia, transphobia and ableism still play a role in societal and political dynamics. These discriminatory attitudes have actually forged the legal approach towards certain criminal phenomena. In the past, some of the behaviours that are nowadays framed as bias-motivated offences were actually socially accepted and law enforcement authorities tended to ignore or dismiss victims' complaints. For example, certain violent behaviours carried out against women, children, the elderly or persons with disabilities were understood as normal means of correction on the part of husbands, parents or carers. However, things have changed notably in the past decades. Not without difficulty, a number of legal reforms have been put in place to implement equality and non-discrimination in different areas of law, including in the area of bias-motivated offences.

The legal response to hate crimes has mostly—if not exclusively—focussed on the enactment of criminal law provisions that can be in part properly framed as hate crime law, and in part more correctly understood as covering hate speech, discrimination or hate incidents more in general.[29] As to hate crime law proper, it consists of a number of measures that either increase the base sentence of an already existing offence when this is committed with a "discriminatory or hate purpose," or create a new offence when the conducts of violence or incitement to violence are committed with a bias motive.[30] The constitutional legal basis of this type of provision is the principle of "equal dignity", which has been elaborated by combining the principle of equality (art. 3 of the Italian Constitution[31]) with the concept of dignity (implicitly embodied in art. 2 of the Constitution[32]).

As it stands, Italian hate crime legislation covers a small number of grounds, namely race, religion, ethnic origins, nationality and belonging to a national linguistic minority. This approach diverges notably from the legal developments that have taken place in other European and non-European countries. Just to name a few examples, Croatian law now includes disability, gender, sexual orientation and gender identity along with the more traditional grounds.[33] Spanish legislation also covers motives related to the victim's ideology, social exclusion or illness, or due to the offender's aporophobia.[34] The Parliament of South Africa is currently discussing a bill to introduce hate crime legislation that, if approved, will include age, albinism, birth, colour, culture, disability, ethnic or social origin, gender or gender identity, HIV status, language, nationality, migrant or refugee status, occupation or trade, political affiliation or conviction, race, religion, sex (including intersex) and sexual orientation.[35]

---

[29] See, in particular, arts. 604-bis and 604-ter of the Penal Code as well as the so-called Reale–Mancino Law, which will be discussed in Chap. 4.

[30] Arts. 604-ter and 604-bis of the Penal Code, respectively.

[31] Art. 3 reads: "All citizens have equal social dignity and are equal before the law, without distinction of sex, race, language, religion, political opinion, personal and social conditions."

[32] Art. 2 reads: "The Republic recognises and guarantees the inviolable rights of the person, both as an individual and in the social groups where human personality is expressed."

[33] Penal Code of Croatia, art. 87 (21).

[34] Penal Code of Spain, art. 22(4).

[35] Parliament of the Republic of South Africa, *Prevention and Combating of Hate Crimes and Hate Speech Bill* (B9-2018), Definitions 3(1), available at https://pmg.org.za/bill/779/ (accessed 25 July 2022).

In the past twenty years, Italian Parliament has discussed a huge number of bills proposing the inclusion of sexual orientation and gender identity in hate crime law (as well as, in some cases and somehow "incidentally", also sex, gender, disability and age), with no success. More in general, the implementation of equality and legal protection measures for LGBTI people has been very difficult, and it is still incomplete in several fields of Italian law. Thus, it comes as no surprise that the proposal to include sexual orientation and gender identity in existing hate crime legislation has been rejected so many times. If one takes into account the more general social and cultural context in Italy, as well as the current situation of LGBTI rights in other countries with a similar profile (e.g. Spain), it may be even argued that the arguments used to reject these bills—which have been *normalised* by certain parts of Italian politics—would be elsewhere probably discharged as homo-transphobic.

Gender-motivated violence, and violence against women in general, is also a difficult topic in the Italian context. Nowadays, social sciences research explains this phenomenon in connection with a more general sexist and patriarchal social context. Moreover, some specific forms of gender-based offences can be theoretically framed as hate crimes as they present certain features and patterns similar to racist or religious-motivated violence. However, the debate is often reduced to terms of private, interpersonal or stranger violence. The misogynist roots of the offender's motivation and the more general social context are usually overlooked. Gender-based violence against men, on the other hand, is not even taken seriously in most cases.

The discussion with regard to other grounds—disability and age, for example—is timidly surfacing. Criminal law mainly conceives these characteristics in terms of *objective vulnerability*, in the sense that a person with a disability, or very old, is considered vulnerable regardless of other personal circumstances. This approach towards these personal characteristics leads, in turn, to a more general perception of their holders as purely *passive* subjects.[36] Moreover, the specific issues raised from the intersection

[36] In other areas of Italian law, and in social sciences more in general, the understanding of *disability* is however slowly changing according to a vision that puts the person in question at the centre of the debate as an *active* subject and does not reduce them to their disability (see Marra, 2013; Paolini & Paolini, 2022).

of two or more grounds (for example, when someone is targeted because she is a woman belonging to an ethnic minority, or for being a trans man with a disability) are also disregarded in the current debate on hate crimes.

5 Hate Crime Law and the Limits of Criminal Law

The law, including criminal law, cannot remain neutral before hate crimes, as neutrality in the context of discrimination produces itself more inequality. With regard to criminal law, however, another important issue has to be considered: the moral boundaries of the State to exercise its powers to limit and punish its citizens' conducts. Hate crime law often consists of only criminal law measures that enhance a base sentence when a given offence is committed out of hate. In other words, what these provisions do is to *criminalise* the bias element of the base crime. In principle, the use of criminal law in this context is not necessarily incorrect or wrong. After all, bias crimes are crimes. However, criminal law is too often employed as an easy token to provide a quick and strong state response to certain criminal phenomena that are profoundly embedded in more transversal social issues that would probably be better tackled by implementing a more holistic approach.

The human and social costs of overcriminalisation are well known, albeit they are often ignored at the legislative level (see, e.g., Moccia, 1997; Husak, 2007; Corral Maraver, 2016; Ouwerkerk, 2017). To start criminal proceedings against someone—even if they are ultimately found to be innocent, or even though their involvement in a crime has merely been investigated—means that that person's life will be inextricably changed. Proceedings are long, costly and consume phenomenal energy, both physically and psychologically. Even though the sentence is ultimately in favour of the accused, the media and the public will have already labelled them as guilty, particularly when they belong to an ethnic or other disadvantaged minority.

Hate crimes lie thus at the centre of a delicate balance. States must provide legal protection to victims of hideous offences enrooted in a more widespread context of inequality and discrimination and strive to limit the use of criminal law only when it is really necessary and properly justified.

In common law and civil law contexts, a number of different legal theories have been developed to decide when criminalisation can be considered legitimate. The concept of *legitimacy* itself has been elaborated in different ways according to the frame of reference adopted. One may look at the legitimacy of a given piece of legislation with regard to a certain country's constitution, or other kind of supranational binding legal documents such as international treaties or conventions (although the language used to describe the provision's accordance with a superior norm would differ). Or, one may look for a philosophical concept or set of principles that understands legitimacy as a benchmark external to the positive-law of a given jurisdiction.[37]

One of the possible approaches to examine the legitimacy of criminalisation, and the one this work has decided to adopt, focuses on the moral limits of the State to criminalise expressed in terms of *normative and external principles of criminalisation*. This expression was first used with regard to Anglo-American principles, such as the harm principle, the offence principle, legal moralism and legal paternalism. According to Feinberg's version of the harm principle, the criminalisation of a given conduct can be *prima facie* warranted only if it causes some sort of serious harm to other persons than the offender (Feinberg, 1984). In Europe, the counterpart of the harm principle has been identified in the German *Rechtsgut* ("legal good") theory (Peršak, 2007), which has been compounded by the *offensività* ("injuriousness" or "harmfulness") principle in Italy (Donini, 2013) and in other jurisdictions following the Italian approach, such as Spain and Portugal (see Micheletto, 2021). Under this paradigm, criminalisation is legitimate only when the conduct at hand seriously affects ("*offende*") a legal good, i.e. an interest that the State considers important enough to be warranted criminal law protection.

Both the Anglo-American and the German-Italian approaches have been heavily criticised as being ultimately unable to limit

[37] For an overview of the different concepts of criminal law legitimacy, see De Coensel (2020, pp. 57–68).

overcriminalisation. These two sets of principles were initially welcome as useful theoretical and normative tools to secularise criminal law by binding it to some kind of *empirical*, and not merely *moral*, rationales. However, in both contexts the interpretation of some of these paradigms' components (e.g. the scope of the terms *harm* and *others*, or the definition of *legal good*) has been too often overstretched in order to criminalise certain conducts that either cause harm only very remotely (e.g. drug abuse), or affect an *immaterial* interest that pertains to a very generic collectivity (e.g. religious feelings).

These criticisms are certainly grounded and must be taken in due consideration. However, both the harm principle and the legal good/*offensività* paradigm still have something to offer to the criminalisation debate—including as regards the legitimacy of hate crime law. This book adopts and applies a novel approach that merges the key features of both theories—the so-called *Integrated Legitimacy Test* (ILT) (Micheletto, 2021). The ILT analyses the *prima facie* legitimacy of criminal law by gauging the degree of intrusion of the conduct at issue into a standard victim's quality-of-life interests—and thus, by determining whether it is sufficiently harmful—and by examining whether the behaviour at stake can be considered wrongful. In practice, the ILT examines the added harmfulness and wrongfulness of hate crimes *vis-à-vis* their parallel counterparts—the base offences committed *without* a bias motive. The ILT uses an approach that is explicitly *dialectic*, as it requires the balance and analysis of different interests and arguments. This aspect allows it to address, and get rid of as inappropriate or purely morally-based, many of the arguments that are often put forward in the hate crime debate (e.g. as regards the extension of hate crime law to LGBTI people), in order to focus only on arguments based on social-democratic and liberal premises that are supported by evidence. To obtain meaningful results, this work applies the legitimacy test by chiefly anchoring it to data obtained through empirical research on the impact of hate crimes on direct victims and their communities.

References

Brax, D., & Munthe, C. (2013). *Introduction to the Philosophy of Hate Crime. When Law and Hate Collide*. University of Gothenburg. Retrieved July 25, 2022, from https://www.uclan.ac.uk/research/activity/perspectives-on-hate-crime

Brudholm, T. (2015). Hate Crimes and Human Rights Violations. *Journal of Applied Philosophy, 32*(1), 82–97. https://doi.org/10.1111/japp.12079

Centro Risorse LGBTI. (2020). *Hate Crimes No More Italia*. Retrieved July 25, 2022, from http://risorselgbti.eu/progetto-hate-crimes-no-more-italia/

Corral Maraver, N. (2016). La irracionalidad de la política criminal de la Unión Europea. *Indret: Revista para el Análisis del Derecho, 4*. Retrieved July 25, 2022, from https://indret.com/la-irracionalidad-de-la-politica-criminal-de-la-union-europea/?edicion=4.16

De Coensel, S. (2020). *Counter-Terrorism & Criminal Law: A Normative Legitimacy Test of Terrorism-Related Offences on Expression, Information and Movement*. Maklu.

Donini, M. (2013). Il Principio di Offensività. Dalla Penalistica Italiana ai Programmi Europei. *Diritto Penale Contemporaneo, 4*, 4–43.

Feinberg, J. (1984). *Harm to Others. The Moral Limits of the Criminal Law 1*. Oxford University Press.

Godzisz, P., & Viggiani, G. (Eds.). (2018). *Running Through Hurdles: Obstacles in the Access to Justice for Victims of Anti-LGBTI Hate Crimes in Europe*. Lambda Warsaw.

Hall, N. (2013). *Hate Crime*. Routledge, Taylor & Francis Group.

Harris, D., O'Boyle, M., Bates, E., & Buckley, C. (2018). *Law of the European Convention on Human Rights*. Oxford University Press.

Hathaway, J. C. (2005). *The Rights of Refugees under International Law*. Cambridge University Press.

Husak, D. (2007). *Overcriminalization: The Limits of the Criminal Law*. Oxford University Press.

Mačkić, J. (2018). *Proving Discriminatory Violence at the European Court of Human Rights*. Brill Nijhoff.

Marra, A. D. (2013). Le Persone con Disabilità. In P. Cendon & S. Rossi (Eds.), *I Nuovi Danni alla Persona: I Soggetti Deboli, Volume II* (pp. 467–518). Aracne.

Micheletto, L. (2021). Towards an Integrated (and Possibly Pan-European?) Prima Facie Legitimacy Test: Merging the *Rechtsgut* Theory, the *Offensività* Principle, and the Harm Principle. *European Journal of Crime, Criminal Law and Criminal Justice, 29*(3–4), 241–263. https://doi.org/10.1163/15718174-bja10025

Moccia, S. (1997). *La Perenne Emergenza: Tendenze Autoritarie nel Sistema Penale*. Edizioni Scientifiche Italiane.

ODHIR (Office for Democratic Institutions and Human Rights). (2009). *Hate Crime Laws—A Practical Guide*. Organization for Security and Co-operation in Europe.

Ouwerkerk, J. W. (2017). Criminalization Powers of the European Union and the Risks of Cherry-Picking between Various Legal Bases: The Case for a Single Legal Framework for EU-Level Criminalization. *Columbia Journal of European Law, 23*(3), 503–550.

Paolini, E., & Paolini, M. C. (2022). *Mezze Persone. Riconoscere e Comprendere l'Abilismo*. Aut Aut Edizioni.

Perry, J. (2019). *Facing All the Facts. Connecting on Hate Crime Data in Italy*. Facing all the Facts Project. Retrieved July 25, 2022, from https://www.facingfacts.eu/final-italy-country-report/

Peršak, N. (2007). *Criminalising Harmful Conduct: The Harm Principle, Its Limits and Continental Counterparts*. Springer.

Peršak, N. (2022). Criminalising Hate Crime and Hate Speech at EU Level: Extending the List of Eurocrimes Under Article 83(1) TFEU. *Criminal Law Forum, 33*, 85–119. https://doi.org/10.1007/s10609-022-09440-w

Pezzella, F. S., Fetzer, M. D., & Keller, T. (2019). The Dark Figure of Hate Crime Underreporting. *American Behavioral Scientist*, January. https://doi.org/10.1177/0002764218823844

Wickes, R. L., Pickering, S., Mason, G., Maher, J. M., & McCulloch, J. (2016). From Hate to Prejudice: Does the New Terminology of Prejudice Motivated Crime Change Perceptions and Reporting Actions? *British Journal of Criminology, 56*(2), 239–255. https://doi.org/10.1093/bjc/azv041

2

A Framework to Analyse Hate Crime Law

1 Introduction

This chapter identifies and elaborates normative criteria to classify hate crime law according to the main characteristics of hate crimes. The purpose of this exercise is five-fold. First, it allows for a better understanding of the structure of bias crime provisions, their explicit or implicit aims, and their potential effectiveness and impact. Second, it can be used to compare different legislations. Third, the combination of legal analysis with relevant sociological and criminological research provides a thorough knowledge of the most important criminological characteristics of these types of crimes. This is in turn necessary to understand the possible impact that hate crime law may have on the investigation and prosecution of bias offenders. Fourth, albeit this research predominantly refers to Anglo-Saxon literature on hate crimes (mainly due to the limited research carried out so far on other legislations), the criteria are shaped in an abstract way not linked to any specific legislation. Fifth, these criteria will allow us to identify and classify different hate crime law models that will constitute the object of a further legitimacy analysis in Chap. 3. In fact,

L. Micheletto, *Assessing Hate Crime Laws*, Palgrave Hate Studies,
https://doi.org/10.1007/978-3-031-19020-9_2

by referring to the framework developed in the present chapter we will be able to apply the Integrated Legitimacy Test (ILT) to abstract paradigms of hate crime law.

The chapter consists of two sections.

By drawing on interdisciplinary research, the first part explores the sociological and criminological roots of bias crimes and distinguishes them from other similar but distinct concepts. In particular, it identifies and describes the specific features that characterise this phenomenon and that have been observed in criminological and victimological studies. The main aim of this section is to provide a first overview of hate crimes in terms of causes, impacts, and connections with other similar phenomena.

By building on these premises as well as on a more elaborate philosophical conceptualisation of bias crimes, the chapter's second section elaborates a framework to analyse hate crimes and hate crime law. The framework consists of four variables that represent the constituent parts of bias offences, and links them to four parts of hate crime provisions that reflect these components. Each variable, in turn, can be implemented in a number of ways, each one having a particular impact on the investigation and prosecution of hate crimes. The claim—which reflects Brudholm's (2015, p. 84)—is that any hate crime law can be analysed as a combination of different interpretations of these four variables. These four parts are analysed in depth by identifying and examining the different ways each tier can be developed to reflect a wide, intermediate or narrow concept of bias offence. Concrete examples of how these different drafting methods are employed by different legislations are also included.

2 Hate Crimes: Context and Features

Hate crime is a recent field of research, particularly in Europe. Nonetheless, interdisciplinary studies have been able to agree on a number of criminological characteristics of hate crimes that allow us to consider them as a specific type of offence. This section first provides a contextualisation of hate crimes in the realm of other bias-motivated acts. Then, it examines "contingent" features of hate crimes—i.e. characteristics that are often observed in the occurrence of hate crimes, but are neither necessary nor sufficient to frame a crime as a bias offence (Brudholm, 2015, p. 88). This preliminary analysis provides a better overview of this phenomenon, with a view to singling out the features of hate crimes that will constitute the pillars of the hate crime law framework in the second part of the chapter.

2.1 Contextualisation of Hate Crimes

2.1.1 Hate, Bias and Prejudice

Hate crimes differ from *parallel* offences because of the *hate* or *bias* component that accompanies the perpetrator's choice of the victim. Along with other authors (e.g. Lawrence, 1999; Perry, 2001; Wickes et al., 2016), Brudholm addresses the issue of whether the expression *hate crime* is a misnomer. He observes that while the concept of bias offence embeds by its very nature "a concern with the state of mind of the offender … conceptions differ in their more detailed definition of the required mental state" (Brudholm, 2015, p. 85), and so does hate crime law. As a matter of fact, many hate crime provisions do not even mention the term *hate*. The mere existence of hateful thoughts and emotions on the offenders' part towards their victims, even when hatred is the only motive of the crime, does not suffice to qualify the offence as a hate crime. What is needed, instead, is a connection between the offence and the offender's hostility towards a certain social group or towards an individual for its membership in that group (Lawrence, 1999, p. 9).

Moreover, not all hate crimes are motivated (only or mainly) by the emotion of hate in the stricter sense. Quite the opposite; the mental attitudes that trigger the criminal act can be more nuanced (prejudice, hostility, loath…), although they all underline a negative perception of the victim by the perpetrator. Perry highlights another problem related to the use of *hate* in hate crime literature:

> a great deal of crime probably is motivated by some emotion akin to 'hate'. However, such reductionist accounts, I would argue, miss the point. They are consciously used to minimize the import and impact of violent and discursive forms of bigotry. They occlude the distinction between the pop-

> ular 'dictionary' meaning of hate, and the sociological meaning that underlay the adoption of the term in the first place. In such cases, 'hate' is divorced from its cultural and political context. (Perry, 2005, p. 123)

In other terms, according to Perry the word *hate* seems to focus on an inner state of mind, or impulse of the perpetrators, that leads them to act in a way disconnected to the external environment. This "reductionist understanding" of the term *hate*, in Perry's opinion, allows critics to depoliticise the phenomenon.

> While hate is a strong sentiment, it is a relatively *safe* one that does not imply rigidly structured patterns of oppression. It does not require us to admit that bias-motivated violence is constituted of and by difference; that it is about race and racism; sex and sexism and heterosexism, for example. Rather, this interpretation of hate crime removes it from the realm of 'cultures of violence', placing it instead in the realm of the psychology of violence. (Perry, 2005, p. 124)

Therefore, it is important to bear in mind that when we speak about the *hate* component of hate crimes, we are actually referring to a number of negative and hostile emotions, which may perhaps be better described by the term *prejudice* in a wider sense.[1]

Hate crimes constitute one of the most serious aspects of "a more general problem of social prejudice" (ODHIR, 2009, p. 24). As shown in Allport's Scale of Prejudice (Allport, 1958),[2] as well as by the US Anti-Defamation League (ADL)'s Pyramid of hate (2021),[3] prejudice and hate

[1] See also Laurenzo Copello's similar remarks as regards how Spanish authorities have 'manipulated' the term hate to apply hate crime law to certain controversial cases (Laurenzo Copello, 2019). For an overview of the evolution of the terms *hate* and *prejudice* from their generic meanings to more restricted and specific ones in the context of hate crimes studies, see Levin and Rabrenovic (2009, pp. 41–42).

[2] According to Allport, we can classify expressions of prejudice in a 5-stages scale, ranked according to the increasing harm they produce: Antilocution (hate and derogatory speech); Avoidance (isolation and exclusion); Discrimination (denial of equal opportunities); Physical attack (violent attacks to property or person); Extermination (physical elimination of the group) (Allport, 1958).

[3] The ADL classifies expressions of prejudice in a 5-level pyramid, and, as with Allport, ranks them according to the degree of harm they produce. Thus, from the bottom to the top of the pyramid we will find: biased attitudes, acts of bias, discrimination, bias-motivated violence and genocide.

manifest themselves in society across a spectrum, from the least serious but most frequent expressions of hate/prejudice (anti-locution/biased attitudes), to the most serious but less frequent phenomena (extermination/genocide).

As the ADL explains, the five levels of the pyramid/scale are closely interrelated. At each level, the behaviours described therein negatively affect the individuals concerned, and their harmfulness grows as one moves up to the top of the pyramid. Moreover, the behaviours described in the upper levels of the pyramid are supported by the conducts included in the lower levels. Social and institutional acceptance of the lower level behaviours as *normal* results, in turn, in a growing *normalisation* of the behaviours described in the upper levels (Anti-Defamation League, 2021). Under both Allport and the ADL's classifications, hate crimes are considered among the most serious expressions of prejudice, coming right before the top of the scale/pyramid occupied by extermination/genocide acts. As Perry observes,

> [h]ate crime … is much more than the act of mean-spirited bigots. It is embedded in the structural and cultural context within which groups interact … It does not occur in a social or cultural vacuum; rather, it is a socially situated, dynamic process, involving context and actors, structure, and agency. (Perry, 2001, p. 1)

2.1.2 Distinguishing Hate Crimes from Related Concepts

Albeit very useful to provide a first contextualisation of the issue under examination, Allport and the ADL's progressive scales are of course mere theorisations of more complex and interrelated societal issues. In particular, hate crime studies have pointed out a number of phenomena that present strong similitudes with bias offences and that need to be conceptually distinguished from them. This, in turn, allows us to distinguish legislation specifically tackling hate crimes, which will constitute the object of the present study, from the law addressing these related, but conceptually distinct, expressions of hate and prejudice. The boundaries between hate crimes and other related notions are not always straightforward and clear. They sometimes depend of the very definitions of the concepts under comparison that we decide to adopt. However, hate crimes, and hate crime law, present a distinct characteristic that will constitute our main tool to distinguish them from other, related, acts motivated by prejudice: hate crimes are "always and necessarily a crime" (Brudholm, 2015, p. 84). This means that "the same conduct, without a bias motivation, could still be prosecuted as a crime" (ODHIR, 2009, p. 24).

Bearing this in mind, the following sections will examine the relationship between hate crimes and hate incidents, discrimination, hate speech, terrorism and genocide, as well as hate crime law from the provisions tackling these phenomena.

Hate Crimes and Hate Incidents

The expression *hate incident* is not a legal one. It is mainly used in anti-hate policy measures to describe "an incident or act committed with a bias motive that does not reach the threshold of a hate crime, either because a criminal offence was not proven or because the act may not have been a criminal offence under a particular state's legislation" (ODHIR, 2013, p. 15). These incidents can consist of name-calling, bullying, harassment or similar negative attitudes that are perpetrated in connection to one of the victim's characteristics. Therefore, only those hate incidents which involve an act already criminalised under the legislation at issue can be considered as hate crimes, but all hate crimes are, ultimately, hate incidents. Moreover, hate incidents "may precede, accompany or provide the context for hate crimes (ODHIR, 2013, p. 15). Hate incidents, in their non-criminal form, correspond to the *acts of bias* of the ADL's pyramid of hate.

Hate Crimes and Discrimination

Hate crimes and discriminatory acts are closely linked. As noted by Levin and Rabrenovic (2009, p. 42), "[n]ot all instances of discrimination are hate crimes, but all cases of hate crimes are discriminatory." Indeed, human rights doctrine (e.g. Swiebel & Van der Veur, 2009; ODHIR,

2009) and bodies (e.g. the European Court of Human Rights[4]) frame hate crimes as a form of discrimination rendered more serious by offenders' use of violence against persons or property.

In some jurisdictions discriminatory acts are punished not only through private law measures, but also by way of criminal sanctions.[5] However, the two phenomena are conceptually and legally separated. In the case of hate crimes, the same conduct committed without a bias motive already constitutes a punishable criminal offence, while in the case of discriminatory acts, it is the discrimination itself that renders the conduct unlawful (see ODHIR, 2009, p. 25; Brudholm, 2015, p. 85).

Hate Crimes and Hate Speech

The distinction between hate speech and hate crime is crucial to define the scope of the present study. In many legislations the two phenomena are neither defined nor well distinguished, and it is not always easy to draw a precise line between the legal provisions addressing them.

So far, there is still disagreement among scholars about how to define hate speech (Pejchal, 2020). For the limited purposes of the present study, we can refer to the United Nations' definition of hate speech that describes it as

> any kind of communication in speech, writing or behaviour, that attacks or uses pejorative or discriminatory language with reference to a person or a group on the basis of who they are, in other words, based on their religion, ethnicity, nationality, race, colour, descent, gender or other identity factor. (United Nations, 2019, p. 2)

This wide definition includes, for example, intimidation of or incitement to hatred against particular social groups, genocide denial or the dissemination of ideas based on the alleged superiority of a social group over others.

---

[4] See, for instance, the case law of the ECtHR cited in Chap. 1, and Mačkić (2018).

[5] This is the case of Italy, for example, where art. 604-bis of the Penal Code punishes those who commit "discriminatory acts based on racial, ethnic, national, or religious motives" with a sentence of either maximum one year and six months' imprisonment or a fine up to € 6000.

Hate speech law, on the other hand, consists of the criminalisation of certain speech acts. Such limitations to free speech can be either grounded solely on the content of the speech at stake, or depend on how these ideas are conveyed and the intention of the speaker (Brax & Munthe, 2013, p. 34). Moreover, the wording and scope of hate speech laws vary widely across states.

As with discriminatory acts, what really distinguishes hate crimes from hate speech is the respective *non-bias element* of the two phenomena. While the non-bias element of hate crimes is an action that has already been criminalised in a given jurisdiction, hate speech's parallel conduct is the expression of thoughts, an activity that—in democratic societies—can be criminalised only under very strict conditions. Thus, if a given kind of speech (e.g. insult or defamation) constitutes a crime according to a given State's law, it will be considered as a hate crime if it has been uttered with a bias motivation (see Lawrence, 1993, p. 679). Otherwise, if a certain form of discriminatory or hateful speech does not constitute an offence, it will at most be framed as hate speech if the legislation at issue has decided to criminalise this particular form of speech when expressed with a bias motivation or intent. Lawrence's distinction has been backed in literature (e.g. Brax & Munthe, 2013, pp. 34–37) as well as by international organisations working on hate crimes, such as the ODHIR (2009, pp. 25–26).

It is important to note, however, that although hate speech may not be criminalised *per se* in a given legislation, it can nevertheless constitute evidence of the offender's motive in the context of the criminal investigation surrounding the commission of a hate crime (ODHIR, 2009, pp. 25–26).

Hate Crimes and Terrorism

Hate crimes and acts of terrorism are "legally distinct but conceptually overlapping crimes" (Deloughery et al., 2012, p. 664). Some scholars have pointed out a number of similarities between the two phenomena that led some authors to define hate crimes as "close cousins" to terrorism (Krueger & Maleckova, 2003, p. 28). For example, it has been highlighted that in both cases "the target of an offense is selected because of his or her group identity, not because of his or her individual behavior" (Krueger & Maleckova, 2003, p. 28); that both phenomena constitute criminal activities that aim to terrorise not only the particular victim but also the whole victim's group (Krueger & Maleckova, 2003, p. 28; Deloughery et al., 2012, p. 664; Brax, 2015; King et al., 2016); that both crimes reflect "certain attitudes and/or political ideals" (Brax, 2015); and that "both are expression of intergroup conflict" (King et al., 2016). Some authors even suggest to frame hate crimes as a form of terrorism (Rosga, 1999) or "domestic terrorism" (Hamm, 1994; see also Perry, 2005, p. 133).

However, studies have pointed to a number of differences between hate crimes and terrorism that make them look more as "distant relatives" than analogous phenomena (see, for example, Deloughery et al., 2012; King et al., 2016). For example, Brax (2015) highlights three main conceptual and practical discrepancies between the two issues. First, while bias crimes differ from parallel crimes for their bias motive element, and do not need to express or be based on a clear political purpose, what distinguishes terror attacks from other crimes is precisely perpetrators' intentions to "spread fear in a society in order to instigate political change." Second, while terrorism is usually understood as a planned and organised phenomenon, bias crimes are often impromptu acts. Third, while the "ideology expressed in an act of terrorism is typically considered to be alien to the system that is being attacked … hate crimes are seen as expressions of the same sort of attitudes that led to institutionalized violence and discrimination against minority groups." Furthermore, beside these conceptual differences, the two phenomena are usually addressed by distinct legal provisions, having different aims and scopes.

Hate Crimes and Genocide

Genocide constitutes the most serious expression of hate and prejudice and it is often preceded and accompanied by hate crimes and hate speech. Conceptually speaking, genocide can be understood as the most extreme form of hate crime. In literature, it has also been suggested that hate crimes be reconfigured as crimes against humanity. As noted by Perry (2005, p. 134), Goldberg calls for the explicit recognition that the perpetrators, along with the specific victim of the hate crime and society in abstract, have also "harmed the entire group—the body of particular people with whom the object of the injustice identifies. In this sense, racist wrongs are wrongs ... against an entire class of people (Goldberg, 1995, p. 273)."

However, acts of genocide present specific characteristics that distinguish them from hate crimes. In particular, the recognition of the crime of genocide requires proof of specific intent to destroy, in whole or in part, a national, ethnic, racial or religious group, which goes "beyond the proof of bias required for hate crimes" (ODHIR, 2012, p. 10). As pointed out by the ODHIR, genocide "is qualitatively and quantitatively different from hate crimes, as are all crimes under international law that require widespread, systematic acts of violence (ODHIR, 2009, pp. 24–25). Since genocide constitutes a crime under international law, "[t]he legislative, investigative and prosecutorial issues arising from such [crime] are very different from those which arise in hate crimes" (ODHIR, 2009, pp. 24–25), which, in turn, are addressed only by way of national criminal law.

2.2 "Contingent" Characteristics of Hate Crimes

2.2.1 Hate Crime Offenders' Motivation(s)

In bias offences, hate and prejudice influence the commission of a crime in a number of ways. Although bigotry usually is the main motive behind the offence, Levin, McDevitt and Bennet have identified four main kinds of offender motivations beyond, and related to, bigotry, which in turn correspond to four categories in which hate crimes can be classified (Levin & McDevitt, 1993; McDevitt et al., 2002). These categories consist of the so-called *thrill*, *defensive*, *retaliatory* and *mission* hate crimes, respectively. The difference between these groups is both quantitative and qualitative, and refers to both psychological and environmental conditions "that ultimately lead to a violent attack" (McDevitt et al., 2002, p. 306). According to their study,

> in thrill crimes … the offender is set off by a desire for excitement and power; defensive hate crime offenders are provoked by feeling a need to protect their resources under conditions they consider to be threatening; retaliatory offenders are inspired by a desire to avenge a perceived degradation or assault on their group; and mission offenders perceive themselves as crusaders who hope to cleanse the earth of evil. (McDevitt et al., 2002, p. 306)

They also observe that, despite the similarities between the categories *defensive* and *retaliatory*, what distinguish them are "the different precipitants that spark violence in each" (McDevitt et al., 2002, p. 306).

Their study also shows that thrill hate crimes are by far the most frequent type of hate crime, as they constitute 66% of the offences they have examined (McDevitt et al., 2002, p. 307). Albeit these crimes are mostly committed by young males out of boredom, or out of "an immature desire to display power and to experience a rush at the expense of someone else" (McDevitt et al., 2002, p. 308), these authors stress that these offenders' target "was not selected randomly but was chosen because the offender perceived that the victim was somehow different" (McDevitt et al., 2002, p. 307). Defensive hate crimes are the second most frequent kind of hate crimes (25%). They are usually "committed, from the offender's prejudiced point of view, in order to protect his neighborhood from those he considered to be outsiders or intruders" (McDevitt et al., 2002, p. 308). The other two motivations appear to be much rarer. Retaliatory hate crimes, which the authors define specifically as "incidents in which offenders act in response to a hate crime, whether real or perceived" constitute only 8% of all case-files analysed. Mission hate crimes, in which the "perpetrator seeks to rid the world of evil rather than to respond to any specific event that threatens him," also creating or joining hate groups for that purpose, constitute in turn less than 1% of all crimes.[6]

[6] By contrast, a recent study conducted in Poland has shown that almost 70% of the hate crimes analysed had been perpetrated by members of extremist groups. However, these results can be possibly explained by the large definition of hate group that research has adopted (Stefaniak & Winiewski, 2022, p. 98).

These results are also reflected in Iganski's, 2008 study. By focussing his research on hate crime victims' personal experience of the offences they have suffered, Iganski concludes, on the one hand, that most bias crime are *low-level* offences, and that, on the other hand, they're predominantly committed by common, ordinary individuals, and not by extremists as one may initially presume. This, in turn, helps to explain hate crimes as the consequence of society's deeply enrooted prejudices. In his words,

> many offenders are not out-and-out bigots, hate-fuelled individuals who target their victims in premeditated violent attacks. Instead, many perpetrators of 'hate crime' are people like 'us', our friends, relatives, neighbours and work colleagues. Not only that, but many incidents are committed by such 'ordinary' people in the context of their ordinary 'everyday' lives. The prevalence of incidents of 'hate crime', combined with the ordinariness of offenders and offending, indicates that the sentiments that inform offending are intricately woven into the structural fabric of society and constitute a key component of 'common sense', which for many individuals lies below the surface of coherent cognition, but given the right circumstances, bursts to the surface. (Iganski, 2008, p. 42)

2.2.2 Victim's Interchangeability and Previous Knowledge Between Victim and Offender

It has been widely observed that one of the salient features of hate crimes is that perpetrators do not target the victims for *who* they are, but for *what* they are. Since what motivates hate crime offenders is the hate/prejudice towards the groups to which the victim belongs, or is perceived to belong, in their minds the victim is usually "interchangeable with any other member of the same group" (Al-Hakim, 2015, p. 1759). However, this is not always the case. Under certain circumstances, the choice of the victim might not be random. Taking Al-Hakim's example, a racist hate crime offender who decides to target Martin Luther King Jr., and only him, because he considers King an important representative of the black community in the US, is making an explicit choice as to which black person to attack. The offender might not want to target any other black person, but this does not mean that the crime they commit is not a hate crime indeed (Al-Hakim, 2015, p. 1779, footnote n. 3).

Another frequently stressed characteristic of hate crimes, linked to the previous one, is that victims and perpetrators are often strangers to each other. Albeit this is certainly the case in many instances of bias crimes, this is not always true. For example, hate crimes against trans persons are often committed by acquaintances of the victims, and sometimes even by members of their family (Turner et al., 2009; Jamel, 2018, pp. 60–61).

Some authors have considered the interchangeability of victims and lack of previous knowledge between victims and perpetrators as foundational features of the phenomenon. This has led some to exclude from the hate crime model those crimes committed by an acquaintance of the victim, as it often happens in gender-, disability- or age-related crimes. However, researchers investigating the possible conceptualisation of offences motivated by one of these latter personal characteristics as hate crimes have pointed to the fact that, while interchangeability and lack of previous knowledge are indeed common in hate crimes, they are by no means *necessary features* of the phenomenon (Weisburd & Levin, 1994; Mason-Bish, 2014).

2.2.3 Hate Crimes Hurt More Than Parallel Crimes

It is commonly argued that hate crimes are somehow worse than their parallel crimes in that they cause greater harm to their victims. Moreover, not only do these crimes appear to more negatively affect their victims, they also seem to have greater impact on the community the victim belongs to and the society at large.

As to direct victims, "there is some evidence that the psychological and physical harms of hate crimes are likely to be more serious or more widespread than those of parallel crimes" (Kauppinen, 2015, p. 1725). As regards physical harm, some authors argue that hate crimes are more brutal in nature, as the parallel crimes often constitute acts of serious physical violence (Levin & McDevitt, 1993; Lawrence, 1999; Hall, 2013). Other authors, however, have criticised this assumption on the ground that there would be not enough evidence to prove it (Dimock & Al-Hakim, 2012, p. 590), or that most hate crimes actually constitute low-base offences which have an "ordinary" nature (Iganski, 2008, p. 42). On the other hand, an increasing number of studies show that "as a group, victims of 'hate crime' collectively experience a greater degree of negative psychological impacts when compared with victims of parallel crimes" (Iganski & Lagou, 2015, p. 1697).

The main reason why these types of crime have a greater impact on their victims is that they attack the core of the targeted persons' identity (Iganski & Lagou, 2015, p. 1711). Let's take the example of a person targeted for the colour of their skin. Skin complexion and physical features are almost impossible to hide, and constitute not only an immutable, but also an evident aspect of a person's identity (Hall, 2013, p. 67 referring to Craig-Henderson & Sloan, 2003). If someone is attacked for no apparent reason, and the only characteristic that distinguishes them from other surrounding people is, for instance, the colour of their skin, this person is very likely to suspect that they were targeted only for this very reason. This is particularly true if victims live in a place which has a history of racial oppression and discrimination against the group they belong to. The same cannot be said as regards other personal features which can distinguish a person from their peers but do not, and never have constituted, a "a group antipathy with a social context" (Lawrence, 1999, p. 11). By using Lawrence's own example, people with blue eyes might well be targeted because of the colour of their eyes, but this cannot generally be said to be a core part of one's identity, nor have blue-eyed people been subjected to a historical pattern of discrimination only because of the colour of their eyes. Our society does not consider race as a neutral characteristic, as eye colour is. Race matters when one looks for a job, or wants to rent an apartment, purchase goods, or step past a cop, or want to engage in a romantic relationship with someone. It should not matter, but it actually does. Moreover, this line of reasoning applies not only to race, but also to other personal characteristics such as ethnic origin, gender, sexual orientation, gender identity, disability, and so on.

Furthermore, many authors have argued that one of the main characteristics of hate crimes is that they convey a message of prejudice, hate, contempt not only towards the direct victim, but also to "those who share the same identity as the primary victim" (Iganski & Lagou, 2015, p. 1697). Hate crimes are said to have an *in terrorem* effect on this wider community, as other members who may not even know the victim personally feel nevertheless to be potential targets of the offender because of the common feature they share (Hall, 2013, p. 166). Moreover, it is argued that hate crimes also affect the society at large, as they would "heighten community tension" and have a socially divisive nature (Hall, 2013, pp. 164, 169).

The analysis of the added harmfulness of hate crimes in comparison with parallel offences, both in qualitative and quantitative terms, is key to determine the legitimacy of hate crime law. For this reason, this topic will be thoroughly dealt with in Chapter 3.

2.2.4 Minority-On-Majority and Minority-On-Minority Hate Crimes

Until recent years, hate crimes have been understood as inevitably requiring victims to belong to "traditionally marginalized minority groups" (Chakraborti & Garland, 2012, p. 500). Members of majority communities, on the other hand, have been excluded from the debate, although the nature and consequences of this kind of victimisation may be very similar. This perspective is understandable, since the debate on this phenomenon was born out of the civil rights movement in the US during the 1960s and 1970s. However, research has shown that the reality of hate crimes is far more complex. Bias crimes committed by a member of a minority group against a member of the majority are not uncommon, and neither are those committed by a member of a minority against a member of another minority, with whom they share the same protected ground (e.g. ethnic origin).

As to minority-on-majority hate crimes, the concerns surrounding their exclusion from hate crime law appear to have some basis (see Lawrence, 1999). If we conceptualise hate crimes as stemming out of a relation based on oppression and discrimination of a group against another, it appears to make little sense to provide enhanced protection also to members of the dominant majority. However, if we consider instead the *vulnerability* and *situational disadvantage* that characterise the victim in the eyes of the perpetrator, or on the *hostility* expressed by the criminal act, the focus shifts completely, and it becomes reasonable to include minority-on-majority hate crimes in the framework (in this regard, see the below Section on vulnerability, disadvantage, and hostility).

Let's think, for example, of an Italian of Roma ethnicity beating up a non-Roma Italian in Italy. There is no doubt that Roma people in Italy still suffer daily discrimination, oppression and exclusion in all aspects of their lives (Associazione 21 luglio, 2022). If we conceptualise hate crimes as requiring an historical, or current, pattern of discrimination, an Italian non-Roma can hardly prove to be a victim of a hate crime, and the perpetrator will be prosecuted at most under the criminal provision covering the parallel crime (assault, in this case). However, if we look closely at the victim and the perpetrator's respective situations, we might find that the offender strongly dislikes non-Roma people; that they attacked the victim because of them being non-Roma, and they made their hate crystal clear by uttering insults to their victim; that, in the perpetrator's mind, any non-Roma person could have been a suitable victim; that the post-victimisation effects of the attack on the direct victim were worse than those that would have occurred following a parallel crime committed without the *hate* component; that the attack caused wider fear within the victim's community, and had the potential to increase the hostility between Roma and non-Roma people in a given place. Under these premises, it is difficult not to frame this particular crime as a hate crime, and possibly as a *retaliatory* crime (see Sect. 2.2.1 above). As put by Chakraborti and Garland, there is now "ample evidence … suggesting that the kinds of biases, prejudices and stereotypes that form the basis of hate crimes are not the exclusive domain of any particular group" (Chakraborti & Garland, 2012, p. 505).

This approach has been followed both in the US and in some European countries. For example, in a 2013 judgment concerning an assault committed by several persons of Roma origin against a non-Roma person, the Supreme Court of Hungary maintained that to establish whether someone can be considered as a hate crime victim, the decisive factor is whether they can be considered as part of a minority in the concrete circumstances of the offence, regardless of the situation of social disadvantage they may find themselves in.[7] Albeit it may appear conceptually logical and coherent, this approach can lead to very dangerous consequences, particularly in those countries that suffer from institutional racism. In those contexts, biased courts can be tempted to construe a base crime as a hate crime whenever a member of a minority group commits a crime against a member of the majority, thus depriving of protection the very social groups that hate crime law was conceived for (see Bárd, 2020, p. 262).

As to the second typology (minority-on-minority hate crime), let's consider the case of a member of a minority ethnic group who attacks a member of another minority ethnic group. For example, hostilities between different religious or ethnic groups that live in a given country can easily be transferred to a new country as a result of migration processes. A failure to cover these kind of crimes under the hate crime legislation umbrella overlooks the important implications of these processes (Hall, 2013), and leaves the victims defenceless and even more vulnerable. This, in turn, may exacerbate the hostility between the two groups concerned, which can give rise to a succession of retaliatory hate crime crimes.

From a stricter criminal law viewpoint, lawmakers often prefer to shape the protected characteristics in neutral terms, in order to avoid encroachment with the principle of equality before the law, and to enhance public acceptance of hate crime law. Usually, in fact, the protected characteristics are defined as, to name just few, *ethnic origin*, *sexual orientation* or *gender*, even though the concrete social groups that the law aims to protect are ethnic minorities, homosexuals and women.

[7] Supreme Court of Hungary (Kúria), judgment no. Bfv.II.590/2012/18, 7 February 2013 (Tavaszmezö case).

3 A Four-Tier Framework to Analyse Hate Crime Law

The first part of this chapter has examined, from a purely descriptive point of view, different aspects that characterise hate crimes and distinguish them from other similar, and sometimes overlapping, phenomena. By building on this background overview of bias offences, as well as on specific, relevant research, this second part will elaborate a framework to connect the key elements of hate crimes to the correspondent components of hate crime law. The aim of this exercise is both descriptive and normative. On the one hand, it allows us to categorise hate crime provisions and their key components according to the scope of the hate crime concept they reflect, as well as to make explicit the rationales behind the enactment of these provisions, their scope and their possible impact on the phenomenon of hate crimes. On the other hand, the solid criminological research this framework is built on can assist lawmakers in making informed choices and designing more effective law to tackle hate crime.

3.1 Elements of the Framework

In hate crime literature, there is still no agreement on the definition of the concepts of hate crime and hate crime law (Brax & Munthe, 2013, p. 5; Brudholm, 2015, p. 83). The definition adopted by this research refers to criminal law provisions that foresee a penalty enhancement when a conduct that already constitutes a criminal offence has been committed in connection "to a negatively biased attitude of the offender towards the victim in virtue of a perceived social group-membership of the latter" (Brax & Munthe, 2013, p. 45). Moreover, the nexus between the perpetrator's bias and the offence "has to take the form of either a state of the offender that contributes to the explanation of the offence (such as an intention, a motive or a disposition), or something expressed by the offender through or in connection with the offence" (Brax & Munthe, 2013, pp. 45–46).

For his part, Brudholm observes that there is no actual need for more definitions; what is necessary is a "more comprehensive conceptual framework" that explains and categorises the different definitions of bias offences in terms of their structure, transversal issues and alternatives (Brudholm, 2015, p. 82). By synthesising the different hate crime conceptions proposed in literature, Brudholm eventually elaborates a four-tier concept of hate crime—a framework consisting of four variables which represent the four constitutive features of bias offences. His claim is "that any conception of hate crime can be analysed as a specific combination of different interpretations of these four features" (Brudholm, 2015, p. 84). According to his framework, "[d]ifferent definitions of hate crime count intelligibly as such, because they differ by their positions in relation to the four core features. Variation between conceptions can be analysed as combinations of different elaborations of the four elements" (Brudholm, 2015, p. 88). According to Brudholm, the four constitutive features of hate crimes are: (1) the inherently criminal nature of hate crimes: the same act without the *hate* component is already a criminal offence; (2) a connection between the offence and the mental attitude of the offender that can be explained in terms of *hate* or *bias* motive; (3) the choice of the *amount* of bias motivation that shall count as sufficient evidence to prove that an offence is a hate crime; and (4) the choice of which grounds should be protected.

In a similar exercise, the ODHIR has examined how the concept of hate crime is *translated into law* through the analysis of the OSCE participating States' hate crime law. Then, it has identified the constituent parts of these provisions, expressed in the form of five "Policy Questions" (ODHIR, 2009, p. 31): (1) Should the law create a new substantive offence or operate as a penalty enhancement for existing crimes? (2) Which characteristics should be included in the law? (3) How should motive be defined in the law? (4) How should association, affiliation and mistakes in perception be dealt with? (5) What evidence is needed and how much motive is required?

Neither Brudholm nor the ODHIR provide final answers as to how the concept of hate crime and hate crime law should be defined. They both recognise the diversity of opinions in academic studies as to the former and the great number of existing possibilities as to the latter. Their approaches have the merit of trying to connect and classify in a consistent and rational way the different conceptions of hate crimes proposed in literature and the various forms hate crime law existing in the OSCE region. In the following sections the main characteristics of hate crime and hate crime law identified by Brudholm and the ODHIR are further developed in a four-tier framework that can be applied to analyse and compare different models of hate crime law. The framework consists of the following four variables or tiers:

- Tier I: the drafting method or provision's structure chosen to increase a base offence's sentence when it is committed in connection with a bias motive;
- Tier II: the personal characteristics or group memberships included in the law;
- Tier III: the kind of evidence and the amount of hate or bias required; and
- Tier IV: the definition of the nexus between the offender's mental attitude and the crime.

3.2 The Four Variables/Tiers in Detail

This section elaborates each of the four variables/tiers that constitute the hate crime law framework and critically examines their most relevant aspects. Each variable can be implemented in a number of ways, depending on the scope of application lawmakers intend to provide that specific provision with—which corresponds, in turn, to the width of the concept of hate crime explicitly or implicitly adopted by the legislator. The variables are developed and critically assessed by drawing on interdisciplinary research on hate crimes and by providing concrete examples from the OSCE jurisdictions.

3.2.1 Tier I: Drafting Method to Increase the Base Sentence

A growing number of studies show that hate crimes are more harmful and wrongful than parallel offences (see Sect. 2.2.3 above and Chap. 3). Accordingly, the typical criminal law response to hate crimes across the

OSCE region is to foresee a penalty enhancement when a base offence is committed out of a bias motive. This is justified—among other things—by referring to the proportionality principle, according to which hate crimes offenders deserve to be punished *more* than otherwise motivated offences of the same nature because the former types of crimes are somehow *worse* than the base/parallel offences. Increasing the sentence for a conduct that already constitutes a criminal offence is also one of the key elements that distinguishes hate crimes from other, similar phenomena such as hate speech and discrimination. The base conduct of the latter, in fact, does not represent, *per se*, a violation of criminal law (see Sect. 2.1.2 above).

Punishment enhancement for hate crime offenders can be introduced in criminal law in a number of ways: by means of new substantive offences, general or specific aggravating circumstances, or other legal policies allowing for motive to be considered as a sentencing factor (ODHIR, 2009, pp. 32–37; Brudholm, 2015, pp. 84–85). Each drafting method reflects a different concept of hate crimes and presents both advantages and disadvantages.

Substantive Offences

Substantive offences are separate criminal law provisions in which bias is considered as a constitutive element of the offence's legal definition. In the OSCE region, these types of hate crime provisions are not very common (ODHIR, 2009, p. 32).

The Penal Code of the Czech Republic, for example, punishes with a sentence ranging from six months to three years' imprisonment whoever uses violence against a group of people or an individual, or threatens to kill or to harm them "for their real or perceived race, ethnic affiliation, nationality, political opinion, religion or belief or real or perceived lack thereof."[8] In the United Kingdom, the 1998 Crime and Disorder Act (as amended by 2001 Anti-Terrorism Crime and Security Act) introduced a number of new substantive offences criminalising racially or religiously

---

[8] Czech Republic's Penal Code, § 352(2).

aggravated assault (Section 29), criminal damage (Section 30), public order offences (Section 31), and harassment (Section 32) in England and Wales, and racially aggravated harassment (Section 33) in Scotland.

According to the OSCE, the primary advantage of drafting a law in the form of substantive offences is that they specifically and explicitly address motives based on the victim's membership to a certain group. Thus, they allow the offence to be more visible and more correctly labelled. This, in turn, better fulfils the expressive function of criminal law, and makes data collection easier and more precise (ODHIR, 2009, p. 33; Brax & Munthe, 2013, p. 29; Gião Hanek, 2017, p. 490).

Furthermore, this drafting method allows legislators to rationally limit the use of the criminal law. Penalty enhancement is applied only to those base conducts that are empirically shown to be committed out of a bias motive with a certain frequency or in which the resulting harm caused to victims appears to be particularly serious.

However, there are also a number of disadvantages related to this kind of measure. First, in those jurisdictions allowing courts to adjudicate only the offence with which the accused is indicted, prosecutors might consider it tactically more convenient either to press charges only with regard to the parallel crime, or to "accept a guilty plea to the base offence in order to ensure the offender is convicted," due to the inherent difficulty of proving the bias element of the hate crime (ODHIR, 2009, p. 35). Second, it has been noted that considering motive as a constitutive part of an offence would encroach on the *mens rea*/*actus reus* dichotomy. If motive becomes a definitional element of a crime this "would be a break with the tradition that motive is relevant only in relation to the gravity of the punishment to be imposed" (Hare, 1997, p. 435). However, this argument is not very convincing. On the one hand, the distinction between motive, intention or purpose is not clear-cut. On the other hand, there already exist offences in with motive is a constitutive part of the crime, both in the UK and in other common law and civil law legal systems (Hare, 1997, p. 485).

Aggravating Circumstances

Aggravating circumstances increase the penalty foreseen for a base offence when this is committed with a bias motive (ODHIR, 2009, p. 33; Brax & Munthe, 2013, p. 29). Across the OSCE region, they constitute the most common types of hate crime provisions (ODHIR, 2009, p. 33). Penalty enhancements can, in turn, be divided into two categories: general aggravating circumstances, which apply to all criminal offences, and specific aggravating circumstances, that apply only to specific criminal offences.

For example, both Danish[9] and Spanish[10] Penal Codes consider as a general aggravating circumstance the fact that the perpetrator has committed an offence for reasons related to specific personal characteristics of the victim or the discriminatory attitude of the offender.

As to specific aggravating circumstances, the Belgian Penal Code provides for the penalty enhancement of the base sentence foreseen for a wide number of crimes when these are committed with a bias motive: voyeurism, indecent assault and rape (art. 377-bis); murder, intentional injury and manslaughter (art. 405-quater); non-assistance to a person in danger (art. 422-quater); violation of personal liberty and trespass (art. 438-bis); libel and defamation (art. 453-bis); arson (art. 514-bis); and destruction of personal possessions or property (art. 532-bis).

Luxembourg, on the other hand, foresees a specific penalty enhancement only for the crimes of violation of the integrity of a corpse and violation or desecration of tombs, graves or monuments erected to the memory of the dead, when these offenses are committed out of racist or religious bias (art. 457-2 of the Penal Code).

Aggravating circumstances, especially in their general form, present an undeniable appeal for legislators because they are very practical and easy to incorporate in a penal code. Moreover, if the prosecution fails to sufficiently prove the offender's bias motive this will not jeopardise a possible conviction based on the underlying offence (ODHIR, 2009, p. 37). Furthermore, as with substantive offences, specific aggravating

[9] Danish Penal Code, Section 81(6).

[10] Spanish Penal Code, art. 22.

circumstances allow restraining the penalty enhancement only to those base offences that can be empirically shown to cause more harm. Conversely, general aggravating circumstances elude this empirical verifiability unless courts' interpretation eventually requires it.

However, this drafting method also presents some relevant drawbacks. First, public criminal records might not take into account the application of aggravating circumstances when labelling an offence, which will then be recorded only with reference to the base offence and not as a hate crime. This means, in turn, that official data collection will omit that particular crime, and that the offender's criminal record will not report it either. Second, procedural rules in place in a given jurisdiction may prevent the application of the aggravating circumstance (Gião Hanek, 2017, p. 479). For example, aggravating factors must usually be balanced with other mitigating circumstances. If the latter are found to prevail, the sentence will not be enhanced and the offence will not be considered as a hate crime. More in general, the ODHIR observes that "[w]ithout explicit recognition of the bias motive, the hate crime law loses much of its symbolic weight. Thus, a penalty enhancement, while easier to implement, may not fulfil the expressive function of recognizing and condemning a prohibited bias" (ODHIR, 2009, p. 36; on the same line, Gião Hanek, 2017, p. 479).

Other Sentencing Provisions

Besides the drafting options analysed so far, States can decide to enact a policy or law which allows judges to take into account hate motives in order to increase the amount of penalty to apply in a given case. More in general, all jurisdictions leave room for judicial discretion for imposing sanctions within the range foreseen in the criminal code, and the judicial interpretation of these provisions can also include the consideration of bias motives as an aggravating factor, even though the law does not explicitly mention them. While hate crime provisions drafted in the form of substantive offences or aggravating circumstances foresee a penalty increment that exceeds the maximum penalty provided for in the base offence, these kinds of provisions have a more limited impact. Judges can consider hate motives only to determine the amount of penalty *within* the penalty range foreseen for the base crime.

In Germany, for example, the criminal law does not explicitly foresee either substantive offences or aggravating circumstances for crimes committed with a bias motive. However, under general sentencing principles, judges may take into account racist, xenophobic and other discriminatory motives when determining the amount of sentence to apply (Section 46(2) of the Penal Code). Moreover, German case-law and literature have interpreted the notion of *base motives* listed in § 211 of the Penal Code as one of the subjective circumstances that "upgrade a killing from manslaughter (*Totschlag*) to murder (*Mord*)" (Dubber & Hörnle, 2014, p. 539) so to include motivations based on bias against political, social or ethnic groups.

Mixed Approach

A number of States have also introduced a combination of substantive offences and general and/or specific aggravating circumstances. The Maltese Criminal Code, for example, foresees a number of specific penalty enhancements (Section 222A) as well as a general aggravating circumstance (Section 83B) for crimes motivated by bias. As it was mentioned in the above sections, England and Wales' hate crime legislation foresees both substantive offences (Sections 28–31 of the 1998 Crime and Disorder Act) and a general aggravating circumstance (Section 66 of the Sentencing Act 2020).

Classification of Drafting Methods under the Concept of Hate Crime Adopted

The first three legal drafting approaches examined above reflect a different degree of understanding of the concept of hate crime: substantive offences correspond to a narrow understanding, while specific and general aggravating circumstances reflect an intermediate and a wide understanding, respectively (Table 2.1).

Table 2.1 Tier I: Methods to draft hate crime law

Narrow understanding of hate crime concept	Intermediate understanding of hate crime concept	Wide understanding of hate crime concept
• Substantive offence	• Specific aggravating circumstances	• General aggravating circumstances • Other sentencing rules that allow bias motives to be considered

The fourth type of provisions—those allowing the judge to consider bias motive when determining the amount of the sentence—are difficult to classify. On the one hand, they are applicable to all kinds of offences, likewise general aggravating circumstances. On the other hand, however, they lie somehow outside of the hate crime concepts analysed so far, as they do not directly link the added harm caused by these crimes to a proportional increase of sentence. Instead, the bias motive is just one among other concurring basic circumstances surrounding the offence that must be taken into account when gauging the amount of sentence, such the offender's *modus operandi*, the consequences caused by the offence, or the offender's prior history, and personal and financial circumstances.[11] These types of provisions are thus better understood as rules of criminal procedure. With some caveats, they can be classified as corresponding to a wide concept of hate crime, because they apply to any offences committed out of a bias motive.

3.2.2 Tier II: Protected Grounds

Criteria to Include Personal Features or Group Memberships

Hate crime law varies considerably as to which personal characteristics or social groups are protected. It is also possible to identify different generations of hate crime laws according to the grounds they cover. Hate crime law was first passed in the US following the civil rights movement in the

[11] See § 46(2) of the German Penal Code.

1960s, and they initially addressed race, ethnic origin, national origin and religion (Al-Hakim, 2015, p. 1776). In Europe, although research focussing specifically on hate crimes is relatively recent, racism and religiously motivated discrimination, speech and violence have been on the legislative agenda of most States since the end of World War Two. At present, race, ethnicity, nationality and religion still constitute the most commonly protected personal characteristics (ODHIR, 2009, p. 40; Gião Hanek, 2017, pp. 480–481). The debate on the inclusion of gender, sexual orientation and gender identity came afterwards, and in many countries legislators are still reluctant to recognise these grounds as worthy of the specific protection provided by hate crime law (Al-Hakim, 2015, p. 1776). Nowadays, hate crime studies—in parallel with studies addressing discrimination and inequality—are focussing on the suitability of disability, age, homelessness and socio-economic status, and other personal characteristics for their inclusion in hate crime law. Moreover, the research on the intersectionality of personal characteristics—in contrast to the "'silo' approach to identity, where groups are added to policy as time goes on" (Mason-Bish, 2014), which has been followed so far—is opening up to a new conception of hate crime victimisation, which focuses on the multi-layered identity of victims rather than on their belonging to one, specific social group.

Why do we need criteria to select protected grounds that should be covered? Jacobs and Potter observe that a principled approach is necessary to avoid that the selection of protected groups ends up being the result of "identity politics" (Jacobs & Potter, 1998);[12] in other words, "an outcome of a process of political lobbying and bargain, where those most disadvantaged usually have poor chances to become recognised" (Brax & Munthe, 2013; Al-Hakim, 2015). Al-Hakim, on his part, warns against the risk of under- or over-inclusiveness, as "hate crime legislation that protects everyone runs the risk of protecting no one" (Al-Hakim, 2015, p. 1758). The use of principled criteria in the selection of protected

[12] Jacobs and Potter (1998, p. 5) describe the term "identity politics" as referring to "a politics whereby individuals relate to one another as members of competing groups based upon characteristics like race, gender, religion, and sexual orientation. According to the logic of identity politics, it is strategically advantageous to be recognized as disadvantaged and victimized. The greater a group's victimization, the stronger its moral claim on the larger society."

grounds would ensure that hate crime law remains "open and flexible, able to encompass new groups in light of scientific, social, economic, moral, and political changes" and that "those who are granted enhanced protection are included for justifiable reasons" (Al-Hakim, 2015, p. 1758). Moreover, using a more transparent and grounded approach can better feed the debate on whether, and how, minority-on-majority and minority-on-minority hate crimes should also be covered by hate crime law (see Sect. 2.2.4 above).

Hate crime studies have developed a number of criteria to identify which personal characteristics should be included in the concept of hate crime and, in turn, in hate crime legislation. Here, six principles are examined. The first criterion—innocence and desert—is a negative one, as it constitutes a preliminary test before deciding to include a given ground. The remaining five criteria provide positive benchmarks that should be satisfied for a characteristic to be included. Furthermore, these criteria partly overlap and are not mutually exclusive; in fact, a criterion can be applied in combination with one or more other ones.

Innocence and Desert

The first criterion provides that, although certain crimes committed against a member of a given social group could theoretically be framed as hate crimes, the victims of these offences cannot claim to be entitled to the special protection provided by hate crime law. This is so because they have been targeted on the ground of a characteristic that society considers very negative and not worthy of special protection. For example, if a member of the Camorra (one of the most powerful criminal organisations in Italy) is assaulted because the perpetrator considers the victim's membership to that crime group a despicable act, the offender certainly commits a crime, and will be prosecuted according to the relevant criminal provision on assault. However, belonging to a criminal organisation cannot be considered as a characteristic that should be protected under hate crime law. This line of reasoning has been developed, in particular, in the study of crimes committed against (alleged) perpetrators of sex crimes against children (Brax & Munthe, 2013, pp. 30–31; Mason,

2007, 2014; see also Al-Hakim, 2015 on the problem of excluding people targeted for being excessively rich from hate crime law).[13]

The problem with this boundary is that the concepts of innocence and desert vary widely across time and space. In some countries, for example, homosexual acts are prosecuted and can be punished with life imprisonment or the death penalty. In those contexts, sexual orientation can hardly be seen as a ground deserving to be included in hate crime law. However, this problem can be reduced if we limit our analysis to hate crime legislation enacted in liberal-democratic societies, in which criminalisation is (at least theoretically) conditioned by the respect of normative principles of criminalisation and fundamental rights. This solution is partial, though, because it does not affect liberal-democratic democracies in which, due to a number of cultural and social reasons, homosexuality (or other features that appear worthy of protection), is still considered as an undesirable personal characteristic (to say the least). The decision on which grounds to include is ultimately political, and inevitably linked to the specific characteristics of each country.

Previous History of Persecution, Exclusion or Discrimination

This criterion requires a given personal characteristic to relate to "divisions that run deep in the social history of a culture" that Lawrence calls "societal fissure lines" (Lawrence, 1999, p. 12). These divisions are the result of a history of persecution, exclusion or discrimination suffered by that social group (see Brax & Munthe, 2013, p. 30; Lawrence, 1999, pp. 11–20). Ethnic origins, race, colour, national origin, religion, sexual orientation, gender identity, gender and disability generally fit the description. Other features, which are relevant in a specific given country, can also be included. For example, membership to a trade union, or the absence thereof, might be an important characteristic to include in bias crime law in a country with a history of strong conflict between members and non-members (Lawrence, 1999, p. 13).

---

[13] For a thorough analysis and discussion of the concept of 'innocence' and 'desert' in relation to the harms caused by hate crimes, see Chap. 3, Sect. 4.2.2.

However, there have been a number of important criticisms against this criterion. First, it is strongly linked to identity politics, as it would further empower lobbyist groups, thus leaving the most vulnerable and disadvantaged groups out of the game (Al-Hakim, 2015, p. 1765). Second, it would allow the legislation to discriminate between victim groups (Schweppe, 2012, p. 175). Third, it does not cover groups lacking a history of oppression and discrimination, which are nevertheless at high risk to be targeted (Al-Hakim, 2015, p. 1765). Fourth, it does not provide a clear tool to understand "minority on majority hate crimes where no fissures can be properly identified" (Al-Hakim, 2015, p. 1765). Fifth, it potentially includes undeserving groups proven that there is a societal fissure line between them and other groups of the society.

High/Actual Risk or Trend of Persecution, Exclusion or Discrimination

This criterion refers to the current spread and seriousness of hate crimes against a certain group in a given country. It is argued that, if the group is at high risk of victimisation because of being more frequently or more severely targeted, it deserves to be included in hate crime law (Brax & Munthe, 2013, p. 30). The problem with this criterion is that available data on hate crimes is usually limited, as many countries have enacted unsatisfactory policies to collect sound and reliable information on the occurrence of hate crimes, which often fail to cover all possible grounds. This problem is compounded by the fact that many bias motivated offences remain unreported, as victims are often reluctant to contact the police, particularly when they belong to the society's most disadvantaged groups (see FRA, 2018, p. 27; and Pezzella et al., 2019). Moreover, this criterion might be over inclusive, as it would encompass crimes against *underserving* groups, proven that they show a "high risk of being attacked based on what they are" (Al-Hakim, 2015, p. 1770).

Vulnerability

This criterion does not focus on the victim's belonging to a certain social group, but addresses instead the perpetrator's perception that the victim is somehow vulnerable due to a certain personal characteristic.

The vulnerability-based approach proposed by Chakraborti and Garland (2012) "acknowledges"—in the authors' own words—"the heightened level of risk posed to certain groups or individuals that can arise through a complex interplay of different factors, including hate, prejudice, hostility, unfamiliarity, discomfort or simply opportunism or convenience" (Chakraborti & Garland, 2012, p. 506). This criterion allows one to draw "attention to those groups of victims, whose experiences have been marginalized in conventional hate crime frameworks," such as the homeless, the elderly, members of subcultures, foreign nationals, refugees, asylum seekers, migrant workers or overseas students, and so on. Moreover, it helps to recognise the diverse experience of victims "who fall within the parameters of a particular group label." Furthermore, it is argued to be more suited to capture the "intersectional nature of identity" and the specific vulnerability that stems thereof (Chakraborti & Garland, 2012, p. 504).

Yet, criticisms to a vulnerability-based approach have been numerous. The main concern lies on the negative connotations surrounding the term *vulnerability*, which reminds one of a state of helplessness, defenceless, and need of external care, and leads inevitability to a paternalistic response by the State.[14] In reply to this, Chakraborti and Garland propose a definition of vulnerability that shifts the focus from an assumed permanent and helpless status of the victims to the offenders' *perception* of their targets' vulnerability. In other words, a certain personal

[14] Harel and Parchomovsky, for example, define individual vulnerability to crime as the probability of harm resulting from a crime multiplied by its magnitude as regards a given person. They explain that "[i]ndividuals may be particularly vulnerable to crime for two different reasons: a greater sensitivity to harm and a greater likelihood of becoming a victim. Individuals who fall into the former category may be labeled 'extra-sensitive victims', and individuals who belong to the latter may be called 'high-risk victims'" (Harel & Parchomovsky, 1999, pp. 509–510). Thus, the second type of crime vulnerability would also encompass the category high risk/actual risk or trend of persecution, exclusion or discrimination examined above.

characteristic or a combination of features does not render *per se* the victim vulnerable all the time. More importantly,

> it is not someone's identity (their disability, their sexuality, and so on) per se that renders them vulnerable in the context of hate crime. Rather, they may become a victim because of how that aspect of their identity intersects with other aspects of their self, and with other situational factors and context, to make them vulnerable in the eyes of the perpetrator. (Chakraborti & Garland, 2012, p. 507)

It follows that hate crimes should not be construed as inevitable phenomena that are irremediably connected to a presumed inherent passivity of victims (Chakraborti & Garland, 2012, p. 507). Moreover, not all offences committed against persons in vulnerable positions can be framed as hate crimes. Those presenting some sort of bias motivation in the form of prejudice, hate or hostility on the part of the offender will be; offences merely committed out of convenience (e.g. robbing a person on a wheelchair assuming that they will not be able to oppose resistance) are usually conceptually and legally framed differently.

Disadvantage

In the context of the analysis of hate crimes against homeless people, Al-Hakim (2015) proposes the use of a ground-selecting criterion that refers to the condition of disadvantage hate crime victims find themselves in.

Al-Hakim first considers Reidy's concept of disadvantage, which includes only historically oppressed groups (Reidy, 2002). He dismisses it on the grounds that it would exclude "newly formed minorities who may not be historically disadvantaged" and "denies, as an implication, minority-on-majority hate crimes" (Al-Hakim, 2015, p. 1771). Al-Hakim instead adopts Wolff and De-Shalit's concept of disadvantage, which is defined as "a lack of genuine opportunity for secure functioning" (Wolff & De-Shalit, 2007, p. 9). Thus, disadvantage is not limited to economic matters, but "has to be understood in a pluralist form" instead (Wolff &

De-Shalit, 2007, p. 8). According to the capability approach developed by Sen (1999) and Nussbaum (2006), and adopted by Wolff and De-Shalit, "to assess an individual's wellbeing we need to attend to a variety of such things as life span, bodily health, bodily integrity, affiliation, control over the environment, and many other categories" (Wolff & De-Shalit, 2007, p. 8). Using disadvantage as a criterion to identify which groups should be protected under hate crime legislation leads to a shift of focus. The law would not protect "identity groups qua identity group but rather in terms of the disadvantage such identification highlights" (Al-Hakim, 2015, p. 1776).

There are a number of pros in adopting this approach. First, it provides a sound explanation as to what the "protected groups and identities" (Al-Hakim, 2015, p. 1755) have in common that make them deserving to be included in hate crime legislation. Second, disadvantage constitutes a "neutral justificatory approach for the choice of selection, thereby remaining consistent with political liberal normative constraints" (Al-Hakim, 2015, p. 1758). Third, while disadvantage usually includes social groups who have been historically oppressed, it also encompasses high-risk groups which have been only recently targeted. At the same time, it sets a boundary between deserving and underserving groups. For example, members of a criminal organisation or paedophiles cannot be said to be disadvantaged because of what they are, albeit they may well be vulnerable and be at high risk of being victims of targeted crimes.

Hostility

The hostility criterion, developed by Schweppe (2012), transfers the choice as to which grounds to cover from the legislator to the judge/jury called to decide a concrete case. To do so, she relies on the common-law legal technique used to identify and develop a *similar factor* element. Under this approach courts do not look to victim features, but develop a case-by-case ruling based on the hostility that motivates the offender. This allows the process to be de-politicised. The decision as to whether a given conduct constitutes a hate crime shifts to judges and jury who will have to determine this on the basis of concrete evidence "rather than curtailing the operation of the legislation to a limited number of (albeit fully deserving) victim groups" (Schweppe, 2012, pp. 182–183). Schweppe argues that the underlying legislation could be drafted by taking into account the concept of *defining* or *personal* characteristics. More specifically, judges would have to determine whether "the motivation behind the criminal offence was based on hostility towards the victim, hostility which was directed at the victim because of their personal characteristics (or presumed characteristics), characteristics of which he or she shares with an identifiable social group" (Schweppe, 2012, pp. 182–183).

This approach has the merit of highlighting the prejudicial nature of bias crimes, thus enlarging the perspective usually focussed on *hate* in the stricter sense. This, in turn, would allow the judge to consider as victims of hate crimes a range of groups that do not fit the *social fissures* or *high risk* criteria, as well as to consider intersectionality issues usually ignored. However, there are also important concerns related to it. First, it does not set a boundary between *deserving* and *underserving* groups. Second, by letting the choice of which groups to include to judges and juries, it encroaches with the principle of legal certainty, particularly in those legislations in which this principle is applied more narrowly and requires criminal provisions to be extremely precise. However, this second concern could be overcome by conceiving hostility as a criterion addressed to the legislator, and not to adjudicating bodies. This, in turn, would nonetheless fall foul of one of the major aims of this criterion as developed by Schweppe, that is to say, to depoliticise the choice of which grounds to protect.

Different Approaches in the OSCE Region

Across the OSCE region, examples vary greatly as to how legislators concretely frame the protected grounds part of hate crime provisions. Differences concern various aspects as to how a certain ground can be included in hate crime legislation.

The first variable concerns the number and kind of chosen protected features. Race, national origin, ethnicity and religion are the most commonly included characteristics, while gender, age, mental or physical disability and sexual orientation are covered by a lesser number of legal systems. Gender identity, along with other features that relate, for example, to marital status, wealth or political affiliation, are included only in a small number of cases (ODHIR, 2009, pp. 41–44; Gião Hanek, 2017, pp. 480–481). These differences reflect the so-called *generations of hate crime law* mentioned above. As to the number of protected characteristics included in the legislation, while Belgium's penal code, for example, lists a very wide number of grounds,[15] the EU's Framework Decision on racism and xenophobia only covers race, colour, descent, national and ethnic origins, and religion.[16]

A second aspect that is key to classify different drafting techniques in relation to the chosen protected characteristics regards the closed or open nature of the list of protected grounds. While some legislations provide for a closed list of characteristics (e.g. Spain[17]), others leave judges the possibility to decide, in a concrete case, whether a personal characteristic not included in the list may nevertheless be considered as a protected ground. This is the case, for example, in Canada (Section 718.2 of the Criminal Code), Czech Republic (§ 42 of the Penal Code), and Denmark (Section 81(6) of the Penal Code). On its part, North Macedonia's criminal law provision on hate crimes provides a long list of grounds and a final clause that includes any other ground provided in law or ratified international agreement (art. 39(5) of the Penal Code).

The ODHIR has singled out a fundamental issue related to the use of open-ended lists of grounds. While this approach has the undoubtable appeal of allowing the legislation to evolve over time to address new categories of hate crime victims, it nevertheless encroaches with the criminal law principle of legal certainty as it renders the provision vague and

[15] Arts. 377-bis, 422-quater, 438-bis, 453-bis, 514-bis, and 532-bis of the Belgian Penal Code include race, colour, descent, national or ethnic origin, nationality, sex, sexual orientation, marital status, birth, age, fortune, religious beliefs or philosophy of life, current and future state of health, disability, language, politic beliefs, trade union, physical or genetic characteristic, or social origin. Along with these grounds, art. 405-quater(6) includes also gender reassignment ('*changement de sexe*').

[16] Art. 4 of Council Framework Decision 2008/913/JHA of 28 November 2008 on combating certain forms and expressions of racism and xenophobia by means of criminal law, O.J. L 328 of 6 December 2008.

[17] Art. 22(4) of the Penal Code.

generic. Moreover, by taking away from lawmakers the power to decide which groups to include, and by handling it to judges, it transforms an otherwise political decision into a case-by-case one (ODHIR, 2009, pp. 46; 55).

Another variable concerns the way the relation between the bias motivation and the targeted victim's personal feature is expressed. Some hate crime provisions define the protected characteristic with reference to the *victim's relevant feature* (e.g. the victim's ethnic origin, disability or gender), while others focus instead on the discriminatory nature of the *perpetrator's motives* (e.g. a racist, xenophobic or homophobic motive). An example of the first type can be found in the Croatian Penal Code, which defines hate crimes as those offences "committed on account of race, colour, religion, national or ethnic origin, language, disability, gender, sexual orientation or gender identity of another person" (art. 87(21)). Conversely, the Austrian Penal Code considers it an aggravating circumstance if the perpetrator "acted out of racist, xenophobic or other motives considered particularly condemnable" (§ 33 (1)(5)). The choice between these two approaches may have practical implications, particularly in terms of evidence. The former adopts a more objective stance, by focussing on a real or perceived characteristic of the victim, while the latter requires proof of a prejudice-based mental attitude of the offender, which may be harder to prove in court. Hate crime law can also adopt a mixed approach. Spain, for example, foresees as an aggravating circumstance the commission of the offence "for racist, anti-Semitic, or anti-Roma reasons, or another kind of discrimination related to ideology, religion or belief of the victim, ethnicity, race or nation to which they belong, their sex, age, sexual orientation, sexual or gender identity, gender motives, aporophobia or social exclusion, illness suffered or disability" (art. 22(4) of the Penal Code).

Fourth, the protected characteristics can all be listed either in a single hate crime provision (e.g. in Finland[18]), or be covered by different criminal law provisions (e.g. in the United Kingdom[19]). The second approach

[18] Penal Code of Finland, Chapter 6, Section 5(4).

[19] Arts. 28–32 and 33, of the 1998 Crime and Disorder Act and Section 66 of the Sentencing Act 2020.

reflects the fact that, in many countries, hate crime legislation has been progressively introduced to include an increasing number of grounds.

Fifth, besides motives based on hate and prejudice, criminal laws can also foresee the application of a penalty enhancement when perpetrators take advantage of a certain condition of their victims that render them particularly vulnerable (see Chakraborti & Garland, 2012, p. 507). If these provisions do not require evidence of a bias motive behind the crime, they can be framed as hate crime law only *implicitly*, under a wide and formalist conception of bias offence, as they may encompass *also* conducts that actually are hate crimes. In Austria, for example, judges can consider as an aggravating factor the commission of an offence by "taking advantage of the defencelessness and helplessness of the victim" (§ 33 (1) (7) of the Penal Code). Disability, for example, is rarely included in hate crime legislation, but the criminal law often provides for a penalty enhancement when the crime has been committed against a person with disabilities due to her or his perceived vulnerability. This is the case, for example, in Italy, where Article 36 of Act 104/1992 foresees a penalty enhancement when certain offences (gross indecency, crimes against persons and property, and crimes related to exploitation of sex workers) are committed against a person having a physical, psychic or sensory impairment.

Finally, the possible intersectionality of two or more grounds is usually not considered by hate crime law, with some, isolated, exceptions. California's Criminal Code's definition of hate crimes, for instance, includes also those crimes committed because of *one or more* protected characteristics of the victim (Section 422.55 of the Criminal Code).

Classification of the Grounds Included under the Concept of Hate Crime Adopted

This section presents the analyses of the different criteria available to legislators to choose which personal characteristics or group memberships to include in hate crime legislation. Even when the law is silent in this respect, the choice itself of protecting certain grounds instead of others reflects an underlying and implicit selecting criterion. Moreover, different aspects concerning the method used to include and express the chosen protected grounds in the law have been identified. Among them, two interrelated variables appear to be useful to categorise hate crime law with regard to the choice of grounds: *the type and number* of protected grounds and the *open or closed nature of the list* of protected characteristics. Each drafting category is connected to a given understanding of the concept of hate crimes, and encompasses different underlying selection criteria. In this way, it is possible to classify hate crime law according to both the drafting technique used and the selecting criteria that may or may not be made explicit by lawmakers, and connect them to a certain concept of hate crimes (Table 2.2).

Innocence and desert, previous history of persecution, exclusion or discrimination, and high/actual risk or trend of persecution, exclusion or discrimination were the first criteria identified in literature to choose among protected grounds. They provide pragmatic solutions and guidance for legislators and researchers and can thus be very helpful. However, recent research has shown that these three criteria are ultimately inaccurate and do not seem to properly reflect the actual impact of hate crimes.

Table 2.2 Tier II: Protected grounds

Narrow understanding of hate crime concept	Intermediate understanding of hate crime concept	Wide understanding of hate crime concept
• **Few characteristics and *closed* list** Selection criteria employed: • Innocence and desert • Previous history of persecution, exclusion or discrimination	• **Many characteristics but *closed* list** Selection criteria employed: • Innocence and desert • Previous history of persecution, exclusion or discrimination • High/actual risk or trend of persecution, exclusion or discrimination • Vulnerability • Disadvantage • Hostility	• **Many characteristics and *open* list** Selection criteria employed: • Innocence and desert • Previous history of persecution, exclusion or discrimination • High/actual risk or trend of persecution, exclusion or discrimination • Vulnerability • Disadvantage • Hostility

Al-Hakim's concept of *disadvantage*, Garland and Chakraborti's *vulnerability and difference*, and Schweppe's *hostility* are at the forefront of the debate on which grounds/personal characteristics should be covered. They all highlight the importance of going beyond the more traditional view of seeing traditional vulnerable groups as victims, in order to encompass those who are excluded from the traditional view (such as people with disabilities, the elderly, the homeless, those belonging to subcultures or other marginalised groups). Moreover, they address important issues such as the intersectionality of identities, the ordinariness of hate crimes, hate crimes committed by a member of a minority against a member of the majority, as well as those committed by members of a minority against a member of another minority (Chakraborti & Garland, 2012, p. 44; Schweppe, 2012). The *innocence and desert* criterion, on the other hand, can be viewed as a boundary delimiting which groups deserve to be included in hate crime law and which do not.

These criteria can also be combined, in the sense that a social group must satisfy all, some, or at least one of them, to be included in hate crime legislation. For example, we may decide that if a group can demonstrate either "an actual trend of persecution or vulnerability in the face of such persecution," it can be included in the law (Brax & Munthe, 2013, pp. 30–31). This decision is eventually political, and will depend on how wide lawmakers intend the protection offered by hate crime law to be.

3.2.3 Tier III: Kind of Evidence and Amount of Hate/Bias Required

The third and fourth variables address two features of hate crimes, and of hate crime law, which are strictly connected and partially overlapping. The third variable describes some evidentiary issues posed by hate crimes that are relevant for the drafting of hate crime law, namely what is the minimum amount of *hate* or *bias* motive required to frame a given offence as a hate crime. The fourth tier explains how the nexus between the bias component and the crime is defined in hate crime law.

What distinguishes hate crimes from parallel crimes is the bias/hate motive that influences the choice of the victim by the perpetrator. The very nature of this element—a mental disposition, attitude or belief—makes it impossible to detect unless it is somehow expressed by the offender before, during or after the hate incident. In fact, the proof that a crime has been committed out of a bias motivation is paved with difficulties that are, sometimes, unsurmountable.

Criminological studies have pointed to a number of circumstantial factors that may indicate that a crime has been committed out of bias. Apart from the case in which perpetrators admit it, these factors can be that offenders clearly express their bias by way of uttering, or displaying, discriminatory insults during the attack; that the crime seems otherwise meaningless or inexplicable, as "the victim personally did nothing that could explain the gravity of the violence" (Brudholm, 2015, p. 86); that the perpetrators did not previously know their victims, and that they have apparently chosen their target randomly; the lack of prior history of hostility between victim and offender (ODHIR, 2009, p. 55); or the present or past belonging of the perpetrator to an extremist group.

However, these factors are merely indicative and by no way conclusive. As pointed out in Sect. 2.2 above, relevant research has observed that most hate crimes actually are low-level offences committed by *ordinary* people in their everyday lives (Iganski, 2008, p. 42) who act out of boredom (Levin & McDevitt, 1993; McDevitt et al., 2002) and only a small number of bias crimes can be described as *mission crimes* committed by perpetrators belonging to extremist groups (see Sect. 2.2.1 above).

Specific Evidence Required by Hate Crime Law

With the aim to assist the investigation and prosecution of hate crimes, some bias crime provisions state explicitly what facts or circumstances can be regarded as proof that a bias crime has occurred.

In England and Wales, for example, hate crime law provides a definition of what constitutes a racially, religiously, homophobic, transphobic or ableist aggravated offence. For instance, an offence is considered as racially or religiously aggravated either if "at the time of committing the offence, or immediately before or after doing so, the offender demonstrates towards the victim of the offence hostility based on the victim's membership (or presumed membership) of a racial or religious group," or "the offence is motivated (wholly or partly) by hostility towards members of a racial or religious group based on their membership of that group" (Section 28 of the UK's Crime and Disorder Act 1998). This provision further specifies the meaning to be attributed to the terms *membership*, *presumed*, *racial group* and *religious group*.

The French Penal Code provides for an aggravating circumstance when an offence is "preceded, accompanied or followed by written or spoken words, images, objects or actions of whatever nature which either damage the honour or the reputation of the victim, or of a group of persons to which the victim belongs, on account of their actual or supposed membership or non-membership of a given race, ethnic group, nation," religion, sex, sexual orientation or gender identity, "or establish that the offence has been committed against the victim for one of these reasons" (arts. 132-76 and 132-77 of the Penal Code).

Amount of Hate Required by Hate Crime Law

A specific—and fundamental—evidentiary issue highlighted by hate crime studies is that of what is, or should be, the *minimum amount of hate or bias* required for an offence to fit the hate crime paradigm and for hate crime law to apply to a concrete case. Brudholm observes two opposite positions in that regard. According to the most restrictive stance the crime must be motivated or caused *solely* by hate. The less restrictive (and more common) position states that the crime should be caused *at least in part* by hate (Brudholm, 2015, pp. 86–87).

The first stance reflects a narrow concept of hate crime. It includes only the so-called mission crimes committed by hate-filled extremists, which in turn constitute only a minority of overall hate crime incidents. The second approach covers a wider range of bias-motivated crimes, particularly the so-called thrill, retaliatory and defensive hate crimes. Research shows that most hate crime offenders are moved by a number of different motivations, among which hate or bias plays only a partial—albeit usually fundamental—role (see Sect. 2.2.1 above).

A law adopting the more inclusive position can, in turn, require that the hate or bias element be just one among other motivations, *or* the predominant or substantial motivation behind the offence. In literature, this second option is commonly preferred. The *substantial motivation* requirement appears, in fact, to be a necessary boundary for the hate crime concept not to lose its fundamental characteristic and to keep the scope of hate crime law reasonably circumscribed. Lawrence, for example, suggests that "to constitute a bias crime, the bias motivation must be a substantial motivation for the perpetrator's criminal conduct. We might assess the role of bias motivation in a crime by asking the 'but for' question: but for the ethnicity of the victim, would this crime have been committed?" (Lawrence, 1999, p. 10).

Across the OSCE region the first, more restrictive position explicitly requiring hate to be the *sole motivation* of the crime has not been identified in any of the hate crime laws adopted by participating States.

Many statutes actually do not usually mention hate, bias or hostility in their provisions, but simply require some kind of connection to exist between the criminal act and the victim's protected characteristic. In these legislations, therefore, the existence of multiple motives will be addressed by prosecutors and courts under the applicable general criminal law provisions. The Penal Code of Luxembourg, for example, foresees a penalty enhancement for the crimes of violation of the integrity of a corpse and violation or desecration of tombs, graves or monuments erected to the memory of the dead, when they are committed "because of membership or non-membership, real or supposed, of the deceased person to a particular ethnic group, nation, race or religion" (art. 457-2).

Most legislations have adopted a *mixed motive* approach, allowing bias/hate to be just one among the motives behind the commission of a crime. Malta, for instance, provides for the penalty enhancement of the punishment foreseen for the base offence when this is motivated "wholly or in part by hatred" against a number of protected characteristics (Section 83B of the Criminal Code of Malta). On the same line, the Belgian Penal Code uses the more nuanced expression "when one of the motives of the crime or offence is hatred against, contempt for or hostility to a person on the grounds of …" (art. 377-bis).

Within the *mixed motive* approach, the ODHIR (2009, p. 54) further observes that many United States' courts apply the *substantial factor* requirement, meaning that hate or prejudice must be the predominant motive behind the crime. For example, California's Criminal Code defines hate crime as a "criminal act committed, in whole or in part, because of one or more ... actual or perceived characteristics of the victim" as listed therein (Section 422.55). It further specifies that, "when multiple concurrent motives exist, the prohibited bias must be a substantial factor in bringing about the particular result. There is no requirement that the bias be a main factor, or that the crime would not have been committed but for the actual or perceived characteristic" (Section 422.56).

Classification of the Amount of Hate under the Concept of Hate Crime Adopted

Among the different evidence-related issues examined above, the most important requirement is the one concerning the amount of bias or hate motivation that shall be proved to apply a hate crime provision. Although in practice many hate crime laws do not *explicitly* mention hate or prejudice, this element nevertheless constitutes the core factor that differentiates bias offences from parallel crimes. Furthermore, the different drafting approaches here identified can be easily linked to different conceptions of hate crimes, and can be thus classified under a wide, intermediate or narrow understanding of hate crime, respectively (Table 2.3).

Table 2.3 Tier III: Amount of hate or bias

Narrow understanding of hate crime concept	Intermediate understanding of hate crime concept	Wide understanding of hate crime concept
• Crime motivated *only* by hate	• Mixed motives—Crime motivated *mostly* by hate	• Mixed motives–Crime motivated *in part* by hate

3.2.4 Tier IV: Nexus Between the Offender's Mental Attitude and the Offence

The Hostility Animus and the Discriminatory Selection Models

To be normatively adequate under a general definition of hate crimes, the nexus between the bias component and the offence shall be expressed either as a mental attitude of the perpetrator "that contributes to the explanation of the offence (such as an intention, a motive or a disposition), or something [the offender conveys] through or in connection with the offence" (Brax & Munthe, 2013, pp. 45–46). In other words, the "negatively biased, disparaging and/or discriminatory attitude on part of the offender towards a social group to which the offender links the victim" must be "in some qualified way connected to, play a role in or explain the occurrence of the crime" (Brax & Munthe, 2013, p. 5).

As to how hate crime provisions differ as regards this particular variable, Brudholm recalls Lawrence's distinction (Lawrence, 1999, p. 9), according to which we can distinguish "roughly" between hate crime law that focuses either on the emotional attitude of the offender (*racial/hostility animus model*) or on the intentional selection of the target because of a protected characteristic (*victim selection model*) (Brudholm, 2015, p. 86). Lawrence has elaborated the two categories after examining US bias crime provisions and observing how "the mental state of the perpetrator is critical in distinguishing" them (Lawrence, 1999, p. 29). Although Lawrence's analysis only focussed on racist crimes, his reflections can be widened to encompass bias crimes against other social groups or personal characteristics.

On the one hand, the *discriminatory selection* model frames hate crimes with regard to the mere *intentional* discriminatory selection of the victim by the offenders, regardless of their actual motive (Lawrence, 1999, p. 30). For example, Wisconsin's hate crime statute provides for the enhancement of the maximum sentence and/or fine for certain crimes of violence if offenders "*[i]ntentionally selects*" their victim "*because of* the [victim's] race, religion, color, disability, sexual orientation, national origin or ancestry" (§ 939.645 of Wisconsin Statutes and Annotations).

North Macedonia considers as hate crimes those criminal acts that are committed "entirely or partially *because of* the actual or presumed characteristic of the victim that refers to race, colour of skin, nationality, ethnic belonging, religion or religious belief, mental or physical disability, sex, gender identity, sexual orientation or political affiliation" (art. 112(41) of the Penal Code). These provisions thus merely require the intentional selection of the victim on the basis of one of the protected characteristics listed therein.

The *hostility animus* model, on the other hand, considers an offence as a hate crime precisely because of the perpetrator's hostile animus against the victim's group. Thus, hostile animus is considered central in the offender's motivation for committing the offence (Lawrence, 1999, p. 30). According to Lawrence, this model

> is consonant with the classical understanding of prejudice as involving more than differential treatment on the basis of the victim's [characteristic]. This understanding of prejudice … requires that the offender have committed the crime with some measure of hostility toward the victim's [social] group and/or toward the victim because he is part of that group. (Lawrence, 1999, p. 35)

Belgium's hate crime provisions, for example, enhance the penalty "when one of the motives of the crime or offence is hatred against, contempt for or hostility to a person on the grounds of" one of the protected characteristics.[20]

Many hate crime provisions, however, do not fit exactly one of the two models. In this regard, Brax and Munthe argue that Lawrence's binary distinction does not fully capture the way different hate crime concepts have been developed in literature as regards the nexus between the bias and the crime. By using different types of nexus as distinguishing criteria, they then propose to classify hate crimes, and hate crime law, into six broad categories, depending on whether the crime is

[20] Belgium's Penal code, arts. 377-bis, 405-quater, 422-quater, 438-bis, 453-bis, 514-bis, 532-bis.

> (1) Motivated by hate/bias/prejudice; (2) Caused/explained by hate/bias/prejudice; (3) Intended by the offender to cause a certain harm/have a certain effect more generally (e.g. incite fear); (4) Causing/risking additional harm of a particular sort; (5) Involving a discriminatory selection of victims; (6) Involving expressions of hate/bias/prejudice towards the victim's group. (Brax & Munthe, 2013, p. 20)

While the first three criteria fall under the hostile animus model, the fifth corresponds to the discriminatory selection model, and the fourth and sixth ones belong to either models depending on the concrete interpretations given to the terms *hostile animus* and *discriminatory selection* (Brax & Munthe, 2013, pp. 21–22). These more detailed categories raise, in turn, a number of further issues. They are abstract reconstructions of a wider number of hate crime concepts and laws, and they allow for further internal variations. Moreover, although these concepts are related, they do not necessarily have the same scope, and "they may sometimes pull in blatantly opposite directions. An action that is not motivated by bias may nevertheless express bias, for example" (Brax & Munthe, 2013, p. 20).

In the United States, for example, bias crime statutes often employ the expression "crime committed *because of* a protected characteristic of the victim" (Lawrence, 1999, pp. 35–36). They do so either by mentioning only the *because of* connection—which requires "only that the defendant has committed the parallel crime and that the crime be committed because of the victim's" characteristic—or augmenting this "element of the bias crime with an additional element of 'maliciousness'" (Lawrence, 1999, pp. 35–36) or using the motivational phrasing "intent to harass and intimidate" (Pezzella, 2017, p. 46). An example of the first kind can be found in the Criminal Code of California, which defines hate crimes as criminal acts "committed, in whole or in part, because of one or more of the following actual or perceived characteristics of the victim" (Section 422.55). The Revised Code of Washington, conversely, requires harassment to be committed "maliciously and intentionally" because of the perpetrator's perception of one of the victim's protected characteristics (Section 9A.36.080). These formulations can hardly be straightforwardly classified into one of the two models proposed by Lawrence. Nonetheless, the *simple because of* model presents more similarities with the discriminatory selection model as "it looks to an actor's actual discriminatory choice rather than to his reasons for making that choice" (Lawrence, 1999, pp. 35–36). On the other hand, the formulation of *because of* requiring also proof of *maliciousness* seems more consistent with the hostility animus model, as it suggests "a greater concern with the motivation of the offender" (Lawrence, 1999, pp. 36–37). However, this is ultimately a matter of interpretation; even a *because of* provision requiring maliciousness can be ultimately construed to be consistent with a discriminatory selection model (Lawrence, 1999, pp. 36–37).[21]

Each of the two models proposed by Lawrence reflects, in turn, a different concept of hate crime and leads to different outcomes in terms of the feasibility of the investigations and prosecution of these crimes. The hostility selection model appears to cover a narrow concept of hate crime, in which the hate/hostility component plays a pivotal role. By recalling Levin, McDevitt, Bennett and Iganski's studies (see Sect. 2.2.1 above), while this model seems more consonant the popular idea of what a hate crime is (ODHIR, 2009, p. 47), it encompasses only a small number of hate crimes, namely those committed by hate-filled perpetrators in the context of the so-called *mission* hate crimes. Moreover, this typology may be difficult to implement in practice. These provisions require evidence that the offender has acted out of hate or hostility towards a given social group as an element of the offence, which is very hard to prove (ODHIR, 2009, p. 47). The discriminatory selection model, on the other hand, has a broader scope and should be easier to apply. It merely "requires a causal link between the characteristic and the offender's conduct," without the need of assessing the offender's mental attitude (ODHIR, 2009, p. 48). This typology can thus reach "those offenders who harbored no hostility but selected their victims based on prejudices or stereotyped information about victim vulnerabilities" (ODHIR, 2009, p. 49).

[21] Lawrence refers to, and comments, the Washington Supreme Court's judgment Washington v. Talley, 858 P. 2d 217 (Wash. 1993), which reviewed Section §9A.36.080 of the Revised Code of Washington (Lawrence, 1999, pp. 36–37).

Table 2.4 Tier IV: Nexus between mental attitude and offence

Narrow understanding of hate crime concept	Wide understanding of hate crime concept
• **Hostility animus model** Law that requires the crime to be: • Motivated by hate/bias/prejudice • Caused/explained by hate/bias/prejudice • Intended by the offender to cause a certain harm/have a certain effect more generally (e.g. incite fear) • Committed *because of* a protected characteristic of the victim and with maliciousness	• **Discriminatory selection model** Law that requires the crime to: • Involve a discriminatory selection of victims • Be committed *because of* a protected characteristic of the victim
Depending on how the notion of hostile animus is interpreted, also those provisions that require the crime to: • Cause/risk additional harm of a particular sort • Involve expressions of hate/bias/prejudice towards the victim's group	Depending on how the notion of discriminatory selection is interpreted, also those provisions that require the crime to: • Cause/risk additional harm of a particular sort • Involve expressions of hate/bias/prejudice towards the victim's group

Classification of the Nexus between the Bias Element and the Offence under the Concept of Hate Crime Adopted

To wrap up the above thoughts, the wording used by hate crime law to express the connection between the bias element and the crime can be ultimately classified according to a narrow and a wide understanding of the hate crime concept, respectively (Table 2.4).

4 Conclusions

In this chapter, we elaborated a framework to examine hate crime law in a way that is not limited to strict legal issues. The framework embeds and applies interdisciplinary research carried out in hate crime studies on the concept and phenomenology of bias crimes.

To this end, Brudholm's and the ODHIR's studies have been used as starting points to identify and develop four main variables. These represent the four main characteristics of bias crime law, which reflect the most important decisions that lawmakers have to make when drafting hate crime law.

Each variable has been further elaborated by drawing on relevant criminological, sociological and legal literature on the field. A number of different possible ways in which each variable can—abstractly—been implemented have been highlighted and discussed. Moreover, concrete examples of hate crime provisions in force in the OSCE region accompany the theoretical options. This pursues the twofold aim of linking the normative discussion carried out so far to the practical challenges that lawmakers have to face when drafting bias crime law, and to classify these provisions under the four variables previously identified.

By paraphrasing Brudholm's explanation on how to implement his framework to analyse hate crime concepts, the present work argues that we can use our concept of hate crime law to map these laws. As shown in the table below (Table 2.5), the scope of the implementation of each of the four variables can be positioned on a line leading from a narrow to a wide understanding of that specific characteristic of bias crime law. If a given statute or provision "can be positioned on the far left of [the table], we have in view the narrowest conception. It correlates only to certain substantial offenses," directed towards a group displaying a history of, or being currently subject to, oppression and discrimination, which are motivated solely by hatred, and in which the perpetrator's mental attitude in committing the crime is defined only by her or his hostility towards the social group the victim belongs to. "On the far right of [the table], we find a conception that accommodates a larger group of offenses. It applies to any crime, and includes a wide range of protected characteristics." It requires the crime to be committed only in part by hate, and the nexus between the bias motive and the crime can consist of the mere selection of the victim because of a protected feature (Brudholm, 2015, p. 88). Moreover, hate crime law can combine the four variables according to the different concepts of each variable explicitly or implicitly adopted by legislators. Therefore, a given law cannot usually be classified under a single model, but will belong instead to two or more models.

Table 2.5 Hate crime law framework

	Understandings of hate crime concept		
	Narrow	Intermediate	Wide
TIER I Drafting method	• Substantive offence	• Specific aggravating circumstances	• General aggravating circumstances • Other sentencing rules that allow bias motives to be considered
TIER II Protected grounds	• Only some (identity politics) characteristics (short, closed list)	• Many characteristics but closed list	• Many characteristics and open list
TIER III Amount of bias motive required	• Crime motivated *only* by bias/hate	• Mixed motives: Crime motivated *mostly* by bias/hate	• Mixed motives: Crime motivated *in part* by bias/hate
TIER IV Nexus between bias and crime	• Hostility Animus model	Not applicable	• Discriminatory Selection model

But what is the best approach to follow? If we want the law to reflect to the largest possible extent the phenomenon of hate crimes and be ready to adapt to social changes, the four variables should probably be drafted following the wide understanding of hate crime. However, these are not the only aspects that should be taken into consideration. Rule of law constraints prevent the criminal law from being imprecise and indeterminate and from applying *in malam partem* analogy in criminal law. There are also legitimacy boundaries that require the legislator to justify the creation or expansion of criminal law under a number of different criteria. Drafting methods that can be considered feasible and effective from a practical point of view may not be justified if analysed under one or more principles of criminalisation. Chapter 3 will examine these issues in detail.

References

Al-Hakim, M. (2015). Making a Home for the Homeless in Hate Crime Legislation. *Journal of Interpersonal Violence, 30*(10), 1755–1781.

Allport, G. W. (1958). *The Nature of Prejudice*. Doubleday & Co.

Anti-Defamation League. (2021). *Pyramid of Hate*. Retrieved July 25, 2022, from https://www.adl.org/sites/default/files/pyramid-of-hate-web-english_1.pdf

Associazione 21 Luglio (2022). *L'Esclusione nel Tempo del Covid. Comunità Rom negli Insediamenti Formali e Informali in Italia*. Retrieved July 25, 2022, from https://www.21luglio.org/2018/wp-content/uploads/2021/10/Rapporto_2021_web_con_indice.pdf.

Bárd, P. (2020). Prerequisites for the Effective Fight against Hate Crimes. *Hungarian Journal of Legal Studies, 61*(3), 255–268.

Brax, D. (2015, December 22). On Hate Crime and Terrorism. *The International Network for Hate Studies*. http://www.internationalhatestudies.com/on-hate-crime-and-terrorism/

Brax, D., & Munthe, C. (2013). *Introduction to the Philosophy of Hate Crime. When Law and Hate Collide*. University of Gothenburg. Retrieved July 25, 2022, from https://www.uclan.ac.uk/research/activity/perspectives-on-hate-crime

Brudholm, T. (2015). Hate Crimes and Human Rights Violations. *Journal of Applied Philosophy, 32*(1), 82–97.

Chakraborti, N., & Garland, J. (2012). Reconceptualizing Hate Crime Victimization through the Lens of Vulnerability and 'Difference'. *Theoretical Criminology, 16*(4), 499–514.

Craig-Henderson, K., & Sloan, L. R. (2003). After the Hate: Helping Psychologists Help Victims of Racist Hate Crime. *Clinical Psychology: Science and Practice, 10*(4), 481–490.

Deloughery, K., King, R. D., & Asal, V. (2012). Close Cousins or Distant Relatives? The Relationship between Terrorism and Hate Crime. *Crime & Delinquency, 58*(5), 663–688.

Dimock, S., & Al-Hakim, M. (2012). Hate as an Aggravating Factor in Sentencing. *New Criminal Law Review (Formerly Known as Buffalo Criminal Law Review), 15*(4), 572–611.

Dubber, M. D., & Hörnle, T. (2014). *Criminal Law: A Comparative Approach*. Oxford University Press.

FRA (European Union Agency for Fundamental Rights). (2018). *Hate Crime Recording and Data Collection Practice Across the EU*. Publications Office of the European Union.

Gião Hanek, A. (2017). International Legal Framework for Hate Crimes: Which Law for the 'New' Countries? In A. Haynes, J. Schweppe, & S. Taylor (Eds.), *Critical Perspectives on Hate Crime*. Palgrave Macmillan. https://doi.org/10.1057/978-1-137-52667-0_24

Goldberg, D. T. (1995). Afterword: Hate or Power? In R. Kirk Whillok & D. Slayden (Eds.), *Hate Speech* (pp. 267–276). Sage.

Hall, N. (2013). *Hate Crime*. Routledge, Taylor & Francis Group.

Hamm, M. S. (Ed.). (1994). *Hate Crime: International Perspectives on Causes and Control*. Anderson Publications.

Hare, I. (1997). Legislating against Hate—The Legal Response to Bias Crimes. *Oxford Journal of Legal Studies, 17*(3), 415–440.

Harel, A., & Parchomovsky, G. (1999). On Hate and Equality. *Yale Law Journal, 109*, 507–539.

Iganski, P. (2008). *'Hate Crime' and the City*. Policy Press.

Iganski, P., & Lagou, S. (2015). Hate Crimes Hurt Some More than Others: Implications for the Just Sentencing of Offenders. *Journal of Interpersonal Violence, 30*(10), 1696–1718.

Jacobs, J. B., & Potter, K. (1998). *Hate Crimes: Criminal Law & Identity Politics*. Oxford University Press.

Jamel, J. (2018). *Transphobic Hate Crime*. Springer International Publishing.

Kauppinen, A. (2015). Hate and Punishment. *Journal of Interpersonal Violence, 30*(10), 1719–1737.

King, R. D., DeMarco, L. M., & VandenBerg, R. J. (2016). Similar from a Distance. In G. LaFree & J. D. Freilich (Eds.), *The Handbook of the Criminology of Terrorism* (pp. 385–401). Wiley Blackwell.

Krueger, A. B., & Maleckova, J. (2003). Education, Poverty and Terrorism: Is There a Causal Connection? *Journal of Economic Perspective, 17*(4), 119–144.

Laurenzo Copello, P. (2019). La Manipulación de los Delitos de Odio. In E. Pomares Cintas, J. L. Fuentes Osorio, G. Portilla Contreras, & F. Velásquez Velásquez (Eds.), *Un Juez Para la Democracia: Libro Homenaje a Perfecto Andrés Ibáñez* (pp. 453–468). Dykinson.

Lawrence, F. M. (1993). Resolving the Hate Crimes/Hate Speech Paradox: Punching Bias Crimes and Protecting Racist Speech. *Notre Dame Law Review, 68*(4), 673–721.

Lawrence, F. M. (1999). *Punishing Hate: Bias Crimes under American Law.* Harvard University Press.
Levin, J., & McDevitt, J. (1993). *Hate Crimes: The Rising Tide of Bigotry and Bloodshed.* Plenum Press.
Levin, J., & Rabrenovic, G. (2009). Hate as Cultural Justification for Violence. In B. Levin (Ed.), *Understanding and Defining Hate Crimes, 1* (pp. 41–53). Praeger.
Mačkić, J. (2018). *Proving Discriminatory Violence at the European Court of Human Rights.* Brill Nijhoff.
Mason, G. (2007). Hate Crime as a Moral Category: Lessons from the Snowtown Case. *Australian & New Zealand Journal of Criminology, 40*(3), 249–271.
Mason, G. (2014). Victim Attributes in Hate Crime Law: Difference and the Politics of Justice. *British Journal of Criminology, 54*(2), 161–179.
Mason-Bish, H. (2014). Beyond the Silo: Rethinking Hate Crime and Intersectionality. In N. Hall, A. Corb, P. Giannasi, J. G. D. Grieve, & L. Neville (Eds.), *The Routledge International Handbook on Hate Crime* (pp. 24–33). Routledge Handbooks Online.
McDevitt, J., Levin, J., & Bennett, S. (2002). Hate Crime Offenders: An Expanded Typology. *Journal of Social Issues, 58*(2), 303–317.
Nussbaum, M. C. (2006). Poverty and Human Functioning: Capabilities as Fundamental Entitlements. In D. B. Grusky & R. Kanbur (Eds.), *Poverty and Inequality* (pp. 47–75). Stanford University Press.
ODHIR (Office for Democratic Institutions and Human Rights). (2009). *Hate Crime Laws—A Practical Guide.* Organization for Security and Co-operation in Europe.
ODHIR (Office for Democratic Institutions and Human Rights). (2012). *Understanding Hate Crimes: A Handbook for Albania.* Organization for Security and Co-operation in Europe.
ODHIR (Office for Democratic Institutions and Human Rights). (2013). *Hate Crimes in the OSCE Region—Incidents and Responses: Annual Report for 2012.* Organization for Security and Co-operation in Europe.
Pejchal, V. (2020). *Hate Speech and Human Rights in Eastern Europe. Legislating for Divergent Values.* Routledge.
Perry, B. (2001). *In the Name of Hate: Understanding Hate Crimes.* Routledge.
Perry, B. (2005). A Crime by Any Other Name: The Semantics of 'Hate'. *Journal of Hate Studies, 4*(1), 121.
Pezzella, F. S. (2017). *Hate Crime Statutes: A Public Policy and Law Enforcement Dilemma.* Springer International Publishing.

Pezzella, F. S., Fetzer, M. D., & Keller, T. (2019). The Dark Figure of Hate Crime Underreporting. *American Behavioral Scientist.* https://doi.org/10.1177/0002764218823844

Reidy, D. A. (2002). Hate Crimes, Oppression, and Legal Theory. *Public Affairs Quarterly, 16*(3), 259–285.

Rosga, A. (1999). Policing the State. *Georgetown Journal of Gender and the Law, 1*, 145–171.

Schweppe, J. (2012). Defining Characteristics and Politicising Victims: A Legal Perspective. *Journal of Hate Studies, 10*(1), 173–198.

Sen, A. (1999). *Development as Freedom*. Oxford University Press.

Stefaniak, A., & Winiewski, M. (2022). Differentiating Between Direct and Indirect Hate Crime: Results from Poland. *Journal of Social and Political Psychology, 10*(1), 86–105. https://doi.org/10.5964/jspp.9285

Swiebel, J., & Van der Veur, D. (2009). Hate Crimes Against Lesbian, Gay, Bisexual and Transgender Persons and the Policy Response of International Governmental Organisations. *Netherlands Quarterly of Human Rights, 27*(4), 485–524.

Turner, L., Whittle, S., & Combs, R. (2009). *Transphobic Hate Crime in the European Union*. Press for Change.

United Nations. (2019). *United Nations Strategy and Plan of Action on Hate Speech*. Retrieved June 24, 2022, from https://www.un.org/en/genocideprevention/documents/advising-and-mobilizing/Action_plan_on_hate_speech_EN.pdf

Weisburd, S., & Levin, B. (1994). On the Basis of Sex: Recognizing Gender-Based Bias Crimes. *Stanford Law & Policy Review, 5*, 21–47.

Wickes, R. L., Pickering, S., Mason, G., Maher, J. M., & McCulloch, J. (2016). From Hate to Prejudice: Does the New Terminology of Prejudice Motivated Crime Change Perceptions and Reporting Actions? *British Journal of Criminology, 56*(2), 239–255. https://doi.org/10.1093/bjc/azv041

Wolff, J., & De-Shalit, A. (2007). *Disadvantage*. Oxford University Press.

3

Analysis of Abstract Models of Hate Crime Law

1 Introduction

In Chap. 2 we developed a four-tier framework to analyse hate crime law according to four main variables, which represent the four main characteristics of these pieces of law. The present chapter will analyse this framework, as a whole and in its constitutive parts, to provide an answer to the following question: is hate crime law considered *in abstracto* (i.e. regardless of any specific, concrete legislation) *prima facie* legitimate under a criminalisation theory that embeds both Anglo-American and European substantive criminalisation principles? In other words, are penalty enhancements for crimes committed out of bias justified?

To answer this question, this work will examine the hate crime law framework through the lens of a theoretical approach that, in a previous work, I labelled "Integrated Legitimacy Test" (ILT) (Micheletto, 2021). This test has been elaborated by merging the two most relevant criminalisation theories in Western law: the Anglo-American harm principle, and the German *Rechtsgut* theory compounded with the Italian *offensività*

L. Micheletto, *Assessing Hate Crime Laws*, Palgrave Hate Studies,
https://doi.org/10.1007/978-3-031-19020-9_3

principle.[1] To justify the criminalisation of a given conduct, the ILT requires evidence and strong arguments indicating that the conduct is wrongful and it causes serious harm to a standard victim's quality-of-life interests. In the case of hate crime law, to justify the legitimacy of the enhanced sentences it must be shown that bias crimes are significantly worse than their parallel counterparts—the base offences committed without a bias motive. What one must analyse here is, therefore, the legitimacy of the criminalisation of hate crimes' bias component—the very element that distinguishes them from parallel offences.

To do so, the Test is applied to assess the legitimacy of the different models of hate crime law we have identified in Chap. 2. First, it examines a number of legitimacy issues that are either common to all tiers of the hate crime law framework or that can be analysed only by considering bias offences and hate crime law as a whole. Here, the subject of the analysis is a default model of hate crime provision corresponding to a narrow concept of hate crime in which (i) bias is the only motive and (ii) its connection with the offence falls under the Hostile Animus model. Second, each of the four tiers of the hate crime law framework is examined separately. This allows additionally refining the legitimacy exercise, by identifying which of the three possible understandings (narrow, intermediate and wide) of the four-tier framework's components passes the legitimacy test.

The choice of developing a new paradigm to examine the legitimacy of hate crime law stems from the analysis of the criticisms that surround its "parent" theories, as well as from the preliminary review of hate crime literature. As to the first aspect, merging Anglo-American and European criminalisation doctrines and further elaborating their constitutive elements helps in overcoming some of the issues that weaken their ability to normatively limit overcriminalisation (see Micheletto, 2021). On its part, hate crime scholarship has followed different paths to examine hate crime law. In the Anglo-Saxon context, hate studies have adopted an interdisciplinary perspective that focuses on the harms of hate crime. European research has followed instead a more traditional legal approach that revolves

[1] The German term "*Rechtsgut*" is usually translated as "legal good" in English. The Italian word "*offensività*" can be roughly translated as "injuriousness" or "harmfulness". The Italian concept has been adopted by Spanish and Portuguese legal theories, which have translated it as "*ofensividad/lesividad*" and "*ofensividade/lesividade*", respectively.

around the compatibility of hate crime law with constitutional principles and international human rights standards. Both perspectives have their merits and must be taken into consideration. In this context, the ILT allows one to address hate crime and hate crime law from a comprehensive viewpoint that embeds the two approaches and offers a more inclusive and analytical understanding of this criminal phenomenon and of the criminal law measures that can be implemented to tackle it.

The ILT and, more in general, criminalisation principles, are philosophical constructions that aim to normatively guide the criminalisation process. However, putting them in practice is not so simple. The ILT (along with the harm principle, the *Rechtsgut* doctrine, and the *offensività* principle) requires empirical evidence that the conduct at stake causes significant harm. Therefore, to implement the test the present work relies on the growing number of criminological and victimological studies on the impact of bias offences on direct victims and targeted communities. However, these studies cover only a small number of countries.[2] Some of them—the oldest ones, at least—also suffer from a number of methodological problems, due in particular to the small sample of respondents and lack of proper comparison with non-bias motivated offences. Unfortunately, there appears to be no studies of this kind conducted in the Italian context. The present work is well aware of these limitations, which are nevertheless believed not to be insurmountable. A number of strong trends and patterns have been identified across different countries, which make the results applicable also in the Italian context—with some caveats and with the urgent need to be compounded with local data and analysis.

2 The Concept of *Prima Facie* Legitimacy and the Integrated Legitimacy Test (ILT)

2.1 Philosophical Foundations

The philosophical foundations of the present work are liberalism and humanism in the context of a democratic society based on respect of

[2] Most studies have been conducted in Canada, the United Kingdom and the United States. Specific studies have been carried out also in Australia, Latvia, North Macedonia and Sweden.

human rights, individual freedoms, diversity and solidarity.[3] One of the main reasons behind the adoption of a liberal approach lies in the very nature of hate crimes. These are offences usually committed against members of minority groups, or against members of groups which, albeit cannot be described as minorities proper, have a history of oppression and discrimination, or are currently oppressed and discriminated against in a wider sense. Crimes motivated by hate or bias are usually the tip of an iceberg, the main part of which is constituted by discriminatory attitudes, segregation, hate speech, and victimised groups with little or no voice in the public space. The progressive version of Anglo-American liberalism that has been adopted by numerous criminalisation scholars (Feinberg, von Hirsch, Simester and Peršak, as well as Italian authors Fiandaca, Francolini and Forti) encompasses a pluralistic concept of society, and is aware of the danger that the tyranny of the majority may cause (Francolini, 2014, 34–35).

The present research adopts an *external* and *normative* concept of *prima facie* legitimacy. It is chiefly based on the assessment of philosophical principles along with the empirical analysis of the phenomenon under study. Its underpinning premise is the three-step filtering procedure elaborated by Schonsheck and Peršak to determine whether the criminalisation of a given conduct is justified. By drawing on Schonsheck's filtering approach (Schonsheck, 1994), Peršak has built the following model of ideal criminalisation process (Peršak, 2007, 92–94; Peršak, 2018, 25–28). We can imagine the criminalisation procedure as a funnel where the proposed criminal provision has to pass "successively and successfully" (Schonsheck, 1994, 25) through three filters: the so-called *Principles* Filter, the *Presumptions* Filter and the *Pragmatics* Filter. At the first, *Principles* filter level "the legislator should determine whether the action in question falls within the moral authority of the state and should therefore contain the main substantive criminalisation principle or principles" (Peršak, 2018, 26). The second *Presumptions* filter includes "the following, essentially normative, limiting factors: the rule of law requirements (including human rights), principles of ultima ratio and of legality, other

[3] This section summarises the contents of a previous article that I published in the European Journal of Crime, Criminal Law and Criminal Justice (Brill) in December 2021 (Micheletto, 2021).

constitutional constraints, and quite possibly also … Jareborg's 'humanity principle'" (Peršak, 2018, 27). Finally, the third, *Pragmatic* Filter deals with "the financial costs of criminalisation and enforcement, the social costs of criminalisation, Jareborg's 'utility principle', his 'practical feasibility of enforcement' … the effectiveness, the defiance factor, consonance and consistency of the proposed offence with the extant law, and similar" (Peršak, 2018, 27–28).

The concept of legitimacy this work relies on belongs to the very first filter, which calls for the application of substantive criminalisation principles. This study will focus on the issue of whether there are justified reasons to criminalise the bias component of hate crimes, but will not provide a final answer as to whether the State *should* criminalise it. This is the reason why the expression *prima facie* legitimacy is used. It will not be possible to examine in depth other topics concerning pragmatic, positive-law or constitutional, reasons in favour or against hate crime law. However, the four-tier framework that links hate crime law to the underlying phenomenon does not merely serve as a descriptive tool to categorise hate crime law, but also allows for a preliminary analysis of these provisions from a criminological point of view that may well be situated under the third, pragmatic filter of Schonsheck-Peršak's model.

2.2 Substantive Criminalisation Principles and the ILT

Anglo-American and continental European criminal law theories have elaborated two different sets of substantive criminalisation principles to address the question of which conducts could be *prima facie* legitimately criminalised under a liberal perspective. The harm principle, developed by Anglo-American legal philosophers,[4] focuses on the harm that the offender's conduct causes to another human being—thus excluding moralistic and (under certain accounts of the principle) paternalistic consid-

[4] The Anglo-American's approach to criminalisation finds its origins in John Stuart Mill's harm to others principle (originally called Principle of Liberty). Among the many, different versions of the harm principle developed over time, the present work focuses on the accounts elaborated by Feinberg (1984), Peršak (2007), Simester and von Hirsch (2011), and Francolini (2014).

erations from its scope of application. Continental European doctrine has focused instead on the identification of the interests that the State can consider as sufficiently valuable to be protected through criminal law—the so-called legal goods (*Rechtsgüter* in their original German name) (Binding, 1872; Birnbaum, 1834; Von Liszt, 1883). As with most European legal traditions, Italian criminal law theory has adopted the *Rechtsgut* doctrine. However, in an attempt to provide stronger boundaries to its potential for overcriminalisation, it has linked it with the so-called *offensività* principle, which requires the conduct's intrusion into one or more legal goods to be serious enough to justify its criminalisation (Donini, 2013; Fiandaca, 2014; Manes, 2005; Pulitanò, 2015). The Italian approach is now also followed in other European and Latin-American jurisdictions (Micheletto, 2021, 245).

From a functional and operational perspective, the harm principle can be schematise as requiring the fulfilment of four steps: (1) the identification and measurement of the non-normative (harm *stricto sensu*) and normative (wrongfulness) aspects of harm. This step implies the identification of the affected interest, the assessment of whether there has been a "set-back" of that interest, and the establishment of whether the harm has been produced wrongfully; (2) the establishment of a causal link between the conduct and the harm and the identification of the type of harm involved; (3) the identification of the "others" and the "victims" affected by the crime; and, in those hard cases in which the establishment of serious harm is not straightforward, (4) the application of mediating maxims that can be linked to the non-normative or to the normative elements of the harm principle respectively (see Feinberg, 1984; Peršak, 2007; Simester & von Hirsch, 2011).

In comparison with the harm principle's structure, the legal goods-*offensività* paradigm is much less elaborated. It consists of two phases: (1) first, we shall identify the legal goods affected by the conduct and determine whether they are important enough to warrant criminal law protection; and (2) we shall measure the "*offensività*" of the conduct with respect to the identified legal goods (see Donini, 2013; Manes, 2005; Pulitanò, 2015).

A thorough analysis and comparison of the Anglo-American and continental European criminalisation approaches has shown that, in spite of their "historical, conceptual, and practical differences … they share a number of key features, particularly from a functional and operational perspective" (Micheletto, 2021, 243). More specifically, two important elements have been identified in both theories. First, they both focus on the identification of the "legitimate interests" that the conduct intrudes upon. Second, both the *offensività* principle and the harm principle encompass the principle *nullum crimen sine iniuria*, which demands that a conduct can be legitimately proscribed only if it causes "at least some degree of harm" (Micheletto, 2021, 252). The results of this comparison have allowed the development of a test that merges both theories, the Integrated Legitimacy Test (ILT).

The ILT has been conceived as a succession of three interrelated stages (and a possible intermediate step). First, we identify the standard victim's legitimate interests affected by the conduct. Second, we measure the degree of intrusion into these interests and the level of the resulting standard harm (in its non-normative aspect). The first and second steps apply Peršak's model based on the concept of quality of life (2014) to identify and classify the legitimate interests that the conduct affects, and to gauge the resulting criminal harm. In the third step, we determine whether the conduct is wrongful. If the conduct's harmfulness or wrongfulness cannot be clearly established, we apply supplementary criteria (mediating maxims) to reach a convincing conclusion.

The *first stage* thus requires to classify interests into four categories: physical, material, psychological and normative (Peršak, 2014, 234). Each of these groups corresponds to the victim's quality-of-life dimension the criminal conduct intrudes upon.[5] The *physical* dimension corresponds to the concept of physical health and integrity—it is intruded upon whenever the criminal conduct causes a physical injury to the victim. The *material* category refers to economic losses deriving directly from the crime, such as in the offences of theft and robbery, or indirectly, such as the costs of medical expenses following violent crimes. The concept of *psychological* dimension—and of psychological harm—adopted by Peršak

[5] The identification of the quality-of-life categories of interests intruded upon by the criminal conduct is an exercise akin to that of determining what affected interests are important enough to be criminally protected as legal goods under the *Rechtsgut* theory.

is quite specific and narrower than the common understanding of this kind of harm. In fact, she limits it

> to proper harm, meaning that there should be a setback of interest, making the victim 'worse-off'. Temporary offendedness will not do. Psychological harm would therefore include such harms as lingering (longer-term) adverse psychological consequences caused by physical harm (torture) or emotional manipulation (in kidnapping or in domestic violence), effects of stalking, harms arising out of harmful psychological treatments, trauma (Post Traumatic Stress Disorder) … and other similar harms to the psychological quality of life (Peršak, 2014, 235)

Finally, the *normative* dimension includes "(living conditions that respect) widely acknowledged normative standards and values, which allow the individual to pursue his life choices, express himself and engage in meaningful social interactions" (Peršak, 2014, 234–235). It covers a diverse range of interests, such as respect, equal treatment, dignity, autonomy, individuality, and so on. Psychological harm is often a consequence of the infringement of normative interests. Nonetheless, assessing separately these two types of harm allows "to bring out the fact that, both in our ordinary language and in our ordinary moral judgements we differentiate between what we see as psychological harms, and what we object to as violations of …" normative interests (Peršak, 2014, 236).

Once we have identified and classified the protected interests, the *second phase* aims to measure the level of intrusion and thus the conduct's harmfulness. Here, we apply the Italian concept of *offensività* and, again, Peršak's more elaborated quality-of-life model. Peršak endorses von Hirsch and Jareborg's (2005) suggestion to classify "the conduct's level of intrusion into the interest dimensions affected … into four degrees: subsistence, minimal well-being, adequate well-being, standard well-being" (Micheletto, 2021, 259, referring to Von Hirsch & Jareborg, 2005, 203–204). However, instead of the six-level scale they use to categorise the resulting harm, Peršak (2014, 237–238) ranges it into four degrees—mild, moderate, serious and grave/severe levels of harm. The measurement of the conduct's level of harmfulness on the standard victims requires lawmakers to refer to available data on the phenomenon they aim to criminalise. Unless there exists convincing empirical evidence on the seriousness of the conduct's impact on direct and indirect victims, its harmfulness cannot be established.

The *third stage* of the ILT requires to identify and explicitly examine the reasons why the conduct is, or is not, wrongful. According to Simester and von Hirsch, there exist three main cases in which wrongfulness can be observed: (i) *immediate harm* instances—where the victim's legitimate interests are directly affected (Simester & von Hirsch, 2011, 44–46); (ii) *remote harm* cases—"when … the actor's present conduct (though harmless in itself) shows 'normative involvement' with the eventual harmful choices of actors further down the causal chain" (Von Hirsch, 2014, 252); (iii) *offensive conducts*—they can be considered wrongful when the conduct "expresses gross disrespect or lack of consideration towards the victim" (Micheletto, 2021, 260, referring to Simester & von Hirsch, 2011, 100). It is also important to note that "the behaviour's wrongfulness is usually implied when it intrudes upon normative interests. The wrongfulness of the conduct is actually the most important aspect to consider when these are the only (or the main) interest dimensions affected. Here, the conduct is harmful (or more harmful) *also because* it is socially perceived as wrongful" (Micheletto, 2021, 260).

Whenever the harmfulness and/or wrongfulness of the conduct cannot be clearly established, we shall identify and apply Feinberg's *mediating maxims*. These are ancillary rules necessary to properly apply the harm principle "in practical contexts of special kinds and in conditions of uncertainty" (Feinberg, 1984, 187–188). Therefore, they are not a constitutive element of the principle, but are instead "supplementary criteria, some of which represent 'controversial moral decisions and maxims of justice'" (Peršak, 2007, 56). Unlike "Feinberg's account of the harm principle [where] mediating maxims are applied once some form of harm has already been established," under the ILT mediating maxims are used "whenever the harmfulness or wrongfulness of the conduct are uncertain" (Micheletto, 2021, 261).

Both the Anglo-American and European-Continental approaches have been criticised as being unable to provide an ultimate benchmark to analyse the legitimacy of criminalisation (see, among others, Harcourt, 1999; Smith, 2006; Donini, 2013; Fiandaca, 2014). In comparison with the two original theories taken separately, and while by no means immune from possible shortcomings, the ILT constitutes a step forward that allows to overcoming some of their deficiencies. The components of the ILT (in particular, the concepts of legitimate interests, harm and wrongfulness) are conceptualised more in detail than in their parent theories. Moreover, they are closely linked to an openly dialectic assessment of empirical evidence and moral arguments (see Micheletto, 2021, 262). These characteristics make it a suitable tool to analyse the *prima facie* legitimacy of hate crime law. The ILT allows finding a balance between the need to provide sentence ranges that are proportionate to the seriousness of the overall harm caused to standard victims of hate crimes and that of avoiding the use of criminal law when it is not strictly necessary and justified.

3 Application of the ILT to the Default Model of Hate Crime Law

This section applies the ILT to a default model of hate crime law which corresponds to the most common understanding of bias offences. Under this model, bias is the only motive of the crime and its nexus with the base offence is explained by the Hostility Animus model.

Considering this general model first allows us to address a number of issues that are either common to all four tiers of the framework, or that deserve to be preliminary examined as a whole before considering them under each tier. Therefore, we will (i) examine the impact of hate crimes on victims and the kind of harm involved; (ii) gauge the extra harm of hate crimes considered as a whole; (iii) identify and discuss the reasons why these conducts are wrongful; and (iv) if necessary, identify and apply mediating maxims. Carrying out this exercise will mean, in practical terms, applying the ILT to hate crimes (and hate crime law) overall considered, before turning to the legitimacy assessment of their more specific features.

3.1 How Much Harm Does Hate Crimes' Bias Element Cause?

The first stage of the ILT foresees the identification of the interest dimensions affected by the conduct at stake, and the measurement of the level of intrusion. As we have seen, what conceptually distinguishes hate crimes from ordinary crimes is the perpetrator's selection of the victim on the basis of one or more characteristics. This means that, apart from the legal good/legitimate interest endangered by the commission of the base crime (life, physical integrity, property, and so on), the bias element of hate crimes may affect other interests. In particular, the interest categories that appear, at first sight, to be intruded upon are the psychological and normative ones. Although the physical dimension is not directly affected, it may be so *indirectly* under certain circumstances; this in turn has a bearing on the other dimensions affected. On the other hand, hate crimes do not seem to further affect in a relevant way those interests pertaining to the material dimension of Peršak's quality of life approach, which will not be discussed. [6]

Iganski conceptualises the harm of hate crimes as waves. They spread from the initial, direct victim, to the initial victim's group in the neighbourhood, to the initial victim's group beyond the neighbourhood, to other targeted communities, and, finally, to societal norms and values (Iganski, 2001, 628; 629). Hate crime specialists, however, usually identify and examine only three, simplified levels of harm: that affecting the direct victim, the group the direct victim belongs to, and society in general (see, for example, Weinstein, 1992; Perry & Alvi, 2012; Pezzella & Fetzer, 2017). The degree of intrusion into the interest at issue also depends on the "nature of the victim's experience" (Verdun-Jones & Rossiter, 2010, 616). We will speak of *primary* victimisation when the victims have "personally suffered the consequences of a crime"

[6] It could be argued that, as a consequence of the physical, psychological and normative harm suffered, hate crime victims also experience a more significant economic loss than victims of parallel offences. However, no empirical data has been found in this regard and specific research on this topic would therefore be welcome.

(Verdun-Jones & Rossiter, 2010, 616); *secondary*[7] or *indirect* victimisation, with regard to "the effects of a criminal victimization on the family and friends (loved ones) of a primary or direct victim—the person to whom the criminal event occurred" (Wilson, 2009, 241–142; Condry, 2010, 222); and *vicarious* victimisation, in relation to the "psychological, behavioral, and physiological impact of observing or learning of the violence or crime perpetrated upon others," particularly as regards communities and groups with a history of victimisation (Wilson, 2009, 285).

The harm hate crimes would cause to society is an issue that several authors have raised (e.g. Iganski, 2001; Perry, 2015; Weinstein, 1992). In particular, these crimes would increase hostility and separation between different social groups, and undermine democratic values. Moreover, some studies suggest that bias offences would trigger retaliation and desire for revenge. This would, in turn, increase the level of violence in society (for a review of extant research on the matter, see Williams & Tregidga, 2014, 952) and thus, according to some, constitute a further public health risk (Dunbar et al., 2005, 15). Despite the appeal and reasonableness of these conclusions, the scope of the studied target (society) is very wide; carrying out methodologically sound and consistent empirical research in this field is thus very difficult. For the purpose of the present work, therefore, the possible harm hate crimes cause to society at large will not be considered to gauge the overall harm they produce.

3.1.1 Physical Dimension

One of the main arguments in favour of a penalty enhancement for hate crimes perpetrators is that these crimes are often more violent and cause more physical injuries than parallel, non-bias motivated offences. In other words, they would intrude more severely upon the interest to physical integrity of victims. This is probably the base dimension of one's

[7] In victimology studies, the concept of *secondary victimisation* is defined and used in three different ways: (i) to distinguish the status of primary victim, secondary victim, tertiary victim or indirect victim; (ii) to identify those processes that cause further victimisation or compound the victim's feelings of victimisation; and (iii) as the consequence of a social reaction to "a primary victim's status that leads to that status becoming entrenched and central to that person's identity" (Condry, 2010, 219–220). Here, we will use this expression in its first meaning.

quality of life. Without it, other needs cannot be fulfilled (Von Hirsch & Jareborg, 2005, 191).

When assessing the physical harmfulness of bias crimes, however, one must bear in mind that the physical injuries the victim suffers are already contemplated in the base crime (Harel & Parchomovsky, 1999, 514). The base offence's definition usually embeds the conduct's consequences resulting in physical harm (e.g. the offence *murder* includes the victim's death; the offences of inflicting *actual bodily harm* or *grievously bodily harm* include serious and really serious injures respectively, and so on). Therefore, when we gauge the added harmfulness of the bias component, we cannot also include the physical dimension.

However, this does not mean that this aspect of bias crime should be overlooked. Physical harm is actually a recurrent consequence of hate crimes. It is a direct result of the base offence, but it is also inextricably linked to the bias component. Had the victim not had that particular characteristic, the perpetrator would not have committed the crime. Furthermore, a higher level of physical violence usually increases the psychological harm suffered by victims. Moreover, the choice of *sending a message* by using a violent criminal conduct bears certain relevance when assessing the conduct's wrongfulness.

The number of studies on the impact and severity of hate crimes on victims has grown notably in the past two decades, and so has their scope. While earlier studies focused on "small, localized sample from select jurisdictions," more recent research "analysed larger samples from official police records" as well as "nationally representative sample of self-reported victimizations" (Fetzer & Pezzella, 2019, 3873). Several authors have also analysed differences in the severity of physical injuries between bias and non-bias offences. These studies have produced "mixed results" (Fetzer & Pezzella, 2019, 3872; see also Pezzella, 2017, 32). Some of them show that bias crimes are more likely to result in serious injuries than their non-bias counterparts (e.g. J. Levin & McDevitt, 1993a, 1993b. Levin, 1999; Strom, 2001; Messner et al., 2004; Cheng et al., 2013; Pezzella & Fetzer, 2017; Fetzer & Pezzella, 2019), while others found the opposite (Corcoran et al., 2015; Garcia et al., 1999; Iganski & Lagou, 2015a). It has been argued that this difference might depend on the context in which these studies have been carried out. Research conducted in the US reports more violence than that carried out in the UK or Sweden. Moreover, the degree of physical harm suffered by victims also depends on other variables, such as the use of weapons, the offender's abuse of drugs and/or alcohol, and the fact that the offence was committed by one or more perpetrators. Moreover, research conducted in the US shows that bias crimes committed against persons possessing certain characteristics are usually more violent than those committed against other groups.

3.1.2 Psychological Dimension

In criminalisation theory, psychological harm has given rise to controversies as to its nature. To be sufficiently serious to constitute *harm*, the intrusion into a standard victim's psychological dimension of quality of life must result in the impairment of victims' *resources or coping abilities*, a setback of their interests, and therefore have a long-term effect on their well-being (Peršak, 2014, 235; 2020). This is what distinguishes it from mere affront, which is only temporary and does not cause permanent impairment on the victim's status (Simester & von Hirsch, 2011, 113). Thus, only serious and long-lasting psychological consequences will be considered in the analysis of hate crimes' intrusion into the psychological sphere of victims.

Crimes' Impact on Mental Health in General

Mental health is the main interest with which the quality of life's psychological dimension is primarily concerned. Crimes can trigger a number of negative emotions in victims, but we can properly speak of *psychological harm* only when the interest to *mental health* suffers a setback, i.e. when the crime has a long-term negative impact on the psychological well-being of the victim.

There is no universal agreement on a definition of mental health (see, for instance, Galderisi et al., 2015). The World Health Organization (WHO) defines it as

> a state of well-being in which the individual realizes his or her own abilities, can cope with the normal stresses of life, can work productively and fruitfully, and is able to make a contribution to his or her community (World Health Organization, 2004).

This definition represents a step forward in comparison with the previous concept that defined mental health merely as the absence of mental illness. However, experts have raised several concerns, particularly with regard to the potential misunderstandings stemming from the identification of "positive feelings and positive functioning as key factors for mental health" (Galderisi et al., 2015, 231). This is not the place to discuss different definitions of mental health, and decide which one should be adopted. However, the definition provided by Galderisi and her colleagues may be useful to understand the interest we are dealing with. They define mental health as

> a dynamic state of internal equilibrium which enables individuals to use their abilities in harmony with universal values of society. Basic cognitive and social skills; ability to recognize, express and modulate one's own emotions, as well as empathize with others; flexibility and ability to cope with adverse life events and function in social roles; and harmonious relationship between body and mind represent important components of mental health which contribute, to varying degrees, to the state of internal equilibrium (Galderisi et al., 2015, 231–232).

We can thus derive from this definition that the intrusion into the interest to mental health reaches the degree of *harm* when it is not possible to "timely restore the dynamic state of internal equilibrium" of the person concerned.

Generally speaking, the psychological impact of crimes on victims varies considerably according to a number of factors. These include "the characteristics of the crime itself, the characteristics of the offender, the nature of the victim–offender relationship, and structural and individual-level factors characterizing the victim" (Verdun-Jones & Rossiter, 2010, 611–612). Mental health consequences of crime victimisation can be described as existing on a spectrum, ranging "from relatively mild and short-lived distress to life-altering and debilitating psychiatric disorders" (Verdun-Jones & Rossiter, 2010, 612).

The most common outcomes of crime victimisation include "changes in cognitive schemas, beliefs, expectations, and assumptions about themselves and others," as "[v]ictimization challenges the victims' beliefs about their own invulnerability, their perceptions of the world as an inherently benign and meaningful place, and their trust in others … [and] may cause [them] to see themselves in a more negative light, and trauma may also impair both memory and decision making functions" (Verdun-Jones & Rossiter, 2010, 614).

However, in some cases victims' responses to crime can result in the development of "psychiatric disorders, where sets of symptoms reach clinically significant levels and begin to interfere with victims' daily functioning" (Verdun-Jones & Rossiter, 2010, 612). The most frequent disorder crime victims suffer from is the so-called post-traumatic stress disorder (PTSD) (Verdun-Jones & Rossiter, 2010, 612), consisting of suffering of "recurring and distressing recollections of a traumatic event" (Wilson, 2009, 201) such as a warfare event, a natural disaster, a terrorist act, a violent assault or rape (see also American Psychiatric Association, 2020). This is of course one of the most severe responses to crime victimisation. Crime victims may show a wider range of emotional and psychological problems "which fall along various points on the continuum of psychological responses to victimization," such as "depression, substance abuse, suicidal ideation, and suicide attempts" (Verdun-Jones & Rossiter, 2010, 613).

Impact of Hate Crimes on Mental Health

Research on the impact of hate crimes on mental health points out a distinctive characteristic of these types of crimes, which sets them apart from the parallel, base offences lacking the bias element: they significantly negatively affect not only the direct victim, but also other members of the victim's community. The "message nature" of hate crimes is actually one of their most important aspects. These crimes convey the message that anyone belonging to the victim's group is the target of hate and hostility.

The present analysis will focus on the first and second levels of psychological harmfulness, namely those concerning the direct victim and the persons sharing the same characteristic of the direct victim. While the number of qualitative and quantitative studies on the first level of harm have considerably increased in number and quality in the past twenty years, studies on the vicarious harmfulness of hate crimes are less numerous and paved with methodological difficulties. Yet, they present some interesting inputs.

Direct Victim

A growing number of studies have been focusing on the assessment of the possible greater psychological impact that hate crimes have on direct victims in comparison with parallel offences.[8] While the first studies examined small, non-random samples of selected respondents, in the past decade researchers have started assessing larger samples in the secondary analysis of crime victimisation survey data,[9] as well as comparing the effects of bias crimes with those of non-bias offences (Iganski & Lagou, 2015b, 1698). So far, this kind of research covers a small number of Western—and, particularly, Anglo-Saxon—countries (United States, United Kingdom, Canada, Australia), with the sole exception of Sweden, Latvia and North Macedonia.

The first studies on the matter already pointed out that the direct victims of hate crimes—taken as a whole group, regardless of differences between personal characteristics—seemed to suffer from greater adverse psychological sequelae than non-bias crime victims, in terms of direct, primary harm as well as secondary, reactive harm. These results have later been confirmed by larger-scale, comparative studies (just to name the

[8] For a review of the most relevant studies conducted so far on the added physical and psychological impact of hate crimes, see Mellgren et al. (2017) and Fetzer and Pezzella (2019)

[9] Fetzer and Pezzella (2019, 3871) stress the importance of using victimisation surveys (such as the British Crime Survey and the Crime Survey of England and Wales, and the US National Crime Victimization Survey) to examine "psychological trauma in addition to physical harm." In this regard, see the ODHIR's recommendations (ODHIR, 2014).

more recent research studies: Williams & Tregidga, 2014; Iganski & Lagou, 2015a, 2015b; Corcoran et al., 2015; Iganski & Sweiry, 2016; Mellgren et al., 2017; Fetzer & Pezzella, 2019; Iganski, 2019).

There is a clear consensus among researchers that, in comparison to victims of parallel offences, bias crimes victims suffer heightened psychological trauma (Benier, 2017, 181; Iganski & Lagou, 2015a, 40). In fact, the negative psychological impact of bias-motivated crimes appears to be qualitatively and quantitatively different from that experienced by victims of otherwise motivated offences (Iganski & Lagou, 2015b, 1698; Benier, 2017, 182). In particular, hate crime victims "are more likely to suffer posttraumatic stress type symptoms," such as high "levels of depression and withdrawal; anxiety and nervousness; loss of confidence; anger; increased sleep difficulties; difficulty concentrating; fear; and reduced feelings of safety" (Iganski & Sweiry, 2016, 102).

Further studies have pointed out that the level of psychological harm varies among victims pertaining to the same social group according to personal circumstances and resilience capacity (Funnell, 2015; Iganski & Lagou, 2015b). Overall evidence indicates "that there is not only within- and between-group variability but also crime-type variability. Some hate crimes do hurt some more, but not all" (Mellgren et al., 2017, 18).[10]

The main explanation as to why bias crimes cause more psychological harm to direct victims than their parallel counterparts is that they target a characteristic that is central to victims' identity (Craig-Henderson & Sloan, 2003; Herek et al., 1997; Iganski & Lagou, 2015b; Mellgren et al., 2017) which is either immutable (e.g. one's skin colour; a permanent disability) or in any event constitutes a fundamental part of one's identity (e.g. religion; sexual orientation). Hate crimes send the message that that personal feature/group membership is "devalued, unwelcome, denigrated, despised" (Iganski & Sweiry, 2016, 103). As Lannert (2015, 295) notes, "victimization motivated by bias against an individual's identity may cause the individual to connect existing feelings of vulnerability, powerlessness, and lowered self-worth to their identity, and this

[10] These findings are however in contrast with Iganski and Sweiry's, who noted that the greater psychological harmfulness of hate crimes "even hold when controlling for differences in type of crime experienced" (Iganski & Sweiry, 2016, 103).

association may explain bias crime survivors' higher rates of distress as compared to nonbias crime survivors." Moreover, the often random nature and the high frequency of bias-motivated attacks render the victim powerless. Bias offences do not happen in a vacuum: victimised groups are often already the target of hate speech, discriminated against or oppressed. By reminding their victims that they must remain in their place, hidden if necessary, bias crimes constitute a further element reinforcing the *status quo*. Furthermore, some victims' experiences are further exacerbated by the lack of social and family support resulting from their disadvantaged status in society.

*The Vicarious/*In Terrorem *Effect of Bias Crimes*

Crimes in general, particularly violent crimes, usually have a negative impact that extends beyond the immediate victim. However, in the case of bias crimes this is not a mere collateral consequence, but it is often the perpetrator's intended effect: to send the message to all the persons sharing the same characteristic of the victim that they are potential targets. And this message is usually well understood by other, potential victims. This secondary outcome of bias crimes is referred to as vicarious (Perry & Alvi, 2012, 58) or *in terrorem* (Weinstein, 1992, 10) effect. Researchers agree on the existence of such effects and on the *message crimes* nature of bias offences (Fetzer & Pezzella, 2019, 3865). However, there is also agreement upon the fact that these "consequences are methodologically more difficult to scientifically demonstrate compared with the consequences for individual victims" (Iganski & Sweiry, 2016, 103).

To date, only a few studies have addressed the vicarious effects of hate crimes (e.g. Bell & Perry, 2015; Benier, 2017; Craig, 1999; Lannert, 2015; Lim, 2009; Noelle, 2002; Perry, 2015; Perry & Alvi, 2012). They suffer from a number of methodological problems (e.g. small number of respondents; non-random selection of respondents; lack of comparison with non-bias offences). The few studies conducted so far, however, all agree that the crimes do cause a number of negative psychological reactions on vicarious victims (Mellgren et al., 2017, 5), and that these consequences are straightforwardly linked to the characteristic these individuals have in common with the direct victim. These studies have been realised through in-depth interviews or focus groups with a small sample of respondents. They have highlighted two kinds of psychological impact on vicarious victims: *primary, direct harm* and *secondary, reactive harm*. A project carried out by Paterson et al. (2018) that focuses on the effect of bias crimes on Muslim and LGBT communities in the United Kingdom, is probably the first research publishing data on the *in terrorem* effects of bias offences on aggregated level. Its results are very similar to the previous, smaller studies—bias offences, "whether experienced directly, indirectly, through the media, in person or online were consistently linked to … increased feelings of vulnerability, anxiety, anger, and sometimes shame" (Paterson et al., 2018, 2).

As to why bias crimes also affect vicarious victims, Lannert (2015, 292) suggests that these offences "may serve as a source of severe, probable, ambiguous, and uncontrollable threat, resulting in repeated activation of anticipatory stress responses to bias crime cues. These studies indicate that knowledge of bias crimes serves as a source of periodic and chronic stress that is unique to the minority experience." In turn, the more individuals identify with a social identity that is the target of hate crimes, the more likely they are "to perceive actions as discriminatory and to report greater psychological distress as a consequence" (Lannert, 2015, 293). Paterson and her colleagues describe the vicarious effects of hate crimes as a process. First, these types of crimes would "increase feelings of vulnerability and empathy" among the wider community, which in turn would "increase emotional reactions (anger, anxiety, shame)" that eventually cause a number of specific behavioural responses. Thus, "[a]nger leads to pro-active behaviours and less avoidance … [a]nxiety leads to avoidance and security concerns," and "[s]hame, although not always felt strongly, is linked to avoidance, pro-active behaviours, security concerns, and uniquely to retaliation" (Paterson et al., 2018, 3).

3.1.3 Normative Dimension

Besides, and beyond, intruding upon the victims' physical and psychological spheres, the bias component of hate crimes is said to invade, and setback, their normative interests. These offences' intrusion into direct and vicarious victims' normative sphere is actually considered (particularly by continental European research) one of the characteristics that differentiate bias crimes from other types of offences. Through the commission of a crime, perpetrators express a value judgment towards not only the direct victim, but to all persons sharing the same feature.

Among the normative interests impaired by hate offences, the one that seems primarily concerned is that of equal dignity/equal respect, both for direct and vicarious victims. However, other interests related to one's well-being, such as individuality and autonomy, come also into play.

Dignity, Equal Dignity, Equal Respect

Human dignity is a concept that, in recent years, has encountered a great success both as a fundamental principle and a (criminal law) legal good, particularly in the human rights discourse.[11] Nevertheless, its conceptualisation as a legitimate interest has proven difficult, as it is a meta-legal, philosophical, and social concept whose boundaries are fluid and depend on the interpreter's subjective values (Riccardi, 2013, 16).[12]

In light of the difficulty to establish *a priori* what dignity is and to develop a general concept of human dignity, Nussbaum (2012, 62) suggests we "should probably avoid thinking that dignity has an obvious specific content all on its own: it seems to be a notion that gets fleshed out through its relationship with other notions, such as that of respect (dignity is that attribute of a person that makes the person an appropriate object of respect), and a variety of more specific political principles." The path chosen by Italian courts[13] and doctrine (see, for example, Drigo, 2011; Vedaschi, 2011) to overcome these problems is that of connecting

[11] For an overview of the development of the concept of dignity, see Dan-Cohen (2011); Drigo (2011); Hörnle and Kremnitzer (2011). On the dignitarian conception of human rights violations and hate crimes, see Brudholm (2016).

[12] As a legal good, it has been used to call for the protection of completely different—and sometimes opposite—interests (from women's right to self-determination in case of abortion, to the embryo's "right to life"; from the prohibition of human cloning to possession of pornographic material depicting children; from slavery to sado-masochist practices between consenting adults, and so on) (Tesauro, 2012, 908–909; Fiandaca, 2014, 78).

[13] See, for example, Italian Court of Cassation, judgment no. 37581/2008.

the concept of dignity to those of equality and respect. Under this conceptualisation, equal dignity is seen as the counterpart of the right to equal respect. The former is a characteristic of the addressee, while the latter is the addresser's recognition of the addressee's equal dignity in relation with other human beings. To respect someone *equally* "implies a) to recognise them as a peer, and b) to orientate our behaviour towards that person in a way that does not humiliate, degrade, disregard, or ignore them" (Bacco, 2013, 833; citing Galeotti, 2010, 77; and Darwall, 1977).

Doctrine has highlighted two conceptions of dignity (Tesauro, 2012, 933–936). The first, subjective conception refers to an individual's inner perception of their dignity. According to its second, objective conception, dignity is a pre-constituted fact that does not depend on a given person's autonomy and self-perception. Both conceptions present important side-effects: while the first one risks to over-personalise the concept according to each individual's perceptions, the second one may become a tool for imposing the majority's idea of dignity against personal autonomy (Tesauro, 2012, 933–934). The second, objective conception seems nevertheless more suited to be conceived as a meaningful legitimate interest. Under this account, every human being is entitled to have their dignity respected by others, regardless of whether the individual is not, or cannot be, aware of it (e.g. infants, persons with severe mental illnesses, persons under the temporary effect of drug or alcohol, and so on). This objective conceptualisation of dignity is connected, in turn, to the so-called recognition-consideration type of respect, which is due to all human beings regardless of their personal characteristics and behaviours (Bacco, 2018, 153–157; Dillon, 2018). Equal dignity would thus constitute the premise for a relationship based on equal respect (Bacco, 2018, 160).

By recalling Kant's account of dignity, we can speak of a violation of this interest when someone is treated merely as an object or used as an instrument (see Hörnle & Kremnitzer, 2011, 146). If we apply this line of reasoning to hate crimes, we might argue that in these types of offences perpetrators treat their victims somehow as a mean, by randomly selecting them to communicate a wider message that all the persons *like them* are not welcome. This account, however, does not grasp the full impact of these kinds of crimes on victims' dignity. In the context of hate crimes, the victim's interest to be treated with equal respect is impaired by the selective and symbolic nature of these kinds of crimes (see Goisis, 2015, 44; 47; 51; Iganski & Sweiry, 2016, 105; Laurenzo Copello, 2019, 462). Offenders commit the crime precisely because victims possess a given personal characteristic. Thus, the message that is transmitted is not only one of *lack of consideration and respect*, but a wider statement about the *less worthiness* of victims in comparison with other members of society (and particularly, with regard to the social group perpetrators belong to). Thus, bias crimes impair the interest to equal dignity and equal respect of both direct victims and the social group they belong to. This is not something that happens incidentally; it is a salient feature of these kinds of crimes, and in some case, it is actually offenders' intended effect.

Furthermore, the intrusion into this interest is one of the reasons why bias crimes cause more psychological harm; yet, this kind of normative harm can, and should, be assessed separately from the psychological consequences of these kinds of offences. Psychological harm depends on victim's perception and response to the crime and is thus mainly subjective. On the other hand, the intrusion into standard victims' normative interest to equal dignity and equal respect has a more objective fashion as it takes place even if victims are unaware of it. This means that even if in some cases hate crimes may not cause added psychological harm to their victims, they nevertheless give rise to a severe intrusion into the latter's normative interest to equal dignity and equal respect.

Individuality

Hate crime perpetrators often—albeit not always—choose their targets randomly. Whoever possesses the despised characteristic can be a potential victim. This process negates the victims' individuality: they are merely seen as possessors of a certain, negative feature; their selves are reduced to a synecdoche. By doing so, offenders set back their victims' interest and impair their quality of life as individuality directly contributes to the construction of one's personal identity and, by extension, to one's well-being (Peršak, 2014, 235; citing Mill 1859). Considering the very definition of the concept of *individuality*, hate crimes' intrusion upon this interest regards only direct, and not vicarious victims.

Autonomy

As a result of hate crime victimisation, direct and vicarious victims may adopt avoidance strategies that end up intruding upon their interest to autonomy and self-direction, which are also universal human needs strictly connected to one's well-being (Tay & Diener, 2011, 354). These measures are mainly deployed for fear of future, possible victimisation (Iganski & Sweiry, 2016, 102–103). These strategies include, for instance, avoiding going to certain places altogether or going there only if, and when, accompanied by other people (particularly, people that do not possess the targeted characteristic); or changing important aspects of their behaviour to hide their perceived belonging to a certain social group (e.g. effeminate men forcing themselves to lower their pitch; black persons stopping wearing their hair in an Afro; Muslim women taking off their veil in certain public space, and so on). Autonomy and self-direction are "values or interests that allow us to construct and follow our own life plans" (Peršak, 2014, 235). Von Hirsch and Simester, in turn, understand autonomy "in terms of 'deep' self-determination, namely someone's acting according to a coherent set of goals of his own considered choice. On that view, a person could engage in apparently self-destructive activities, but only if these were part of a fuller life-conception or plan of his own." In the case of avoidance strategies, one can hardly state that the person in question *freely* decides to, for example, get back in the closet, or not wear a crucifix publicly, because this is part of her long-term life-plan. These are survival strategies that hate crimes actual and potential victims eventually decide to adopt to avoid being targets of hate crimes and incidents, at the high price of losing an important part of their autonomy and self-direction.

Secondary, reactive harm resulting from avoidance strategies seems to be a common consequence of hate crimes among direct victims (Perry & Alvi, 2012; K. Smith et al., 2012; Iganski & Lagou, 2015a; Corcoran et al., 2015; Bell & Perry, 2015; Perry, 2015; Iganski & Sweiry, 2016; Benier, 2017; Mellgren et al., 2017; Sharrock et al., 2018; Iganski, 2019). As with direct victims, also members of the community adopt a number of strategies to avoid future victimisation, including through voluntary segregation (Perry, 2015, 53; Pezzella & Fetzer, 2017). These reactions have in turn significant mental health implications for the persons concerned (Lannert, 2015, 292; 296). These strategies result in a worsening of these persons' quality of life, particularly because of the stress and negative impact associated to hiding one's identity, or to the reduced capacity to act autonomously and independently in public spaces (see, for example, Perry & Alvi, 2012; and Bell & Perry, 2015).

3.1.4 Levels of Intrusion into Interest Dimensions and Resulting Harm

In order to gauge the bias element of hate crimes' intrusion into each dimension of quality of life, this study applies von Hirsch and Jareborg's scale (Von Hirsch & Jareborg, 2005) as amended by Peršak (2014). Following their models, the bias element's level of intrusion into each interest dimension affected is classified into four degrees: subsistence, minimal well-being, adequate well-being and standard well-being. These, in turn, correspond to a four-level scale of harm ranging from mild, moderate, serious and grave/severe.

As to quality-of-life's *physical* dimension, it is not possible to gauge the bias element of hate crimes' level of intrusion and resulting harm because it is already covered by the base offence.

With regard to the *psychological* category, the level of intrusion and resulting harm can be measured as follows:

- *Direct victims*—level of intrusion: minimal well-being; degree of harm: serious;
- *Vicarious victims*—level of intrusion: adequate well-being; degree of harm: moderate.

As regards the interests pertaining to the *normative* dimension, we can gauge the degree of intrusion and resulting harm in this way:

- *Equal dignity/equal respect* (direct and vicarious victims)—level of intrusion: minimal well-being; degree of harm: serious;

- *Individuality* (direct victims)—level of intrusion: adequate well-being; degree of harm: moderate;
- *Autonomy* (direct and vicarious victims)—level of intrusion: adequate well-being /minimal well-being; degree of harm: moderate/serious.

The analysis of hate crimes overall considered shows that their bias element intrudes upon the psychological and the normative dimensions of the standard victims' quality of life in a relevant way and thus causes significantly more harm than parallel offences. While some aspects need further research (e.g. the harm caused to vicarious victims), evidence on the added psychological harm to direct victims of hate crimes is nowadays uncontested. Moreover, hate crimes' serious intrusion into both direct and vicarious victims' interest to equal dignity and equal respect is also clearly identifiable. In addition, research points to some common patterns and mechanisms that lead hate crimes to intrude upon the normative interests to individuality and autonomy, although in a less serious way.

It can be concluded that, overall, hate crimes are more harmful than parallel offences, and that this added harmfulness is serious enough to fulfil the first criterion of the ILT. By using the levels of harm identified here as benchmarks, Sect. 4 will analyse in more detail each of the four hate crime law variables under a harmfulness perspective.

3.2 Wrongfulness Issues

Proponents of hate crime legislation argue that the bias element adds a further degree of wrongfulness to the base conduct, thus making hate crimes more wrongful than parallel crimes. This is so because the bias component constitutes *per se* a distinctive moral wrong, linked to the discriminatory nature of these types of offences. Hate crimes represent a form of direct discrimination, as perpetrators single out their victims because of a certain feature they possess. The wrongfulness of discriminatory conducts rests, primarily, on the fact that they treat someone less favourably than another, all things equal, only because of their personal characteristics or group membership.

According to some authors, however, the discriminatory component of hate crimes would not increase the wrongfulness of the base offence. Dillof (1997, 1039–1042), for example, does not recognise that the discrimination that underlies hate crimes produces a distinctive wrong separated from that of the base offence. He conceives the right not to be discriminatorily harmed "as resting on a protectable interest in the thoughts of another". He argues that "to establish a protectable interest, a person must show that a matter she is concerned with is properly viewed as her concern, rather than somebody else's". In his view, however, thoughts are protectable interests only with respect to the person who produces them, not with respect to the addressee. Thoughts are not (or, better, should not be) the business of the criminal law. The discriminatory, biased thoughts that constitute the motive of the perpetrator's conduct would thus not concern the victim, as they "do not amount to protectable interests" (Harel & Parchomovsky, 1999, 516). In sum, discrimination would not constitute a separate wrong because to say so would infringe the perpetrator's freedom of thought and expression.

In the United States, the strict interpretation of freedom of thought and expression has been widely used to oppose hate crime law. In the European context, however, this freedom is conceived differently. It is understood as a constitutional principle and a human right that, albeit fundamental, must be balanced against other principles having an equivalent or superior weight. Thus, under some and well-defined circumstances, freedom of thought and speech is subject to certain limits. On the one hand, it has been shown that the bias component of hate crimes has an independent effect on the level of the added harm caused to direct and vicarious victims, and that this is not just an incidental element of the crime (Andersson & Mellgren, 2016, 231; 246). This makes the offender's mental attitude to be the proper concern of victims, contrary to what Dillof maintains. In this regard, it shall not be overlooked that victim groups already find themselves in a situation of disadvantage that includes, among other things, a weakened and silenced position in society. Hate crimes not only stem from this situation; they also contribute to this unbalanced position among groups in the public debate due to their "silencing effect" (Pelissero, 2015, 24). Another limit to freedom of expression concerns the way thoughts are conveyed to the audience.

Performing a conduct that is considered a crime (such as destroying someone else's property, or threatening, assaulting, sexually harassing, raping or killing them) cannot be reasonably considered a legitimate way of expressing one's thoughts. And the perpetrators' thoughts, being the main or sole reason why they decide to commit a crime, become the business of the victims concerned. Moreover, what hate crime law actually addresses is not the mere ideas of the offender, but the conduct resulting from those thoughts.

Furthermore, according to other authors discriminatory conducts are wrongful not only because they are "based on the victim's membership in a salient social group," but also because they involve "the imposition of a disadvantage … on account of the group membership of the victims" (Altman, 2016). In the case of bias crimes, of course, the disadvantage consists of victimising someone through the commission of an offence. But there is more. In most cases, bias offence victims belong to societal groups already disadvantaged or particularly vulnerable, and they are victimised because they belong to such groups. By drawing on a prioritarianism perspective, Brax points out that "harm done to those people worst off has particular moral weight" (Brax, 2016, 59). Under this perspective the wrong of discrimination is strictly connected with the violation of victims' *equal dignity*. In particular, it is argued that "the essential wrong of paradigmatic acts of direct discrimination seems to be that they violate the equal moral status of persons by treating the victims in ways that would be appropriate only for individuals having a diminished or degraded moral status" (Altman, 2016). In this sense, the (added) moral wrong of bias crimes rests in the negation of victims' (equal) dignity, in their being treated as morally inferior (Hellman, 2011, 172; see also Brax, 2016, 60). The moral wrong of discrimination (and of hate crimes) is thus linked to the gross disrespect perpetrators show to their victims by choosing them on the basis of a characteristic that they consider, to say the least, unworthy. Moreover, when hostile animus is present, there are even stronger reasons to classify the bias as wrongful. Adams (2005, 27) maintains that "[a]n actor who commits an underlying offense and in which his or her conduct is referable to hateful beliefs and desires, other things being equal, demonstrates a distinctive and greater degree of disregard for the worth and dignity of the victim than an actor who commits the same underlying offense and in which his or her conduct is not referable to hateful beliefs and desires."

Other authors also link the higher wrongfulness of bias crimes to the added moral blameworthiness of perpetrators. In their view, discriminatory motives are "more socially condemnable than other motives … because racist crimes (and by analogy other prejudice-motivated crimes) directly undermine democratic values and fundamental human rights, including dignity, respect, and equality" (Schweppe & Walters, 2015, 6).

3.3 Conclusions

This first part of the chapter has applied the ILT to a default model of hate crime law in which hate or bias are the only motives of the offence and their link to the base conduct can be explained with the Hostility Animus model. Hate crime provisions have therefore been considered as a whole, without disaggregating their constitutive parts. It has been shown that these types of crime cause serious intrusion into the psychological and normative dimension of standard victims' quality of life. This results in the causation of direct primary harm and secondary reactive harm, the level of which is significantly higher than that of parallel, non-bias motivated offences. Moreover, bias crimes are also more wrongful than their parallel counterparts because their discriminatory nature makes them a distinctive moral wrong. The added harmfulness and wrongfulness of bias-motivated crimes have been sufficiently demonstrated and thus it is not necessary to apply Feinberg's mediating maxims. We can therefore conclude that these provisions are overall legitimate.

4 Application of the ILT to the Hate Crime Law Framework

The four-tier framework developed in Chap. 2 allows us to disaggregate bias crime laws into four main elements: (i) the drafting method adopted to increase the base sentence; (ii) the protected grounds included; (iii) the kind of evidence and amount of hate/bias required to apply the legal provision; and (iv) the nexus between the offender's mental attitude and the offence. In the next sections, each of these variables will be analysed under the Integrated Legitimacy Test. We will analyse whether, and which of, the different ways to draft their main components pass the ILT and can thus be considered legitimate.

4.1 Tier I: Drafting Method Adopted to Increase the Base Sentence

The first tier of the hate crime law framework allows us to draw a connection between how bias crime provisions are introduced in criminal law and the scope of the underlying hate crime concept that they reflect (see Table 2.1 and Table 2.5 in Chap. 2). Separate, substantive offences correspond to a narrow scope of the concept, specific aggravating circumstances are linked to an intermediate approach, and general aggravating circumstances reflect a wide understanding. A fourth, possible way the criminal law can take bias motives into account is allowing them to be considered only when determining the amount of sentence *within the range* foreseen for the base offence. Albeit these kinds of provisions are applicable to all crimes, and in that sense they reflect a wide understanding of the hate crime concept, it is difficult to properly classify them under one or more concepts of hate crime.

4.1.1 General Aggravating Circumstances and Basic Legitimacy Requirement

General aggravating circumstances are in principle applicable to all kinds of conduct proscribed as criminal law offences that have been committed out of a bias motive. However, not all crimes can be committed with a discriminatory motive (e.g. victimless crimes, or crimes against the State, cannot possibly be conceived as base offences of bias crimes). Moreover, there should be empirical data showing that *all* the categories of base offences the aggravating circumstance can be applied to *can be*, or *have been* committed out of bias in the legal system at issue, and that they cause more harm (and are more wrongful) than their non-bias motivated counterparts.

General aggravating circumstances fall foul of one of the basic requirements of the ILT (as well as of the Italian *offensività* principle and the Anglo-American harm principle): empirical evidence showing that the conduct is sufficiently harmful. It follows that hate crime law in the form of general aggravating circumstances is *in principle* not legitimate. However, at this stage the legitimacy exercise examines hate crime law only in its abstract and literal version, and does not take into account the actual interpretation that courts and other authorities give to these legal provisions. Courts might interpret them as having a narrower scope and apply only to a small number of base offences, or to exclude their applicability to base crimes they are incompatible with.

In many jurisdictions, the use of general aggravating circumstances is widespread and even welcome. From a positive-law and systematic point of view, they can be easily introduced in the criminal law system and they apply to a wide range of base offences; at the same time, they cause less consistency problems than substantive offences. This also applies to hate crime law, which is very often drafted in the form of general aggravating circumstances. There are of course pros and cons in the use of this drafting method (see Chap. 2, Sect. 3.2.1). In any event, the ultimate assessment of their legitimacy has to be carried out with regard to the concrete legal provisions under exam as actually interpreted by the competent legal authorities. Therefore, their legitimacy cannot be excluded in principle.

4.1.2 Substantive Offences and Specific Aggravating Circumstances

Substantive offences and specific aggravating circumstances are distinct drafting techniques which entail different consequences from a criminal law point of view as well as in terms of the hate crime concept adopted. Nonetheless, in both instances lawmakers have to previously decide to which base crimes they shall be applied. Not all conducts criminalised as offences can be committed out of bias; even among those that can be potentially motivated by hate, not all offences actually do. To be legitimate, specific aggravating circumstances and substantive offences should be based on the empirical assessment of which base crimes are actually committed out of bias in a given jurisdiction, with which frequency, and what is the ultimate impact on the quality of life of victims.

Data collection of hate crime incidents is still very limited and methodologically uneven across states. In collaboration with its participating states, ODHIR has been keeping track of bias motivated offences across the OSCE region for some years now. However, it is very difficult to compare data because the approaches adopted by States differ notably. A number of base offences that are more commonly committed out of bias can be nevertheless identified across the OSCE region: property crimes such as robbery, burglary, larceny-theft, arson, vandalism, and damage, and personal crimes such as murder, rape, simple and aggravated assault, and intimidation. These offences are also those more commonly considered in research's analysis on the added harmfulness of bias crimes (see, among others, Noelle, 2002; Iganski, 2008; Dzelme, 2008; K. Smith et al., 2012; Williams & Tregidga, 2014; Corcoran et al., 2015; Mellgren et al., 2017; Pezzella & Fetzer, 2017; Fetzer & Pezzella, 2019). The previous section's findings on the *prima facie* legitimacy of a default model of hate crime law were based on these very studies. We can therefore conclude that substantive offences that embed, and specific aggravating circumstances that apply to, these kinds of base crimes are both legitimate. As with general aggravating circumstances, concrete and geographically pertinent evidence concerning each base offence the penalty enhancement is applied to should however be provided by legislators when enacting hate crimes provisions in a given jurisdiction.

4.1.3 Bias Motive Contemplated Only in Sentencing Phase

The fourth drafting method consisting of the consideration of bias motives only among other sentencing principles, and allowing for the enhancement of the sentence only within the range foreseen for the base offence, appears to be quite unusual; in fact, it has been found only in

Germany.[14] Unlike the other three drafting approaches, the bias component of hate crimes is not treated here as an extra element that adds something to the base offence in terms of extra harm or wrongfulness. These provisions concern instead the sentencing stage; they do not criminalise any new conducts. Therefore, we cannot properly assess them under the ILT as they lie outside the criminalisation stage. However, by drawing on some features of the ILT, some observations as to these provisions' suitability can be nevertheless advanced.

Some researchers have endorsed the use of these types of law. Iganski and Lagou (2015b) observe that, within the same group of race-motivated hate crime victims, the psychological impact of these crimes varied notably among the respondents. Not all victims reported suffering the same degree of psychological harm. Based on these results, these authors highlight some problems as regards the justification of enhanced sentences for bias crime offenders in terms of retributive desert. As they argue, "a blanket uplift in penalty in every case which rests on the offender's motivations cannot be justified if the justification for sentence uplift is to give offenders their just deserts for the harms they inflict" (Iganski & Lagou, 2015b, 1696). They thus propose that penalties be decided on a case-by-case basis, leaving to the judge/jury the assessment of the actual psychological harm suffered by the concrete victim, as well of the actual culpability of the concrete offender for the harm brought about.

This approach, however, suffers from a number of shortcomings. First, it assumes that the only type of harm that justifies the enactment of bias crime provisions is psychological harm. As we saw in the general part of the present chapter, however, bias crimes also intrude upon the normative dimension of the victim's quality of life. The violation of victims' interest to equal dignity and respect takes place even if the victim does not suffer any psychological harm; it is an objective intrusion in that the victim's awareness is not even required. Second, even though the concrete

[14] Section 46(2) of Germany's Penal Code, under the heading *Principles of Sentencing*. However, many jurisdictions leave room for judicial discretion when imposing sanctions within the range foreseen in the criminal code (for example, art. 80(1) of the Hungarian Penal Code, and art. 53(2) of the Polish Penal Code). Albeit not explicitly contemplated in these provisions, bias motives can nonetheless be taken into consideration by courts when deciding the amount of the sentence to be imposed.

direct victims do not actually suffer greater psychological harm, this perspective fails to consider the psychological (and normative) harm caused to vicarious victims (see Mellgren et al., 2017, 8). Third, this approach overlooks the fact that, for criminalisation purposes, we must take into account the harm caused to a *standard* victim. The fact that some, concrete victims suffer a lesser degree of psychological harm than others is sometimes due to their capacity for resilience, or to the fact that they have got so used to be victimised in relation with their personal characteristic that they do actually suffer less. Some victims may also suffer from a certain permanent or temporary mental disability that prevents them from fully emotionally and cognitively realising what has happened to them; does this mean that the perpetrator's conduct is less blameworthy?

Therefore, it is argued that this drafting technique, albeit not assessable under the ILT, is nevertheless not appropriate to properly address hate crimes.

4.1.4 Conclusions

Hate crime law introducing a penalty enhancement for bias-motivated offences can be drafted according to four, distinct approaches, which in turn reflect different conceptions of hate crimes. Substantive offences correspond to a narrow conception of bias offences, while specific and general aggravating circumstances reflect an intermediate and a wide conception, respectively. The fourth technique (other policy of law allowing for motive to be considered as a sentencing factor) falls under the last, wide category.

In the OSCE region, general and specific aggravating circumstances are the most commonly adopted methods, while the introduction of substantive offences is less usual. The fourth method, in turn, has been identified only in one country.[15]

This section has analysed different techniques available to draft hate crime provisions. At the outset, we observed that the *general aggravating circumstances* option does not comply at first sight with the basic evidence

[15] See Chapter 2, Section 3.2.1.

requirement of the ILT. However, it has also been argued that the ultimate conclusion about its legitimacy can only be reached by taking into account the actual interpretation of a concrete legal provision provided by the competent authorities (e.g. a Supreme or a Constitutional Court) of a given jurisdiction. Hence, the legitimacy of this drafting option cannot be excluded *a priori*.

The methods consisting of *substantive offences* and *specific aggravating circumstances*, instead, are legitimate techniques to draft hate crime law and both pass the ILT. However, a need for further research has been identified in relation with concrete geographical contexts. As to the fourth technique, where hate motives are considered only among other sentencing principles, it has been categorised as a measure of procedural nature, which does not imply the criminalisation of any conducts. While opposing this method's suitability as a hate crime provision, the ILT is nevertheless not applicable to it (Table 3.1).

4.2 Tier II: Protected Grounds

4.2.1 Preliminary Considerations

The choice of which personal features to include in hate crime law is probably the most controversial among the four variables under examination. This is due to the almost exclusive role identity politics play in many jurisdictions when lawmakers are called to pass bias crimes law (Jacobs & Potter, 1998). Preliminary discussions about which criteria to use, and the resulting adoption of one or more criteria following a reasoned approach, would be highly beneficial to reduce the impact of political lobbying in the process. Albeit with different perspectives, all criteria identified in Chap. 2 foresee an empirical exam of the relevance of a given characteristic for the purpose of including it in bias crime law.

As we have seen, the standards adopted to decide which groups to protect are not usually explicitly mentioned in the law (although they may be). What we can always "see" in these provisions is the way in which

Table 3.1 Legitimacy assessment of Tier I—Methods to draft hate crime law

	Substantive offences	Specific aggravating circumstances	General aggravating circumstances
Harmfulness	Some hate crimes are significantly **more harmful** than parallel crimes [reference to analysis of hate crime law as a whole]	Some hate crimes are significantly **more harmful** than parallel crimes [reference to analysis of hate crime law as a whole]	Theoretical law does not pass ILT: no empirical verifiability of harmfulness for all base offences Concrete law may be interpreted narrowly; need to assess concrete law
Wrongfulness	Some hate crimes are significantly **more wrongful** than parallel crimes [reference to analysis of hate crime law as a whole]	Some hate crimes are significantly **more wrongful** than parallel crimes [reference to analysis of hate crime law as a whole]	Not applicable for theoretical option Need to assess concrete law
Mediating maxims	Analysis not necessary	Analysis not necessary	Not applicable for theoretical version Need to assess concrete law
Conclusion: ILT Passed?	**Yes**	**Yes**	**Theoretical version: No** **Concrete law: Might be**

the list of protected groups/characteristics has been drafted. This reflects (albeit not univocally) the criteria that have been employed and, in turn, the scope of the understanding of the hate crimes concept adopted.

Thus, we can distinguish between (i) a narrow concept of hate crime, which corresponds to a short, closed list containing the traditional groups/characteristics (reflecting the criteria *innocence and desert* and *previous history of persecution, exclusion or discrimination*; (ii) an intermediate understanding, with a longer, closed list containing many characteristics (reflecting the previous criteria as well as the criteria based on the concepts of *vulnerability*, *disadvantage* and *hostility*); and (iii) a wide understanding corresponding to a an open list of grounds (reflecting all the employable criteria) (see Table 2.2 in Chap. 2).

The aim of the present section is to examine these three categories under the ILT, in order to determine their *prima facie* legitimacy.

From the outset, we can already exclude the legitimacy of the third, wide category. A provision with an open list of grounds leaves the assessment of the harmfulness and wrongfulness of the conduct to the authorities and, ultimately, to judges/juries. While this flexibility can probably be beneficial in the day-by-day fight of hate crimes, it nevertheless fails to comply with the preliminary requirement of the ILT (and of both the harm principle and the *offensività* principle): it does not allow to empirically verify the legitimacy of this part of the provision in the criminalisation phase. In other words, there should be empirical evidence that hate crimes against a given social group or people sharing the same characteristics hurt more than parallel crimes. In order to find and assess such evidence, we must be able to identify the group *before* criminalising the conduct at stake. Moreover, unlike in the case of aggravating circumstances, where judges may interpret these provisions in favour of the offender and narrow down their scope of application, an open list of grounds implies the use of an analogy *in malam partem* (i.e. against the defendant), which is usually proscribed in criminal law.

This does not mean, however, that an open list of grounds should be forbidden *in all areas of law*. It is, in fact, highly useful in developing policies to tackle hate crimes, e.g. by promoting data collection and research on new groups that appear to be targeted in a given context, educational programs, or measures to address the needs of victims, and so on. However, the special features of criminal law (and, particularly, the especially negative effect that condemnatory sentences have on offenders) require its boundaries to be very narrow and strictly harm-oriented. Moreover, this category also falls foul of rule of law requirements, as it allows the criminalisation as a hate crime of a conduct directed against a group that is neither identified nor straightforwardly identifiable.

4.2.2 How Much Harm Does Hate Crimes' Bias Element Cause?

Interest Dimensions Affected

Physical Dimension

The bias component of hate crimes does not directly intrude upon any interests pertaining to the physical dimension of quality of life, which are instead reflected by the base offence. However, the fact that a crime is committed out of bias can *indirectly* affect the severity of the base offence, in terms of the ultimate, physical and psychological harm caused to victims. In particular, in some geographical contexts, research indicates that the severity of the base offences changes in relation to the personal characteristic or group membership of the victim. That is to say, hate crimes against certain groups are more violent than others.

Research on hate crimes against the homeless in the US, for example, shows that bias crimes directed against this part of the population are much more likely to end in fatality than otherwise-motivated bias offences (Al-Hakim, 2015, 1760). Cheng, Ickes and Kenworthy (2013, 780) have found that racist and homophobic crimes are "more likely to be directed against persons, whereas antireligious hate crimes [are] more likely to be directed against property." Moreover, in comparison with antireligious bias offences, homophobic and racist hate crimes are more severe, as they are more likely to involve simple and aggravated assault (Cheng et al., 2013, 785).[16] Other studies show that homophobic hate crimes tend to be more violent than other motivated bias offences. Lantz and Kim (2019) maintain that hate crimes are generally more violent because they are "significantly more likely than other crimes to involve the participation of multiple offenders or co-offending," characteristics that, in turn, are proven to be related to serious injuries to victims (Lantz & Kim, 2019, 438). However, they point out that homophobic crimes constitute an important exception. These kinds of hate crimes, in fact, "are significantly associated with the likelihood of serious victim injury even after

[16] Hate crimes against Muslims constitute an exception to this pattern (Cheng et al., 2013, 780).

accounting for the presence of multiple offenders" (Lantz & Kim, 2019, 448). Similar findings have been put forward by Lannert (2015) and Gruenewald and Allison (2018), as well as in less recent studies (Berril, 1992). Moreover, Pezzella and Fetzer (2017) found higher rates of physical injuries among lesbians, while Williams and Tregidga report that "over a third of victims of transgender and disability hate crimes … stated that violent crimes were the most serious they had experienced" (Williams & Tregidga, 2014, 960–961). Other studies point out how the intersection of different characteristics also plays a role in the physical harm suffered by hate crime victims. Von Schulthess, for example, suggests that non-White lesbians would be more likely than White lesbians to suffer violence (Von Schulthess, 1992).

A higher rate of violent hate-motivated offences against a certain social group, in comparison to other hate crime victims and non-hate crime victims, denotes both a higher/actual risk of hate crime victimisation for the group in question and higher hostility in its regard. Moreover, if these results cover a quite long period of time (decades at least), also the criterion *previous history of persecution, exclusion or discrimination* comes into play. Although the present findings show strong patterns of violent crime against LGBTI people, the homeless and persons with disabilities, the data is limited to the US geographical context and partly contested by other studies. These results cannot be used to gauge the extra harmfulness of bias offences in the criminalisation process. However, they are nevertheless relevant to address the phenomenon at stake under other policy measures, such as when elaborating crime prevention measures, or putting in place restorative justice initiatives.

Psychological Dimension

Most studies agree that hate crimes, as a general category, cause more psychological harm than parallel offences. Although it has been covering an increasing number of personal features, research does not often disaggregate and compare data between grounds. Therefore, the added psychological harmfulness of hate crimes taken as a whole category may be due to the fact that psychological harm may be greater for certain groups and lesser for others. So far, only a few studies have carried out comparative analysis between grounds (Mellgren et al., 2017; Williams & Tregidga, 2014). These studies show that victims targeted because of their sexual orientation, gender identity or disability suffer greater harm in comparison with other hate crime victims (Williams & Tregidga, 2014, 951; 963; Mellgren et al., 2017, 6–7). Further research should assess the harm suffered by each *strand* (or even better, by each subcategory under each strand) in comparison with parallel crimes' victims, possibly divided by type of base offence, too. However, what the present section is interested with is to know whether there is evidence that hate crimes directed against a given group are more harmful than parallel offences; while interesting, comparison between groups is irrelevant for the application of the ILT.

The disaggregated data we have is limited and geographically circumscribed to the United States, the United Kingdom, and Sweden; however, some strong patterns can be identified.[17] From the studies conducted so far it appears clear that, in comparison with parallel offences committed without bias, hate crimes perpetrated on the basis of the following grounds cause more psychological harm to direct victims: *sexual orientation* (e.g. Herek et al., 1997; Herek et al., 1999; Herek et al., 2002; Mellgren et al., 2017; Tiby, 2009); *race* and *ethnic/national origins* (e.g. Craig-Henderson & Sloan, 2003; Iganski & Lagou, 2015b); *religion* (e.g. J. Levin & McDevitt, 1993b); *gender identity* (e.g. Mellgren et al., 2017); *disability* (e.g. Coleman et al., 2013; Iganski & Lagou, 2015b; Nocon et al., 2011); *sex/gender* (e.g. Mellgren et al., 2017; Zempi & Smith, 2021); *belonging to a subculture* (Garland, 2010).

Research on the *vicarious effect* of bias crimes has focused on a limited number of strands. Craig (1999), for example, analysed the different reactions that two groups of US students, Blacks and Whites,

[17] The first studies showing the heightened psychological harmfulness of bias crimes took into account a limited number of grounds: particularly, race, national/ethnic origins (e.g. Iganski & Lagou, 2015b), and religion (J. Levin & McDevitt, 1993b). Further studies started to also incorporate sexual orientation, gender identity and disability (K. Smith et al., 2012; Corcoran et al., 2015; Pezzella & Fetzer, 2017; Sharrock et al., 2018; Fetzer & Pezzella, 2019), and then also gender and age (Williams & Tregidga, 2014). A few studies covered other types of grounds, such as belonging to a subculture (Garland, 2010; Garland & Hodkinson, 2014) and homelessness (Al-Hakim, 2015).

respectively, had after viewing a scripted video of a racist assault. The emotional and cognitive response differed between the two groups. The Black students expressed being angrier and aware that they could be possible victims of the same type of crime, and had desire for revenge. Similar feelings of vulnerability and lack of safety following racist incidents were also reported among members of the Asian community in the United States (Lim, 2009).

Research on the impact of anti-LGBTI crimes evidences an unequivocal, negative effect on non-victims sharing the same characteristic of the direct victim. In particular, Noelle's study evidences "clear shifts in [the participants'] assumptions of benevolence of the world and of people," as well as increased feelings of vulnerability, shock and denial (Noelle, 2002, 45–46). Bell and Perry's more recent study conducted in Canada, and Lannert's research, report similar results (Bell & Perry, 2015; Lannert, 2015).

Perry and Alvi's research addresses the in *terrorem effect* of hate crimes among seven communities identified as vulnerable in Ontario, Canada: Aboriginal peoples, African Canadians, Asians, South Asians, Jews, Muslims, and homosexual, bisexual, and transsexual/transgender persons. The results show that the different groups had "strikingly similar patterns of emotional and behavioural responses" that consisted of "a complex syndrome of reactions, including shock, anger, fear/vulnerability, inferiority, and a sense of the normativity of violence" (Perry & Alvi, 2012, 58).

Similar vicarious impacts were also identified among persons belonging to a subculture (Goths) that has been repeatedly and violently targeted in the area concerned (Garland & Hodkinson, 2014, 622–623).

The core reasons why hate crimes cause more psychological harm are similar across the different victim groups. They reflect a mechanism that does not depend on the personal characteristic *per se*, but that has instead to do with how fundamental the attacked feature is for the victims, the general conditions of disadvantage or vulnerability they find themselves in relation with this feature, and their relation with other people having the same characteristic. However, for some groups there are further, exacerbating factors. For example, in victims belonging to a social group with a history of oppression and discrimination "the crime serves as a painful reminder of the cultural heritage of past and ongoing discrimination, stereotyping, and stigmatization of their identity group" (Iganski & Lagou, 2015b, 1699). Moreover, persons belonging to socially disadvantaged groups (e.g. the homeless, people with disabilities, trans people) are often left in isolation and lack of proper community support, which increases the psychological pain resulting from the crime (Williams & Tregidga, 2014, 959–960). In the case of homosexual and bisexual victims, internalised homophobia or biphobia, and the strength of their connection with a wider LGBTI community play a strong role in their ability to cope with their victimisation (Noelle, 2002, 30; Bell & Perry, 2015, 103). Moreover, in some geographical contexts LGBTI persons are more likely to suffer a violent attack than other hate crime victims, which exacerbates the psychological harm suffered. As regards trans persons, Hardy and Chakraborti (2020, 117) observe that "it is evident that the emotional harm caused to transgender respondents who have experienced both the more 'everyday' and 'extreme' acts of hate referred is acute, with high proportions citing feeling upset, vulnerable, distrustful, angry, depressed and suicidal."

From these reflections we can draw a connection between hate crime's intrusion into the psychological sphere of victims and the ground-selection criteria that can be employed to decide which groups to include in hate crime provisions. As we have seen, increased negative psychological reactions are common across all the social groups analysed by extant research. They do not include only *identity politics* groups, that is to say, those collectivities that, having a history of discrimination and/or oppression, could form strong political alliances to effectively advocate for their rights. On the contrary, even more recently constituted groups (e.g. those belonging to subcultures) present similar patterns of psychological distress in comparison with consolidated hate crime victim groups. Previous history of repeated victimisation and awareness of the overall prejudice they are subjected to are factors that strongly influence the psychological reactions of hate crime victims. These elements are in turn connected with the selecting criteria *high risk/actual trend of victimisation*, *vulnerability*, *disadvantage* and *hostility*. All these criteria capture, albeit from different perspectives, the way in which hate crimes strike at the core of victims' identities. Moreover, the victimisation patterns identified so far can help us to predict which other personal characteristics/group memberships can be considered as hate crime victims. Al-Hakim's work on the inclusion of homelessness under US hate crime law, for example, points to the high rate of crime directed against homeless people, its seriousness, and the condition of disadvantage the homeless find themselves in (Al-Hakim, 2015; see also The National Coalition for the Homeless, 2012; and B. Levin, 2015). All these are indicators of a possible higher level of psychological harm. Specific research on this point is however necessary, because other personal circumstances may counteract the experience of negative psychological reactions.

A similar debate concerns *ageist* hate crime. In the aftermath of the COVID-19 outbreak, discrimination and hate speech against old people have grown exponentially. Concerns have been raised by NGOs (see AGE Platform Europe, 2021) and even by the UN's Independent Expert on the Enjoyment of all Human Rights by Older Persons (United Nations, 2020; see Peršak, 2022, 94). However, specific research on ageist-motivated crime is still limited and needs to be further developed. Most studies either frame crimes against old people as elderly abuse—where the added harm is explained in terms of the consequence of an abuse of power or trust towards an already vulnerable victim—or focus instead on the circumstantial factors that make old people more suitable targets in the eye of the offender, who nevertheless harbours no particular hostility against that specific social group.[18] However, offences actually motivated by the offender's bias or hostility towards the victim's old age do exist and, as with disability offences or crimes against the homeless, present certain patterns that make them very likely to cause added harm to their victims. In turn, this added harm can be explained through the criteria of disadvantage and vulnerability—situations in which old people find themselves *vis-à-vis* the perpetrators (Al-Hakim, 2015; Mason-Bish, 2013).

[18] The latter cases are better understood by referring to *lifestyle/routine activity theory*, which predicts that the probability that an offence be committed arises when a motivated offender and suitable target meet in the absence of capable guardians. See, for example, Payne and Gainey's study on elder abuse in nursing homes (Payne & Gainey, 2006) and DeLiema's work on elder fraud and financial exploitation (DeLiema, 2018).

The negative ground-selection criterion *innocence and desert* does not seem to be applicable to the analysis of the intrusion into hate crime victims' psychological dimension. If members of advantaged groups (such as the rich, members of armed forces, or the White majority) are attacked because of their salient feature, they may suffer higher psychological harm than victims of parallel offences, in a similar manner as persons belonging to disadvantaged groups. Moreover, research on hate crimes committed against child molesters or abusers shows victimisation patterns very similar to those of "innocent" hate crime victims (Mason, 2007, 2014). Social groups that society strongly condemns (e.g. sex offenders, criminals, and so on) can in fact find themselves in a situation of vulnerability, hostility and social exclusion. This criterion, therefore, appears to be irrelevant when analysed through a psychological dimension perspective. However, it will become relevant when assessed under the normative facet of harm as well as under wrongfulness considerations.

Although the studies carried out so far are limited to some geographical areas, their findings are unambiguous in indicating that hate crimes committed towards certain social groups do cause more psychological harm, both to direct victims and to members of their community. This is the case for personal characteristics such as race, ethnic and national origins; sexual orientation; gender identity; disability; religion; sex/gender; and, in certain contexts, also the belonging to a subculture. Research in this field is currently limited to a certain number of grounds. Although certain studies suggest that hate crimes against other personal characteristics such as homelessness and age may present a similar added harmfulness, further specific analysis is needed.

All ground-selection criteria—except for the criterion *innocence and desert*—are compatible with the results so obtained as they all take into account, albeit from different perspectives, one of more fundamental reasons why hate crimes hurt more psychologically than parallel offences.

Normative Dimension

Interest to Equal Dignity and Equal Respect In accordance with their nature of message crimes, hate offences have the effect of intruding upon victims' interest to equal dignity and equal respect (Goisis, 2015;

Laurenzo Copello, 2019; Morassutto, 2015; Pelissero, 2015). When the crime motive is directly connected with a victim's salient characteristic or group membership, the message conveyed to the direct and the vicarious targets is that they do not deserve the same level of respect as those who do not belong to that social group. This is so because the offender would not have committed the crime but for that relevant feature of the victim. The base offence often already contains a violation of the victim's right to equal dignity and respect. The bias component of hate crimes, however, adds further normative harm since the discriminatory treatment is the essence of this phenomenon.

The normative interest to equal dignity/respect is impaired even though the victim does not actually suffer any heightened negative psychological reaction; and even regardless of whether the concrete victim is aware that their right to be treated with respect and consideration has been violated. In gauging a conduct's harmfulness, we must take into consideration the impact that it has on a standard victim. According to the general, objective concept of equal dignity and equal respect that has been adopted, everyone has the right to be treated with respect just for being human. This means that even those persons that do not have, or have lost (permanently or temporarily), the capacity to understand and appreciate their interest to equal dignity and equal respect, are still entitled to it (for example, persons with a serious mental disability due to illness or old age; or very small children). The same goes for those persons that have become so used to being despised and excluded from the general, mainstream community that they do not consider themselves worthy of respect anymore.

How is the interest to equal respect reflected by the different ground-selection criteria?

First of all, not all crimes motivated on victims' personal characteristics or group memberships intrude upon their interest to equal respect in a serious way. Only attacks against certain personal features do. What do these features have in common? First, they constitute a core part of the victim's identity, whether immutable or not. Furthermore, all the positive ground-selecting criteria reflect the fact that hate crimes are not isolated incidents, but constitute instead a fundamental part of a more general negative prejudice directed against the characteristic in question. The criteria *previous history of persecution, exclusion or discrimination*, and *current high/actual risk or trend of persecution, exclusion or discrimination* take into account past and current expressions of prejudice, respectively. The concepts of disadvantage, vulnerability and hostility instead address the way the offender sees the victim and embed the idea of lack of equal respect in a more individualised way.

Previous history and current trends of oppression and discrimination can be interpreted as exacerbating the degree of intrusion into hate crime victims' interest to equal dignity and respect. This is so because these two criteria straightforwardly refer to society's past or present general prejudice and negative attitude towards the social groups victims belong to. Thus, they take explicitly into consideration also the normative harm bias crimes cause to vicarious victims. The group characteristics that fall into these two categories depend on the particular circumstances of time and space in a given country. However, we can point to certain features that in Western countries appear to fulfil these criteria's requirements: race and ethnic origins, religion, sexual orientation, gender identity, sex/gender, disability, and age. They also correspond to the most frequently covered group characteristics in hate crime law across the OSCE region.

On the other hand, the negative criterion *innocence and desert* is more difficult to classify. According to it, crimes committed against undeserving members of the population (child abusers, members of organised crime, etc.) should not be labelled as hate crimes and not covered by hate crime legislation. The same goes for crimes against members of advantaged parts of society (e.g. the rich, members of police and armed forces, majority groups). At first sight, this criterion would seem to mean that some persons are entitled to be treated with respect and others not. However, this argument can be rebutted by observing that these types of crimes are already covered by base offences. In that sense, the law treats victims with the same respect that it accords to other members of society. In the case of hate crimes committed towards vulnerable or disadvantaged members of society instead, the lack of respect is more severe, and deserves to be punished more harshly.

The problem concerns some of the so-called undeserving groups, which can also be described as vulnerable or disadvantaged (e.g. child molesters) due to the very negative attitude society has towards them. Is it legitimate to exclude these groups from the protection offered by hate crime law? Probably yes. The idea that the victim be "innocent" lies at the base of the conceptualisation of hate crimes. This is so because the victim's innocence contrasts with the negative stereotypes that hate crime offenders target. The concept of *innocence* is not used here in an absolute way, but must instead be compared with the prejudice attributed by hate crime offenders to a given personal characteristic. For example, transphobic offenders target trans people because they think that transgenderism is a "bad" feature that takes away the victim's innocence (for example, because they consider it being immoral, or against nature, or an attack against the principles of a given religion). They are motivated by a negative attitude towards transgender identity, based however on stereotyped and prejudice-based ideas. Being trans is not good or bad *per se*, it is just a part of someone's identity, as being cisgender is. In that sense, trans victims are innocent because the prejudice towards them is unfounded. In the case of child abusers, conversely, they are targeted because of a wrongdoing that they have (supposedly) committed, that society considers extremely hideous. In that sense, they are not innocent in the sense used here. This does not mean that people should be authorised to commit crimes against paedophiles; the base offence already covers this criminal conduct, thus respecting the principle of equality before the law. However, in their case, the right to equal respect cannot be said to be intruded upon at the same level as in the case of hate crimes directed against innocent victims.

On the basis of these considerations, we can conclude that all ground-selecting criteria can be in principle legitimately used to determine which personal characteristics should be covered by hate crime legislation, as they all embed the assessment of the intrusion into the victim's interest to equal respect.

Interest to Individuality Hate crimes offenders often choose their victims randomly. They target a certain personal feature, not the individual person *per se*. The fact that sometimes victims know, and perhaps very well, the offender, does not diminish the impairment of their interest to individuality. The criteria *previous history of persecution, exclusion or discrimination, current high/actual risk or trend of persecution, exclusion or* *discrimination*, and *hostility* address more clearly the issue of individuality. They do not refer directly to the direct victim of hate crimes, but, more widely, they focus on how the personal characteristic itself has been the past, or current, target of prejudice. The concepts of *disadvantage* and *vulnerability* address instead the victims in a more holistic way. Their wide scope allows, on the one hand, to capture all the personal circumstances (including one or more personal features) that make victims the target of hate crimes. On the other hand, they also include certain elements that cannot be straightforwardly subsumed under a specific personal characteristic. The assessment of the intrusion into the interest to individuality is more ambiguous, as it is extended to all individuals (each and every person is considered as a single individual in the assessment of whether he has been a victim of a hate crime). However, we can also argue that, in this way, the interest to individuality is intruded upon each time that a person is targeted because of her situation of vulnerability or disadvantage. In fact, what the offender targets is what the victim represents, not who they really are.

Is this also true for advantaged or underserving categories of victims (e.g. the rich, members of criminal organisations, child abusers and so on)? At first sight, their interest to individuality seems to be affected as in other groups' cases. They are targeted for what they are (e.g. the rich), or for the institution they represent (e.g. members of the armed forces), or for the wrongdoing they have committed (in the case of persons criminally convicted), not for their personality. Here the *innocence* criterion, albeit applied in a relative way in relation with the prejudice surrounding the victim's characteristic, does not seem applicable.

In conclusion, all crime victims attacked because of a characteristic they possess have their interest to individuality intruded upon; we are not in the position to make any distinctions among targeted groups.

Interest to Autonomy A further effect resulting from the message nature of the bias component of hate crimes is that of spreading fear of further or future victimisation across the direct victim's community (and towards direct victims themselves). In response to this fear, direct and vicarious victims adopt a range of avoidance strategies. They are specific to each type of personal feature, but they mostly consist of concealing the relevant characteristic and avoiding places where the perceived risk of possible victimisation seems higher. They ultimately result in an impairment to victims' interest to autonomy, because they feel no longer free to express a core part of their identity.

Avoidance strategies have been identified among direct and vicarious victims pertaining to all the most relevant group strands: *race/ethnicity* (K. Smith et al., 2012; Perry & Alvi, 2012; Iganski & Lagou, 2015a; Corcoran et al., 2015; Benier, 2017; Sharrock et al., 2018); *religion* (K. Smith et al., 2012; Perry & Alvi, 2012; Iganski & Lagou, 2015a; Corcoran et al., 2015; Iganski & Sweiry, 2016; Sharrock et al., 2018); *gende*r (Mellgren et al., 2017); *sexual orientation* (Noelle, 2002; K. Smith et al., 2012; Perry & Alvi, 2012; Iganski & Lagou, 2015a; Bell & Perry, 2015; Lannert, 2015; Sharrock et al., 2018); *gender identity* (K. Smith et al., 2012; Perry & Alvi, 2012; Iganski & Lagou, 2015a; Sharrock et al., 2018); *disability* (K. Smith et al., 2012; Iganski & Lagou, 2015a; Sharrock et al., 2018); and *members of subcultures* (Garland & Hodkinson, 2014, 623).

As to a whole social group's deployment of a common avoidance strategy, research has pointed to the recent French Jews migration out of France in the aftermath of an increasing escalation of anti-Semitic hate crimes in that country (Iganski & Sweiry, 2016, 98). Fear of repeated or future victimisation, which triggers the adoption of avoidance strategies, is widespread across the different categories of hate crime victims analysed, and higher in comparison with victims of non-hate motivated crimes. However, comparative research between different groups is scarce; thus, we cannot establish whether certain groups suffer more secondary harm than others.

Each of the positive ground-selection criteria captures the issue of autonomy, albeit with slight differences. *Previous history of discrimination and/or oppression* and *high risk/actual trend of victimisation* focus on specific reasons why hate crime victims present higher levels of fear. The hate offence is not seen as an isolated incident, but as part of a wider pattern of oppression and discrimination and as a very likely possibility, respectively. On the other hand, the concepts of *disadvantage*, *vulnerability* and *hostility* point to the offender's perception of the overall circumstances of the victim, including any relevant element of intersectionality, as well as to the victim's awareness and reaction to this perception. These three concepts allow one to also include in hate crime legislation those strands that do not present a previous history of discrimination and/or oppression, and particularly those groups that do not have enough internal cohesion and power to compete in the identity politics race.

The negative ground-selecting criterion *innocence and desert* does not seem to be applicable here. Unfortunately, there is not sufficient available research on the intrusion into the interest to autonomy resulting from crimes directed against undeserving or advantaged social groups. However, we can *prima facie* argue that the mechanisms that lead to this kind of secondary harm are similar across all groups. The fear stems from the awareness of possessing a characteristic (being it "innocent" or not) that makes people potential targets of crime and in that sense is connected with the intrusion upon the interest to individuality.

Levels of Intrusion into Quality of Life's Dimensions and Resulting Harm

On the basis of the analysis carried out in the previous section, we can classify hate crimes' levels of intrusion into the different interest dimensions identified and the resulting harm as follows.

With regard to quality-of-life's *physical* category, it is not possible to gauge the bias element of hate crimes' level of intrusion and resulting harm. Research has pointed out that in certain geographical contexts (particularly in the US) homophobic and transphobic hate crimes are far more violent than otherwise motivated bias offences and non-bias motivated crimes. However, hate crimes' intrusion into victims' physical dimension of quality of life concerns the base offence and not the bias element of hate crimes (at least, directly). Therefore, these findings cannot be applied in the context of assessing the added harmfulness the bias element brings about.

As to the *psychological* dimension, the level of intrusion and resulting harm can be measured as follows:

- *Direct victims* (sexual orientation; race and ethnic/national origins; religion; gender identity; disability; gender; belonging to subculture;

and possibly homelessness and old age)—level of intrusion: minimal well-being; level of harm: serious;

- *Vicarious victims* (race and ethnic/national origins; religion; sexual orientation; gender identity; gender; belonging to a subculture)—level of intrusion: adequate well-being; level of harm: moderate.

Here we could assess only a limited number of grounds, corresponding to those characteristics covered by existing research on the matter. Studies comparing the degrees of psychological harm between different characteristics are still insufficient to draw sound conclusions. Thus, the psychological harm suffered by groups has been classified at the same level. The same goes for the normative interest to autonomy below.

As regards the interests pertaining to the *normative* category:

- *Equal dignity/equal respect* (direct and vicarious victims)—level of intrusion: minimal well-being; level of harm: serious;
- *Individuality* (direct victims)—level of intrusion: adequate well-being; level of harm: moderate;
- *Autonomy* (direct and vicarious victims belonging to groups based on race/ethnicity; religion; gender; sexual orientation, gender identity; disability, and subcultures)—level of intrusion: adequate well-being/ minimal well-being; level of harm: moderate/serious.

Bias offences' intrusion into the normative interest to equal respect and dignity is an objective consequence of hate crimes that virtually applies to all social groups, except for those that cannot be said to be "innocent". On the other hand, the intrusion into victims' interest to individuality takes place for all social groups, includ those who are underserving or not "innocent".

When analysed through the lens of harmfulness, all the positive ground-selection criteria are legitimate. They all take into account, albeit differently, how hate crimes intrude upon different dimension of victims' quality of life and thus produce harm. The negative, *innocence and desert* criterion is however applicable only as regards the analysis of the intrusion into victims' normative interest to equal dignity and respect. Despite this, the importance of the interest in question, compounded with the liberal aim to limit and contain criminalisation, are sufficient to consider it as a legitimate criterion under harmfulness considerations.

In conclusion, the overall results show that not only traditional, 'identity politics' hate crime victims suffer significant heightened harm (those identified by their race, ethnic or national origins, religion) but also members of other groups (LGBTI people, persons with disabilities, women, members of subcultures, homeless people, the elderly, and so on). Extant research points to some patterns and mechanisms that lead to increased harm under certain circumstances. Therefore, we can assume that also members of other social groups suffer heightened levels of harm provided that certain conditions are met. However, further research is needed in order to draw any conclusions from a legitimacy point of view.

4.2.3 Wrongfulness Issues

Hate crimes, as a whole crime category, are considered to be more wrongful in comparison with parallel crimes as well as crimes committed against undeserving and advantaged groups. This is so, because they constitute a distinctive moral wrong by reason of their discriminatory nature. However, this discriminatory element is not sufficient to conclude that hate crimes are more wrongful than parallel crimes. It also depends on the kind of targeted group characteristics, which must pass a positive and a negative test, respectively.

As to the *positive* prong, what makes the characteristic positively relevant is not only the discrimination implied in the offender's choice to target a given feature, but also the overall situation surrounding the victim's characteristic. This second factor can in turn be explained by using the concepts of disadvantage, vulnerability, hostility, or previous or current oppression and discrimination. Each of the positive ground-selection criteria are therefore acceptable as they all reflect the added wrongfulness of bias crimes and provide an explanation of why it is so. This line of reasoning thus allows us to exclude the extra wrongfulness of those crimes directed against advantaged social groups (e.g. the rich, members of armed forces, members of the government, etc.). As to the *negative* part of the test, the relative concept of 'innocence' comes again into play.

Those group characteristics that cannot be said to be 'innocent' cannot claim a further, distinctive degree of wrongfulness than that of the base offence. The concept of wrong is inextricably connected with the morals and values of a given time and space, which in turn shape the relative notion of 'innocence' that we have adopted under the analysis of hate crimes intrusion into the interest to equal respect. Framing as hate crimes also those offences directed against non-innocent groups would run counter to the concept of wrong as currently perceived by current Western societies. Thus, it appears legitimate to apply the *innocence and desert* criterion also under a wrongfulness perspective.

In conclusion, both the positive and the negative ground-selection criteria reasonably pass the wrongfulness part of the ILT.

4.2.4 Conclusions

Three, different methods to include protected characteristics in hate crimes law have been identified: a short, closed list of strands; a longer, closed list; and a long, open list of grounds. These techniques correspond, in turn, to a narrow, intermediate, and wide concept of hate crimes, respectively. Moreover, each reflects the use of one or more different positive and negative selection criteria.

Across the OSCE region, race, ethnic origin and religion are always covered by hate crime law. Sexual orientation, gender identity, gender and disability are less frequently included. Moreover, a few states provide for a long list of other grounds (e.g. age, social status, health), sometimes with the possibility to include other characteristics not explicitly foreseen by the law.

The application of the ILT to the three drafting methods has given the following results. First, the technique consisting of an open list of grounds has been considered illegitimate from the beginning, as it does not comply with the empirical verifiability of the conduct's harmfulness. Conversely, the other two drafting methods are both legitimate. All the ground-selection criteria are legitimate to decide which grounds to include. As to the specific grounds, not only traditional identity politics group-memberships have passed the test, but also other, more recently debated features (e.g. sexual orientation, gender identity, gender, disability, and possibly, age). In short, offences motivated by bias against individuals possessing certain characteristics that comply with the ground-selection criteria identified in Chapter 2 are indeed more harmful and more wrongful than the respective base crimes. The results concerning this added harmfulness and wrongfulness are clear and there is thus no need to apply further mediating maxims (Table 3.2).

Table 3.2 Legitimacy assessment of Tier II—Protected grounds

	Only some features (short, closed list)	Many features and closed list	Many features and open list
Harmfulness	Bias crimes committed in connection with traditional personal features (race, ethnic origins, nationality, religion) are significantly **more harmful** than parallel crimes	Bias crimes committed in connection with a wider number of personal features (e.g. sexual orientation, gender identity, gender, disability, age) are significantly **more harmful** than parallel crimes	This option does not pass ILT at the outset: no empirical verifiability
Wrongfulness	Bias crimes committed in connection with traditional personal features (race, ethnic origins, nationality, religion) are significantly **more wrongful** than parallel crimes	Bias crimes committed in connection with a wider number of personal features (e.g. sexual orientation, gender identity, gender, disability, age) are significantly **more wrongful** than parallel crimes	Not applicable
Mediating maxims	Analysis not necessary	Analysis not necessary	Not applicable
Conclusion: ILT passed?	**Yes**	**Yes**	**No**

4.3 Tier III: Kind of Evidence and Amount of Hate Required

4.3.1 Preliminary Considerations

The present tier deals with the amount of hate or bias[19] required to accompany the base crime in order to frame the conduct as a hate crime, as well as with whether, and how, hate crime law explicitly mentions the kind of evidence required to prove so. These issues are in turn strictly connected with the fourth tier on the nexus between the bias component and the crime. At the outset, we can already conclude that the second part of the tier—on the kind of evidence the law requires—cannot be properly assessed from a legitimacy point of view. It does not criminalise anything; it is instead a rule of procedural nature that specifies, and must be read in conjunction with, other criminal procedure provisions.

Moreover, the general part of the present chapter has analysed, and concluded in favour of, the legitimacy of bias crime law taken as a whole. In doing so, bias has been considered as the sole motive of the crime. Therefore, on the basis of those findings we can already conclude that the first, narrowest position, requiring the crime to be motivated solely by hate/bias, does pass the ILT. This section will thus focus only on the analysis of the legitimacy of the other two ways this aspect of the law can be theoretically drafted, with hate either as the main motive of the crime or as just one among other motives. These two methods are in turn connected with an intermediate and a wide understanding of the hate crime concept, respectively.

[19] These terms are not used in their literal meanings, but as umbrella words, to indicate all possible negative and hostile emotions and attitudes that can explain perpetrators' reasons why they commit a hate crime (hatred, prejudice, loath, disgust, etc.).

4.3.2 How Much Harm Does Hate Crimes' Bias Element Cause?

Interest Dimensions Affected

Physical Dimension

Research suggests that most hate crimes are low-level crimes committed by ordinary people with a low degree of hate motivation (Iganski, 2008; McDevitt et al., 2002). However, studies conducted in the United States indicate that hate crimes are more likely to result in serious injuries than parallel crimes (particularly for some types of victims). Less recent research suggested that the increased violence and brutality of these types of crimes was due to the offender's hostile animus, the bias element of the offence (J. Levin & McDevitt, 1993b; Perry, 2001). Further studies, however, observed that bias crimes are often associated with high rates of co-offending, a factor that alone increases the level of violence involved in the offence (e.g. B. Levin, 1999; Pezzella & Fetzer, 2017). Lantz and Kim's study analyses whether hate crimes are more violent because of the offender's bias towards the victim or because they are associated with higher rates of co-offending. They conclude that, although co-offending partially moderates this relationship, "bias is still significantly associated with increased likelihood of serious injury after controlling for co-offending" (Lantz & Kim, 2019, 451).[20] Thus, at least in the United States, the higher the level of bias involved in the offence is, the higher the probability is that the crime results in the serious intrusion into the victim's physical dimension of quality of life.

Psychological Dimension

Research carried out on bias crime offenders' motivations and profiles has shown that most hate crimes are committed by perpetrators with a "low

[20] Anti-LGBTI hate crimes, however, constitute a unique case. In fact, Lantz and Kim (2019, 450) have found that they are comparatively more violent than other hate crimes and parallel offences "regardless of the number of offenders involved in the offense."

bias commitment," where prejudice mixes up with other trivial motives, such as "mere boredom or sensation-seeking" (Andersson & Mellgren, 2016, 228). Just a minority of hate crimes are committed by high-motivated offenders, such as those belonging to specific hate groups (Neo-Nazis, White supremacy groups and so on) (J. Levin & McDevitt, 1993b; McDevitt et al., 2002; Iganski, 2008). At the same time, there is plenty of evidence that bias crimes hurt more psychologically. The *hostility* victims perceive—expressed by the bias component of hate crimes—is the main reason why these crimes cause added psychological harm to both direct and vicarious victims (Andersson & Mellgren, 2016, 231; 238; 246). From a theoretical point of view, it would seem logical that a different degree of hate expressed by the crime would correspond to a different level of psychological harm (as we have seen, this is the case in the US for physical injuries). However, this is an element that is methodologically very difficult to assess separately. The direct victim's actual perception of the offender's motives plays a central role in the process. This perception, in turn, is linked to a number of factors: their cognitive ability to understand the motives behind the crime and awareness of what is going on; the correct identification, on the part of the perpetrator, of the victim's targeted characteristic; the victim's resilience capacity, and so on. Moreover, there is evidence that the degree of psychological harm victims suffer does not depend only on the impact on the actual hate crime, but is correlated to their previous and/or repeated history of victimisation (Williams & Tregidga, 2014, 955). This means that the ultimate harm caused to victims results from a combination of the amount of bias expressed by the offender and victims' awareness of the high risk of victimisation they are subject to in connection to their personal features and/or their belonging to *minority groups*[21] in a context of widespread discrimination or oppression (Andersson & Mellgren, 2016, 228).

Therefore, crimes do not need to be motivated only by bias or hate to cause added psychological harm. The intermediate drafting method requiring hate to be, at least, the predominant motive of the crime thus

[21] The expression *minority group* goes beyond numerical considerations; as Akhtar observes, a minority "is defined by the relative weakness of its social praxis, the lack of its governmental representation, the unfairness of the judiciary towards it, and the distorted gaze of the so-called majority on it" (Akhtar, 2014, 138).

passes this part of the ILT. However, the same cannot be said with enough certainty for crimes based on mixed motives. Here, although the bias element of the crime plays a role in that it is one of the reasons why offenders select a given victim, it is not the only factor behind the psychological harm they suffer. Since the burden of proof of harmfulness lies with those who propose the conduct's criminalisation, we can argue that the mixed-motives drafting technique does not pass the psychological harmfulness part of the ILT. This is true at least in theoretical terms. In certain practical contexts, however, it can be shown that some group categories suffer high victimisation rates and find themselves in a particular position of disadvantage or vulnerability in that specific society. This, in turn, results in a higher psychological harm even though it cannot be straightforwardly proved that offenders acted solely or predominantly out of hate or bias.

Normative Dimension

Interest to Autonomy The analysis of the interest to autonomy suffers from similar methodological problems as the ones encountered under the psychological dimension part. This interest is connected to the victim's fear of future victimisation, which is a subjective emotion strongly depending on one's perceptions that is difficult to disaggregate according to the amount of hate motive expressed by the crime. As with psychological harm, victims' previous history of repeated victimisation and perception of high risk of future victimisation are key in their decision to adopt avoidance strategies. We can thus assume that, where hate is at least the predominant motive behind the crime, the intrusion into victims' interest to autonomy reaches a significant level of seriousness. The same cannot however be said as regards those situations in which bias is just one among other motives. The observations made above as regards the higher psychological harm caused to particularly disadvantaged or vulnerable groups apply here as well; to receive a final answer, this issue has to be examined with regard to a concrete piece of law in a specific legal context.

Interests to Individuality and to Equal Dignity and Respect The other two normative interests hate crimes usually intrude upon—individuality and equal respect/equal dignity—have a more prominent objective fashion that can be examined regardless of a standard victim's perception. Even though some hate crime victims do not suffer more psychological harm than victims of parallel crimes (for example, because they have developed a high level of resilience), their normative interest to equal respect and individuality can nevertheless be set back in a serious way.

Crimes motivated only in part by hate might not always infringe the interest to individuality. Let's consider this example. X has a quarrel with her neighbours Y and Z regarding a parking lot that they are supposed to share; X is heterosexual and Y and Z are in a same-sex relationship; X has never liked the idea of living next to a same-sex couple; in fact, she is "a bit" homophobic even though she has never had the opportunity to manifest her thoughts on the matter; she actually never thought about hurting anyone just because of their sexual orientation. However, this time she is so enraged about the parking lot that she decides to paint a homophobic insult on her neighbours' wall. She would have done the same neither to a random same-sex couple, nor to the opposite-sex couple of neighbours living on the other side of the street with which she had a number of similar quarrels in the past. Therefore, X's motives are both connected to her neighbours' sexual orientation and the issue about the parking lot and fall under the mixed-motives category.

What if, however, the parking lot issue is just an opportunity for X to finally express her homophobic views by damaging her neighbours' property? What if she was just looking for an excuse to manifest her prejudice (this is a case in which hate/bias is the main, albeit not the only, motive of the crime)? In this case, we can assume that she would not have committed the base offence had her neighbours not been in a same-sex relationship. Therefore, the mixed-motives hate crime example does not seem to interfere with the interest to individuality in a relevant way. However, when hate is proven to be the main motive of the crime, the victim's interest to individuality is substantially intruded upon.

The same example is useful to illustrate also a similar problem under the interest to equal dignity and equal respect. In crimes committed wholly or mostly out of hate the offence is committed because the victim possesses a given characteristic that perpetrators dislike. They would not commit that crime if the victim did not have that specific characteristic. In crimes committed only partially out of hate motives, perpetrators would perhaps commit the crime in any event, as they have multiple reasons to act. Therefore, in mixed motives cases it is not clear whether the victim's equal dignity is really impaired.

Therefore, it can be concluded that, where hate or bias are the *prevalent* motives of the crime, the interests to individuality and to equal respect are significantly intruded upon. When bias, however, is only *one among other motives*, the level of intrusion into these interests does not seem sufficient to result in the causation of further harm. These conclusions apply when examining theoretical models of bias crime law. As with the intrusion into the psychological interest to mental health and the normative interest to autonomy, it cannot be excluded that in certain practical contexts lawmakers can show that certain disadvantaged groups suffer a higher form of intrusion also into their normative interest to equal dignity.

Levels of Intrusion into Quality of Life's Dimensions and Resulting Harm

The *narrow* drafting technique—in which bias is the *sole motive* of the crime—has been adopted as the default model for the assessment of hate crime law as a whole in Sect. 3 above. Thus, for this method, the identification of the level of intrusion into victims' quality of life dimensions and the gauging of the resulting harm correspond to those indicated in that section.

The adoption of an intermediate or wide drafting method as regards the amount of hate or bias required lead to different results in terms of harm assessment.

Research in the US has pointed out that in that geographical context higher levels of bias on the part of the offenders are correlated to higher levels of intrusion into victims' *physical* dimension of their quality of life. However, we cannot assess under the ILT hate crimes' bias element's level of intrusion into that category, as this is already encompassed by the base offence.

As regards the *intermediate option* (hate/bias as the predominant motive), the analysis of the *psychological* dimension leads to the following results:

- *Direct victims*—level of intrusion: minimal well-being; degree of harm: serious;
- *Vicarious victims*—level of intrusion: minimal well-being /adequate well-being; degree of harm: moderate/serious.

As to the *normative* interests, the assessment of the levels of intrusion and resulting harm is as follows:

- *Autonomy* (direct and vicarious victims)—level of intrusion: adequate well-being /minimal well-being; degree of harm: moderate/serious;
- *Individuality* (direct victims)—level of intrusion: adequate well-being; level of harm: moderate;
- *Equal dignity/respect* (direct and vicarious victims)—level of intrusion: minimal well-being; level of harm: serious.

Here, hate crimes' levels of intrusion into victims' quality of life and the degree of the resulting harm are the same as in the first drafting method. This is so because no significant differences have been identified between crimes committed only out of hate and crimes where hate is the predominant motive. Thus, this drafting technique passes the harmfulness phase of the ILT.

With regard to the wide option (hate or bias as one among other crime motives), a significant intrusion into direct and vicarious victims' psychological dimension has not been sufficiently proven. However, there is an exception for particularly disadvantaged groups in specific practical contexts, which can be assessed in a concrete case.

As regards the normative dimension, the harm assessment gives the following results:

- Equal dignity/equal respect (direct and vicarious victims): no higher degree of intrusion in comparison with base offence (but: exception for particularly disadvantaged groups in specific practical contexts);

- Autonomy (direct and vicarious victims): significant intrusion has not been sufficiently proven (but: exception for particularly disadvantaged groups in specific practical contexts);
- Individuality (direct victims): no higher degree of intrusion in comparison with base offence.

The third, wide technique, does not pass the harmfulness part of the ILT—at least when considered abstractedly from any specific legal system. There is no sound evidence proving that when hate is only one of the offender's motives the resulting intrusion into the victim's interests to mental health and to autonomy is significantly higher than in parallel crimes. Moreover, it has been argued that, in this case, the intrusion into the interests to equal dignity and respect, and to individuality, is not higher than in base offences. When analysing a concrete hate crime law in a specific jurisdiction, however, the mixed-motives approach might be considered legitimate if, and only if, it can be shown that the level of harm suffered by a certain protected group is particularly high due to the victims' specific situation of vulnerability or disadvantage.

4.3.3 Wrongfulness Issues

Let's turn now to the analysis of the different levels of wrongfulness surrounding crimes motivated mostly, or only in part, by bias.

As to crimes committed *predominantly* out of bias, their discriminatory element is strong enough to conclude that they constitute a separate wrong. This is so because perpetrators would not have committed them but for the victim's salient characteristic. Thus, it can be concluded that they are more wrongful than their parallel counterparts.

When bias is only one of the offender's motives, however, things are less straightforward. What differentiates bias offences from parallel crimes is the primary role that prejudice/bias/hate plays in the selection of victims. In the case of mixed motives, however, it is difficult to argue that the crime involves further wrongfulness reasons due to its discriminatory nature. All crimes are committed with some degree of opportunistic thoughts, and involve a choice of which type of person to target. When offenders commit the crime for a number of motives, they would probably commit it even though the victim did not have the particular salient characteristic that is the object of their prejudice.

Therefore, we can conclude that when bias is at least the predominant motive behind the crime there are further wrongfulness reasons to warrant for the legitimacy of hate crime provisions. On the other hand, when hate is only one of the motives of the crime, its added wrongfulness cannot be established.

Here as well, there exists an exception that applies to the legitimacy assessment of concrete pieces of law. According to a prioritarianism approach, in fact, the degree of wrongfulness of a criminal conduct is directly proportional to the severity of the disadvantage victims already find themselves in (see Brax, 2016, 59). Thus, if it can be shown that a given hate crime victim group is in a position of severe disadvantage or vulnerability in a concrete jurisdiction, hate crime provisions adopting a mixed-motive approach can be considered legitimate as they reflect the offence's added wrongfulness.

4.3.4 Conclusions

The third tier of the hate crime law framework concerns the amount of hate motive required to frame an offence as a hate crime. Three options have been identified, which correspond to a narrow, intermediate and wide concept of hate crimes, respectively: that the law requires the offence to be motivated only, mostly or partially by hate.

Research has shown that most hate crimes are committed out of a low amount of hate/bias. Moreover, this part of the law, albeit conceptually important, is rarely explicitly mentioned in hate crime provisions. In addition, none of the hate crime provisions enacted in the OSCE region adopts the narrowest position, foreseeing hate/bias as being the sole motive behind the crime. However, this does not mean that the amount of hate required by hate crime legislation is an irrelevant matter. Even if it is not explicitly mentioned in hate crime law, the present issue must nevertheless be dealt with in the evidentiary stage of the criminal proceedings in accordance with general rules on evidence. Moreover, it is closely linked with the fourth tier of the framework concerning the nexus between the bias element and the crime.

The assessment on whether, and which of, the three different positions on the matter are legitimate has given the following results. The first and the second drafting techniques (hate as the sole or predominant motive of the crime) have both passed the ILT. The assessment of the third method has been more problematic. On the one hand, there is not enough evidence to prove that crimes motivated only partly by hate cause additional harm in comparison with parallel offences. On the other hand, they do not seem to be more wrongful than their non-bias motivated counterparts. We therefore concluded that—at least *under a mere theoretical approach*—the third drafting technique is not legitimate under the ILT. However, there is an important exception to this: in certain cases, even if the law does not require proof of bias/hate/prejudice, it may still be considered legitimate if it nevertheless requires proof that the targeting of certain kinds of victim causes or risks to cause a particularly serious harm. This is so because in some cases hate crime victims may belong to groups that are particularly disadvantaged or vulnerable in a given social context. When these people are targeted by hate crime offenders, even by those having a low bias motivation, and even when the hate motive behind the crime is not so clear, the crime may nevertheless cause a level of harm and wrongfulness that make the conduct's criminalisation justified from a legitimacy perspective. This exception must however be applied narrowly, and be supported by evidence-based and well-argued reasons. In the next section, it will be shown how this exception is connected with the choice to use a Discriminatory Selection model to explain the connection between the offender's mental attitude and the crime.

In any event, it does not appear necessary to identify and apply further mediating maxims to the analysis. As to the intermediate option, the evidence surrounding the added harmfulness and wrongfulness of these kinds of hate crimes seems clear enough. With regard to the narrow option, it has been considered legitimate only if the causation of serious harm and wrongfulness is proven in a *concrete* legitimacy assessment (Table 3.3).

Table 3.3 Legitimacy assessment of Tier III—Amount of hate or bias

	Only hate/bias motive	Mostly hate/bias motive	Partly hate/bias motive
Harmfulness	Crimes committed *solely* out of bias are significantly **more harmful** than parallel crimes [reference to analysis of hate crime law as a whole]	Crimes committed *mostly* out of bias are significantly **more harmful** than parallel crimes	Crimes committed *partially* out of bias are **not significantly more harmful** than parallel crimes. But: exception may apply in concrete contexts (e.g. harm caused is very serious because victims are particularly disadvantaged)
Wrongfulness	Crimes committed *solely* out of bias are significantly **more wrongful** than parallel crimes [reference to analysis of hate crime law as a whole]	Crimes committed *mostly* out of bias are significantly **more wrongful** than parallel crimes.	Crimes committed *partially* out of bias are **not significantly more wrongful** than parallel crimes. But: exception may apply in concrete context (e.g. victims are particularly disadvantaged)
Mediating maxims	Analysis not necessary	Analysis not necessary	Not applicable/ Analysis not necessary
Conclusion: ILT passed?	**Yes**	**Yes**	**Theoretical model: No** **Concrete law: exception in specific contexts** (e.g. harm is very serious because victims are particularly disadvantaged)

4.4 Tier IV: Nexus Between the Offender's Mental Attitude and the Offence

4.4.1 Preliminary Considerations

The fourth tier of the hate crime law framework deals with how the connection between the mental attitude of the offender and the offence, expressed in the law, underlines either a narrow or a wide concept of hate crime. Hate crime law focussing on the emotional attitude of offenders, their hostile animus, reflects the traditional, narrow view of bias crimes (Hostility Animus model). On the other hand, the law can merely require that offenders intentionally select their victims on the basis of a protected characteristic (Discriminatory Selection model) and thus have a wider scope (see Table 2.4 in Chap. 2). In practical terms, the main difference between these two models is the kind of evidence required. The Discriminatory Selection model only asks proof that the victim has been targeted because of a particular characteristic foreseen in the law; the Hostile Animus model, as its name suggests, requires *also* proof of a prejudice-based attitude on the part of the offender toward that personal characteristic, which is much harder to obtain. Thus, a conduct that fulfils the requirements of the first model will be covered also by the second one; but not the other way round (Lawrence, 1999, 73).

The fourth tier is strictly interwoven with the third one concerning the amount of hate. Sometimes, the law does not even mention the amount of bias required to apply hate crime legislation; however, it always specifies the nexus between victims' salient feature and the offence. The choice of the kind of nexus to adopt encompasses also an implicit position as to the amount of hate to take into consideration. The Hostile Animus model, for its part, implies that the motive of the crime be, if not solely, at least predominantly hate/bias/prejudice. The Discriminatory Selection model, on the other hand, is compatible with a provision that foresees hate/bias to be just one of the motives behind the crimes. Actually, it does not explicitly foresee hate/bias at all. It would be contradictory (even though not impossible) to use a Discriminatory Selection model and then require the crime to be motivated solely by hate.

The Hostility Animus model reflects the common concept of hate crimes as prejudice-based offences involving something more than mere differential treatment (Lawrence, 1999, 34). It is the model that has been considered by default when analysing hate crime law as a whole in the general part of the present chapter. Therefore, it can already be concluded that this drafting technique passes the ILT. This section will thus analyse whether the Discriminatory Selection model also fulfils the ILT's requirements.

4.4.2 How Much Harm Does Hate Crimes' Bias Element Cause?

Interest Dimensions Affected

Physical Dimension

As shown in the previous chapter, research in the United States suggests that higher levels of hostile animus may lead to increased level of violence, and thus, of intrusion into victims' physical dimension of quality of life, on the part of bias crimes perpetrators (see, in particular, Lantz & Kim, 2019, 451). In that geographical context, therefore, the Discriminatory Selection model does not seem to capture this particular aspect of the phenomenon.

Psychological Dimension

Hate crimes offenders' hostile attitude, expressed by their attack to a central part of victims' identity, has been suggested as the main reason why these types of crimes cause more psychological harm than their parallel counterparts. However, research shows that most hate crimes are committed by offenders with a low degree of hate motivation. How can we explain the higher level of psychological harm they nevertheless cause? As suggested in Sect. 4.3.2 above, other factors must be considered: the often random nature of the attack, that make the victim powerless; the previous or current context of discrimination and/or oppression surrounding the targeted group, in which hate crimes are only the tip of the iceberg; previous episodes of hate crime victimisation; and the perception of being at high risk of future victimisation resulting from the previous factors and/or from the knowledge of hate crime victimisation of other group members. As the ODHIR (2009, 49) explains, "[a] victim who is targeted because the offender assumes that some protected characteristic of the victim makes him/her especially vulnerable to crime is likely to experience the same trauma as a victim who is targeted because the offender actually hates that characteristic. From the victim's perspective, what matters is that he/she has been chosen because of an immutable or fundamental aspect of his/her identity." This is particularly so when victims belong to groups that are already in a severe position of disadvantage or vulnerability in a given social context, and suffer repeated victimisation due to their specific situation. When they are the target of a criminal conduct, these types of victims can be prone to suffer particularly grievous psychological harm, which is of a "cumulative" nature (Hardy & Chakraborti, 2020, 117).

In this context, both the Hostile Animus and the Discriminatory Selection models can explain the added psychological harm caused to both direct and vicarious victims and we must conclude that both are admissible under this heading.

Normative Dimension

Interest to Equal Dignity/Equal Respect The Hostile Animus model reflects the fact that the crime would not be committed if victims did not have that particular personal characteristic/group membership. It is the prejudice/hostility towards a specific personal feature that explains the conduct of offenders. In turn, that negative attitude reflects offenders' view (and transmits the message that) the victims are not worthy of respect because of that characteristic. Conversely, in the Discriminatory Selection model perpetrators would perhaps commit the base crime in any event; they are only looking for a suitable victim. Hence, in this case it is not clear whether the victims' interest to equal dignity is really impaired more than in parallel, non-bias motivated crimes.

However, there are two problematic issues. First, offenders' choice may be based on victims' perceived vulnerability to that particular type of crime, which in turn may be based on one or more personal features. Second, the specific situation of disadvantage or vulnerability victims may consequently find themselves in can also lead to repeated victimisation. However, while these factors are relevant in the context of psychological harm, they are not so as regards victims' interest to equal respect. Although discriminatory selection can lead to repeated victimisation on the basis of victims' identity, in these cases offenders merely perform a selection based on convenience considerations. But this is true also for most, non-bias motivated crimes. Here, the bias element is just one of the elements behind the crime, it is not the key factor that motivates offenders.

Thus, in these cases the base offence already covers the intrusion into victims' equal respect (in the sense that nobody should be the victim of the base offence). The bias element of the crime does not further intrude upon the victim's interest to equal dignity and respect. Therefore, we can conclude that the Discriminatory Selection model does not reflect a higher degree of intrusion into victims' interest to equal dignity and respect than parallel offences, at least as regards hate crime law considered as theoretical models. In fact, as with the observations made as to mixed-motives types of law in Sect. 4.3, a narrow exception to this conclusion must be conceded when examining a concrete hate crime law in a given social context. One cannot exclude *a priori* that, under certain circumstances, crimes with no explicit bias motive that repeatedly target persons belonging to a seriously disadvantaged group cause them a very serious intrusion into their interest to equal dignity.

Interest to Individuality In both models, offenders target their victims because of a salient feature they possess, regardless of whether perpetrators have strong negative feelings towards them. However, in the case of the Discrimination Selection model this aspect is already covered by the base offence. In the offender's view, in fact, the lack of individuality of the victim is not linked to a despised feature *per se*. That feature is, along with other possible characteristics, a mere proxy of a larger condition of vulnerability to that particular type of crime that makes that person a suitable target. Therefore, crimes based on mere discriminatory selection of victims cannot be said to intrude upon victims' interest to individuality in a relevant way to constitute further harm.

Interest to Autonomy As with psychological harm, hate crimes' intrusion into victims' interest to autonomy is closely linked to their perception of victimisation. Actual and potential victims deploy avoidance strategies because of the victimisation they have previously suffered or fear they may suffer; their behaviour is only indirectly connected with the offender's animus behind the crime. What they take into account is the probability and risk of future harm, based on previous personal experience of the same kind, or what they see happening to persons belonging to the same social group. In turn, risk of future victimisation can also be linked to the discriminatory selection model of bias crimes law. Thus, also in this model's case the intrusion into victims' interest to autonomy, and the resulting secondary reactive harm, seems to be relevantly higher in comparison with parallel crimes.

Levels of Intrusion into Quality of Life's Dimensions and Resulting Harm

Since the *Hostile Animus* model is the default approach considered in the general part of the present chapter, we concluded at the outset that it passes the harmfulness part of the ILT.

The intrusion into victims' quality of life dimensions and the resulting harm reflected by the *Discriminatory Selection* model can be measured as follows.

Again, the analysis of the physical dimension is not applicable because it is already covered by the base offence.

These are the results as regards the level of intrusion into the *psychological* dimension, and the resulting harm:

- *Direct victim*: level of intrusion: minimal well-being; level of harm: serious;
- *Vicarious victim*: level of intrusion: adequate well-being; level of harm: moderate.

With regard to the *normative* dimension's interests, the harm assessment gives the following results:

- *Autonomy* (direct and vicarious victims): level of intrusion: minimal well-being/adequate well-being; level of harm: moderate/serious;
- *Individuality* (direct victims): no higher degree of intrusion in comparison with base offence;
- *Equal dignity/equal respect* (direct and vicarious victims): no higher degree of intrusion in comparison with base offence—but possible narrow exception based on victims' particularly disadvantaged position.

The Discriminatory Selection model reflects a higher level of intrusion only as regards the interests to mental health and to autonomy (and, in some specific cases that have to be demonstrated, also to the interest to equal dignity). We nevertheless consider the resulting harm significant enough to conclude that this approach also passes the harmfulness exam.

4.4.3 Wrongfulness Issues

The Discriminatory Selection model, while passing the harmfulness phase of the ILT, presents however some conceptual problems as regards the wrongfulness implied in criminal conducts motivated by mere differential treatment. A discriminatory selection implies that offenders choose their victim on the basis of the latter's personal features; nevertheless, the proof that perpetrators were motivated by a prejudice-based negative attitude is not needed. Victim selection on the basis of a particular characteristic will do. However, perpetrators of base offences usually choose their target based on certain convenience reasons that have to do with one or more circumstances surrounding the victim.[22] In this case, therefore, the crime does not seem to be more wrongful in comparison with parallel offences. In particular, the offender's motives do not add further blameworthiness to the crime (Lawrence, 1999, 38–39).

[22] These cases could also be explained by referring to lifestyle/routine activity theory (see also Section 4.2.2 above).

There is however another element to consider. As with the reasoning applied in Sect. 4.3 above as regards hate crime law's required amount of bias, under a prioritarianism approach hate crimes targeting victims that already find themselves in a severe condition of disadvantage or vulnerability are more wrongful than bias offences against less disadvantaged groups. In this case, Lawrence suggests that we could "consider discriminatory victim selection, in the absence of [hostile] animus, to be a lower grade of bias crime than true cases of [hostile] animus. Under this approach, discriminatory selection would be seen as a wrong in and of itself but a wrong of less seriousness than that of [hostile] animus" (Lawrence, 1999, 79).

We can therefore conclude that the Discriminatory Selection model also passes the wrongfulness part of the ILT, at least when it can be proved that the groups included in the law are in a position of severe disadvantage in that particular societal context.

4.4.4 Conclusions

Hate crime law can express the nexus between the bias element of the hate crime and the conduct in a number of ways, which have been categorised into two main approaches: the Hostility Animus model (linked to a narrow concept of hate crime) and the Discriminatory Selection model (reflecting a wide concept). The former approach is more in line with the common understanding of bias offences as crimes expressing some sort of hostility towards their victims. However, it is very difficult to apply in practice because it requires proof of the offenders' motives. The Discriminatory Selection model, in turn, merely requires that offenders target their victims on the basis of a protected characteristic and may thus be more effective in the prosecution of hate crime perpetrators. Both models are used across the OSCE region.

From a legitimacy point of view, both models pass the ILT, albeit with some caveats as regards the Discriminatory Selection model. They both reflect the added harmfulness and wrongfulness of hate crimes in comparison with non-bias motivated offences. However, the

Discriminatory Selection model expresses a lesser degree of both harmfulness and wrongfulness than the Hostility Animus approach (but still higher than those of parallel offences, and thus sufficient to pass the ILT even without the application of mediating maxims). In particular, the former approach can be considered legitimate only when the law includes personal characteristics or group memberships that are shown to be in a serious position of disadvantage in that specific jurisdiction, which lead in turn hate crimes to cause or risk to cause to these kinds of victims particularly serious harm. These conclusions must be read in connection with the results of the legitimacy analysis of the third tier, in Sect. 4.3 above. There, it has been suggested that hate crime law that does not require bias to be the sole or predominant motive of the crime is *overall* not legitimate. However, under a narrow exception, it can be considered legitimate if, and when, it can be shown that in a concrete social context the grounds covered refer to significantly disadvantaged groups (Table 3.4).

Table 3.4 Legitimacy assessment of Tier IV—Nexus between mental attitude and offence

	Hostile Animus model	Discriminatory Selection model
Harmfulness	Crimes committed with a hostile animus are significantly **more harmful** than parallel crimes [reference to analysis of hate crime law as a whole]	Crimes committed with a discriminatory selection of victims are significantly **more harmful** than parallel crimes only when they target particularly *disadvantaged* victims
Wrongfulness	Crimes committed with a hostile animus are significantly **more wrongful** than parallel crimes [reference to analysis of hate crime law as a whole]	Crimes committed with a discriminatory selection of victims are significantly **more wrongful** than parallel crimes only when they target particularly *disadvantaged* victims
Mediating maxims	Analysis not necessary	Analysis not necessary
Conclusion: ILT passed?	**Yes**	**Yes—but only law requiring conduct to cause/risk additional harm**

5 Conclusions

This chapter's aim was to assess whether hate crime law *in abstracto* can be considered *prima facie* legitimate—i.e. whether the criminalisation of the bias element of hate crimes through the enactment of penalty enhancements is sufficiently justified.

At the outset, we have limited the scope of the analysis to the assessment of the *external* and *normative* legitimacy of hate crime law through the application of a test (the Integrated Legitimacy Test or ILT) that encompasses the most relevant common features of the Anglo-American harm principle and the European *Rechtsgut* theory and *offensività* principle. The ILT requires lawmakers to examine whether the conduct they intend to criminalise causes significant harm by seriously intruding upon a standard victim's quality of life, and whether there are sufficient reasons to consider it wrongful. This assessment shall be carried out on the basis of empirical studies on the phenomenon under consideration, in an open and dialectical perspective, especially with regard to the moral reasons why the behaviour in question can, or cannot, be considered wrongful.

In Sect. 3 the ILT has been applied to hate crime law considered as a whole, by addressing a model that represents the most common understanding of the phenomenon. The general assessment of bias offences has demonstrated that these types of law are legitimate under the ILT. In particular, hate crimes have been shown to cause more psychological as well as normative harm to both direct and vicarious victims, and to be more wrongful, than parallel, non-bias motivated crimes.

In Sect. 4, each of the four tiers constituting the hate crime law framework has been examined under the ILT. All the approaches reflecting a narrow and intermediate understanding of hate crimes have passed the ILT and are thus legitimate; nonetheless, those drafting techniques reflecting a wide concept of bias offences have posed a number of legitimacy problems. For example, under the *first tier* (method to draft hate crime law) we excluded in principle the legitimacy of general aggravating circumstances as they do not meet evidence-related requirements. However, this conclusion takes into account general aggravating circumstances in their theoretical and literal version; it has been conceded that in certain legal contexts, these types of provision may be interpreted in a narrow way that make them ultimately legitimate (e.g. judges may apply them only to specific crimes). Moreover, we recognised the impossibility to assess the legitimacy of those provisions providing for the exam of motives only in the sentencing phase as they lie outside the field of criminalisation.

Under the *second tier* (choice of protected grounds) the wide option has been considered illegitimate from the beginning. An open list of strands does not allow one to prove at the criminalisation stage that hate crimes directed against social group/personal characteristics that are not explicitly identified by the law are more harmful than parallel crimes. The other two approaches, instead, pass the ILT. This means that not only the *traditional* social groups (such as those based on their members' race, ethnic origins or religion) can be legitimacy included in hate crime law but also other group features, such as gender, gender identity, sexual orientation, disability, and possibly homelessness and old age.

As to the *third tier* (amount of hate), allowing bias to be only a partial motive of the crime has not passed the ILT, at least in principle. Crimes where hate/bias is just one among other motives, in fact, appear to be neither more harmful nor more wrongful than parallel, non-bias motivated offences. However, an exception has been made in those cases in which proof of bias on the part of the offender is not required, but other circumstances are met—especially when it can be shown that hate crimes cause particularly serious harm to victims as these belong to a very vulnerable or disadvantaged group.

Under the *fourth tier* (nexus between the mental attitude of the offender and the crime), both the Hostile Animus model and the Discriminatory Selection model have passed the ILT, albeit with different degrees. The kind of crime reflected by the Discriminatory Selection model, in fact, does not appear to be as wrongful as that committed with a Hostile Animus. However, the level of added wrongfulness is serious enough to eventually conclude for the legitimacy of this model, as well—provided that the law foresees that, along with a discriminatory selection of victims based on their protected characteristics, the bias offence causes or risks to cause a harm of a particular gravity. This allows us to coordinate and make these results consistent with those regarding the amount of hate or prejudice required by the legislation (Table 3.5).

Table 3.5 Legitimacy of the hate crime law framework

	UNDERSTANDINGS OF HATE CRIME CONCEPT		
	NARROW	INTERMEDIATE	WIDE
TIER I Drafting method	• Substantive offence **LEGITIMATE**	• Specific aggravating circumstances **LEGITIMATE**	• General aggravating circumstances a) Theoretical model: **NOT LEGITIMATE** b) Concrete law: **MAY BE LEGITIMATE** • Other sentencing rules that allow bias motives to be considered **ILT NOT APPLICABLE**
TIER II Protected grounds	• Only some characteristics (Short, closed list) **LEGITIMATE**	• Many characteristics and closed list **LEGITIMATE**	• Many characteristics and open list **NOT LEGITIMATE**
TIER III Amount of *hate* motive required	• Crime motivated *only* by hate **LEGITIMATE**	• Crime motivated *mostly* by hate **LEGITIMATE**	• Crime motivated *in part* by hate a) Theoretical model: **NOT LEGITIMATE** b) Concrete law: **MAY BE LEGITIMATE**
TIER IV Nexus between bias and the crime	• Hostility Animus model **LEGITIMATE**	*Not applicable*	• Discriminatory Selection model **LEGITIMATE** only when foresees additional harm

The application of the ILT to the analysis of hate crime law has allowed covering the most important and controversial matters surrounding this topic. The benefits of this novel approach are numerous. For example, it has allowed combining the different viewpoints used to examine hate crimes in European and Anglo-Saxon research, respectively. In fact, European doctrine addressing bias offences has been mainly concerned with these crimes' intrusion into the legal good equal dignity, without taking into account the interest to mental health and the resulting psychological harm. Anglo-Saxon research, on the other hand, has focused chiefly on the added psychological and physical harm caused by these kinds of crimes, encompassing the consideration of victims' normative interests in the assessment of psychological harm. However, a holistic approach that combines both legal cultures allows us to better appreciate the complex ways in which these crimes affect victims. In particular, Peršak's quality of life model allows us to identify more precisely and to properly analyse the different interests affected by hate crimes. Even though psychological and normative interests are strongly interrelated, by analysing them separately, we can better spot the different impacts of these types of crimes on victims.

The most important contribution of the ILT to the study of hate crime law, however, probably lies in the procedure itself that we must follow to perform the legitimacy assessment. The ILT provides a principled and empirical-based method to examine the legitimacy of criminal law that is based on multi-level facets of Western criminalisation theory and which takes into account in a detailed and analytical fashion different, complementary aspects of the criminal conducts under scrutiny. Thanks to its premises, this test can be performed on any legislation that is based on social-democratic premises and respect of human rights. With regard to hate crime, it allows us to elaborate on and discuss evidence-based arguments in relation to an important number of issues that are still central to the hate crime debate across most states in the OSCE region. Therefore, the findings of this study can be usefully employed to examine a concrete piece of law and draw sound conclusions as regards not only its legitimacy, but also its connection with the phenomenon of hate crimes.

References

AGE Platform Europe. (2021). *Response to the consultation on the roadmap on Hate speech & hate crime—inclusion on list of EU crimes*, 20 April 2021, Retrieved July 25, 2022, from https://age-platform.eu/sites/default/files/Hate_speech%26crime-AGE_reply_to%20EC-Apr2021.pdf.

Akhtar, S. (2014). The Mental Pain of Minorities. *British Journal of Psychotherapy, 30*(2), 136–153.

Al-Hakim, M. (2015). Making a Home for the Homeless in Hate Crime Legislation. *Journal of Interpersonal Violence, 30*(10), 1755–1781.

Altman, A. (2016). Discrimination. In E. N. Zalta (Ed.), *The Stanford Encyclopedia of Philosophy, Winter 2016*. Stanford University. Retrieved July 25, 2022, from https://plato.stanford.edu/archives/win2016/entries/discrimination/

American Psychiatric Association. (2020). What Is Posttraumatic Stress Disorder? Reviewed August 2020. Retrieved July 25, 2022, from https://www.psychiatry.org/patients-families/ptsd/what-is-ptsd.

Andersson, M., & Mellgren, C. (2016). Consequences of Bias-Motivated Victimisation among Swedish University Students with an Immigrant or Minority Background. *Irish Journal of Sociology, 24*(2), 226–250.

Bacco, F. (2013). Dalla Dignità all'Eguale Rispetto: Libertà d'Espressione e Limiti Penalistici. *Quaderni Costituzionali, 4*, 823–848.

Bacco, F. (2018). *Tra Sentimenti ed Eguale Rispetto: Problemi di Legittimazione della Tutela Penale*. Giappichelli.

Bell, J. G., & Perry, B. (2015). Outside Looking in: The Community Impacts of Anti-Lesbian, Gay, and Bisexual Hate Crime. *Journal of Homosexuality, 62*(1), 98–120.

Benier, K. (2017). The Harms of Hate: Comparing the Neighbouring Practices and Interactions of Hate Crime Victims, Non-Hate Crime Victims and Non-Victims. *International Review of Victimology, 23*(2), 179–201.

Berril, K. T. (1992). Anti-Gay Violence and Victimization in the United States: An Overview. In G. M. Herek & K. T. Berril (Eds.), *Hate Crimes: Confronting Violence Against Lesbians and Gay Men* (pp. 19–45). SAGE.

Binding, K. (1872). *Die Normen und ihre Übertretung*. W. Engelmann.

Birnbaum, J. M. F. (1834). Über das Erforderniß einer Rechtsverletzung zum Begriffe des Verbrechens. In J. Abegg et al. (Eds.), *Archiv des Criminalrechts*. Halle.

Brax, D. (2016). Hate Crime Concepts and their Moral Foundations: A Universal Framework? In J. Schweppe & M. A. Walters (Eds.), *The Globalization of Hate: Internationalizing Hate Crime?* (pp. 49–64). Oxford University Press.

Brudholm, T. (2016). Conceptualising Hatred Globally: Is Hate Crime a Human Rights Violation? In J. Schweppe & M. A. Walters (Eds.), *The Globalization of Hate: Internationalizing Hate Crime?* (pp. 31–48). Oxford University Press.

Cheng, W., Ickes, W., & Kenworthy, J. B. (2013). The Phenomenon of Hate Crimes in the United States. *Journal of Applied Social Psychology, 43*(4), 761–794.

Coleman, N., Sykes, W., & Walker, A. (2013). *Crime and Disabled People. Baseline Statistical Analysis of Measures for the Formal Legal Inquiry into Disability-Related Harassment.* Equality and Human Rights Commission. Retrieved July 25, 2022, from https://www.equalityhumanrights.com/sites/default/files/research-report-90-crime-and-disabled-people.pdf.

Condry, R. (2010). Secondary Victims and Secondary Victimization. In S. G. Shoham, P. Knepper, & M. Kett (Eds.), *International Handbook of Victimology* (pp. 219–249). CRC Press.

Corcoran, H., Lader, D., & Smith, K. (2015). *Hate Crime, England and Wales, 2014/15.* Home Office. Retrieved July 25, 2022, from https://assets.publishing.service.gov.uk/government/uploads/system/uploads/attachment_data/file/467366/hosb0515.pdf.

Craig, K. M. (1999). Retaliation, Fear, or Rage: An Investigation of African American and White Reactions to Racist Hate Crimes. *Journal of Interpersonal Violence, 14*(2), 138–151.

Craig-Henderson, K., & Sloan, L. R. (2003). After the Hate: Helping Psychologists Help Victims of Racist Hate Crime. *Clinical Psychology: Science and Practice, 10*(4), 481–490.

Dan-Cohen, M. (2011). A Concept of Dignity. *Israel Law Review, 44*(1-2), 9–23.

Darwall, S. (1977). Two Kinds of Respect. *Ethics, 88*(1), 36–49.

DeLiema, M. (2018). Elder Fraud and Financial Exploitation: Application of Routine Activity Theory. *The Gerontologist, 58*(4), 706–718.

Dillof, A. M. (1997). Punishing Bias: An Examination of the Theoretical Foundations of Bias Crime Statutes. *Northwestern University Law Review, 91*(3), 1015–1081.

Dillon, R. S. (2018). Respect. *The Stanford Encyclopedia of Philosophy (Spring 2018 Edition).* Retrieved July 25, 2022, from https://plato.stanford.edu/archives/spr2018/entries/respect/.

Donini, M. (2013). Il Principio di Offensività. Dalla Penalistica Italiana ai Programmi Europei. *Diritto Penale Contemporaneo, 4*, 4–43.

Drigo, C. (2011). La Dignità Umana come Valore (Super)Costituzionale. In L. Mezzetti (Ed.), *Principi Costituzionali* (pp. 239–273). Giappichelli.

Dunbar, E., Quinones, J., & Crevecoeur, D. A. (2005). Assessment of Hate Crime Offenders: The Role of Bias Intent in Examining Violence Risk. *Journal of Forensic Psychology Practice, 5*(1), 1–19.

Dzelme, I. (2008). Psychological Effects of Hate Crime—Individual Experience and Impact on Community (Attacking Who I Am). *Latvian Centre for*

Human Rights. Retrieved July 25, 2022, from https://cilvektiesibas.org.lv/en/publications/psychological-effects-of-hate-crime-individual-exp/.

Feinberg, J. (1984). *Harm to Others. The Moral Limits of the Criminal Law 1*. Oxford University Press.

Fetzer, M. D., & Pezzella, F. S. (2019). The Nature of Bias Crime Injuries: A Comparative Analysis of Physical and Psychological Victimization Effects. *Journal of Interpersonal Violence, 34*(18), 3864–3887.

Fiandaca, G. (2014). *Sul Bene Giuridico: Un Consuntivo Critico*. Giappichelli.

Francolini, G. (2014). *Abbandonare il Bene Giuridico? Una Prospettiva Procedurale per la Legittimazione del Diritto Penale*. Giappichelli.

Funnell, C. (2015). Racist Hate Crime and the Mortified Self: An Ethnographic Study of the Impact of Victimization. *International Review of Victimology, 21*(1), 71–83.

Galderisi, S., Heinz, A., Kastrup, M., Beezhold, J., & Sartorius, N. (2015). Toward a New Definition of Mental Health. *World Psychiatry, 14*(2), 231–233.

Galeotti, A. E. (2010). *La Politica del Rispetto. I Fondamenti della Democrazia*. Laterza.

Garcia, L., McDevitt, J., Gu, J. & Balboni, J. (1999). Psychological and Behavioral Effects of Bias and Non-Bias Motivated Assault, Final Report. *National Institute of Justice, U.S. Department of Justice*. Retrieved July 25, 2022, from https://nij.ojp.gov/library/publications/psychological-and-behavioral-effects-bias-and-non-bias-motivated-assault-final.

Garland, J. (2010). 'It's a Mosher Just Been Banged for No Reason': Assessing Targeted Violence Against Goths and the Parameters of Hate Crime. *International Review of Victimology, 17*(2), 159–177.

Garland, J., & Hodkinson, P. (2014). 'F**king Freak! What the Hell Do You Think You Look Like?': Experiences of Targeted Victimization Among Goths and Developing Notions of Hate Crime. *British Journal of Criminology, 54*(4), 613–631.

Goisis, L. (2015). Omosessualità, Hate Crimes e Diritto Penale. *GenIUS, 1*, 40–53.

Gruenewald, J., & Allison, K. (2018). Examining Differences in Bias Homicide Across Victim Groups. *Crime & Delinquency, 64*(3), 316–341.

Harcourt, B. E. (1999). The Collapse of the Harm Principle. *Journal of Criminal Law and Criminology, 90*, 109–194.

Harel, A., & Parchomovsky, G. (1999). On Hate and Equality. *Yale Law Journal, 109*, 507–539.

Hardy, S., & Chakraborti, N. (2020). *Blood, Threats and Fears. The Hidden Worlds of Hate Crime Victims*. Palgrave Pivot.

Hellman, D. (2011). *When Is Discrimination Wrong?* Harvard University Press.
Herek, G. M., Gillis, J. R., & Cogan, J. C. (1999). Psychological Sequelae of Hate-Crime Victimization among Lesbian, Gay, and Bisexual Adults. *Journal of Consulting and Clinical Psychology, 67*(6), 945–951.
Herek, G. M., Gillis, J. R., Cogan, J. C., & Glun, E. K. (1997). Hate Crime Victimization among Lesbian, Gay and Bisexual Adults: Prevalence, Psychological Correlates and Methodological Issues. *Journal of Interpersonal Violence, 12*, 195–215.
Herek, G. M., Cogan, J. C., & Gillis, J. R. (2002). Victim Experiences in Hate Crimes Based on Sexual Orientation. *Journal of Social Issues, 58*(2), 319–339.
Hörnle, T., & Kremnitzer, M. (2011). Human Dignity as a Protected Interest in Criminal Law. *Israel Law Review, 44*(1-2), 143–167.
Iganski, P. (2001). Hate Crimes Hurt More. *American Behavioral Scientist, 45*(4), 626–638.
Iganski, P. (2008). *'Hate Crime' and the City*. Policy Press.
Iganski, P. (2019). *Hate crime victimization survey report*. Organization for Security and Co-operation in Europe—Mission to Skopje.
Iganski, P., & Lagou, S. (2015a). The Personal Injuries of 'Hate Crime'. In N. Hall, A. Corb, P. Giannasi, & J. G. D. Grieve (Eds.), *The Routledge International Handbook on Hate Crime*. Routledge.
Iganski, P., & Lagou, S. (2015b). Hate Crimes Hurt Some More than Others: Implications for the Just Sentencing of Offenders. *Journal of Interpersonal Violence, 30*(10), 1696–1718.
Iganski, P., & Sweiry, A. (2016). How 'Hate' Hurts Globally. In J. Schweppe & M. A. Walters (Eds.), *The Globalization of Hate: Internationalizing Hate Crime?* (pp. 96–107). Oxford University Press.
Jacobs, J. B., & Potter, K. (1998). *Hate Crimes: Criminal Law & Identity Politics*. Oxford University Press.
Lannert, B. K. (2015). Traumatogenic Processes and Pathways to Mental Health Outcomes for Sexual Minorities Exposed to Bias Crime Information. *Trauma, Violence, & Abuse, 16*(3), 291–298.
Lantz, B., & Kim, J. (2019). Hate Crimes Hurt More, but so Do Co-Offenders: Separating the Influence of Co-Offending and Bias on Hate-Motivated Physical Injury. *Criminal Justice and Behavior, 46*(3), 437–356.
Laurenzo Copello, P. (2019). La Manipulación de los Delitos de Odio. In E. Pomares Cintas, J. L. Fuentes Osorio, G. Portilla Contreras, & F. Velásquez Velásquez (Eds.), *Un Juez Para la Democracia: Libro Homenaje a Perfecto Andrés Ibáñez* (pp. 453–468). Dykinson.

Lawrence, F. M. (1999). *Punishing Hate: Bias Crimes under American Law*. Harvard University Press.
Levin, B. (1999). Hate Crimes: Worse by Definition. *Journal of Contemporary Criminal Justice, 15*(1), 6–21.
Levin, B. (2015). Reassessing Laws on Hate Violence Against the Homeless. *American Behavioral Scientist, 59*(13), 1715–1728.
Levin, J., & McDevitt, J. (1993a). *Hate Crimes*. Springer US.
Levin, J., & McDevitt, J. (1993b). *Hate Crimes: The Rising Tide of Bigotry and Bloodshed*. Plenum Press.
Lim, H. A. (2009). Beyond the Immediate Victim: Understanding Hate Crimes as Message Crimes. In B. Perry & P. Iganski (Eds.), *Hate Crimes: The Consequences of Hate Crime* (pp. 107–122). Praeger.
Manes, V. (2005). *Il Principio di Offensività nel Diritto Penale: Canone di Politica Criminale, Criterio Ermeneutico, Parametro di Ragionevolezza*. Giappichelli.
Mason, G. (2007). Hate Crime as a Moral Category: Lessons from the Snowtown Case. *Australian & New Zealand Journal of Criminology, 40*(3), 249–271.
Mason, G. (2014). Victim Attributes in Hate Crime Law: Difference and the Politics of Justice. *British Journal of Criminology, 54*(2), 161–179.
Mason-Bish, H. (2013). Examining the Boundaries of Hate Crime Policy: Considering Age and Gender. *Criminal Justice Policy Review, 24*(3), 297–316.
McDevitt, J., Levin, J., & Bennett, S. (2002). Hate Crime Offenders: An Expanded Typology. *Journal of Social Issues, 58*(2), 303–317.
Mellgren, C., Andersson, M., & Ivert, A. (2017). For Whom Does Hate Crime Hurt More? A Comparison of Consequences of Victimization Across Motives and Crime Types. *Journal of Interpersonal Violence*. https://doi.org/10.1177/0886260517746131.
Messner, S. F., McHugh, S., & Felson, R. B. (2004). Distinctive Characteristics of Assaults Motivated by Bias. *Criminology, 42*(3), 585–618.
Micheletto, L. (2021). Towards an Integrated (and Possibly Pan-European?) Prima Facie Legitimacy Test: Merging the Rechtsgut Theory, the Offensività Principle, and the Harm Principle. *European Journal of Crime, Criminal Law and Criminal Justice, 29*(3-4), 241–263. https://doi.org/10.1163/15718174-bja10025
Morassutto, L. (2015). Omofobia e Medioevo Italiano. *GenIUS, 1*, 65–81.
Nocon, A., Iganski, P. & Lagou, S. (2011). *Disabled People's Experiences and Concerns about Crime Analysis of the British Crime Survey 2007-08, 2008-09 and 2009-10*. Equality and Human Rights Commission. Retrieved July 25, 2022, from https://www.equalityhumanrights.com/sites/default/files/

briefing-paper-3-disabled-peoples-experiences-and-concerns-about-crime_0.pdf.

Noelle, M. (2002). The Ripple Effect of the Matthew Shepard Murder: Impact on the Assumptive Worlds of Members of the Targeted Group. *American Behavioral Scientist, 46*(1), 27–50.

Nussbaum, M. C. (2012). *The New Religious Intolerance: Overcoming the Politics of Fear in an Anxious Age*. Belknap Press of Harvard University Press.

ODHIR (Office for Democratic Institutions and Human Rights). (2009). *Hate Crime Laws—A Practical Guide*. Organization for Security and Co-operation in Europe.

ODHIR (Office for Democratic Institutions and Human Rights). (2014). *Hate Crime Data-Collection and Monitoring Mechanisms a Practical Guide*. Organization for Security and Co-operation in Europe.

Paterson, J., Walters, M. A., Brown, R., & Fearn, H. (2018). *The Sussex Hate Crime Project: Final Report*. University of Sussex. Retrieved July 25, 2022, from http://www.edf.org.uk/university-of-sussex-hate-crime-project-final-report/

Payne, B. K., & Gainey, R. R. (2006). The Criminal Justice Response to Elder Abuse in Nursing Homes: A Routine Activities Perspective. *Western Criminology Review, 7*(3), 67–81.

Pelissero, M. (2015). Omofobia e Plausibilità dell'Intervento Penale. *GenIUS, 1*, 14–27.

Perry, B. (2001). *In the Name of Hate: Understanding Hate Crimes*. Routledge.

Perry, B. (2015). Exploring the Community Impacts of Hate Crime. In N. Hall, A. Corb, P. Giannasi, & J. G. D. Grieve (Eds.), *The Routledge International Handbook on Hate Crime* (pp. 44–58). Routledge.

Perry, B., & Alvi, S. (2012). 'We Are All Vulnerable': The *in Terrorem* Effects of Hate Crimes. *International Review of Victimology, 18*(1), 57–71.

Peršak, N. (2007). *Criminalising Harmful Conduct: The Harm Principle, its Limits and Continental Counterparts*. Springer.

Peršak, N. (2014). Using 'Quality of Life' to Legitimate Criminal Law Intervention: Gauging Gravity, Defining Disorder. In A. Simester, A. Du Bois-Pedain, & U. Neumann (Eds.), *Liberal Criminal Theory: Essays for Andreas von Hirsch* (pp. 225–247). Hart Publishing.

Peršak, N. (2018). EU Criminal Law and its Legitimation: In Search for a Substantive Principle of Criminalisation. *European Journal of Crime, Criminal Law and Criminal Justice, 26*(1), 20–39.

Peršak, N. (2022). Criminalising Hate Crime and Hate Speech at EU Level: Extending the List of Eurocrimes Under Article 83(1) TFEU. *Criminal Law Forum, 33*, 85–119. https://doi.org/10.1007/s10609-022-09440-w

Pezzella, F. S. (2017). *Hate Crime Statutes: A Public Policy and Law Enforcement Dilemma*. Springer International Publishing.

Pezzella, F. S., & Fetzer, M. D. (2017). The Likelihood of Injury among Bias Crimes: An Analysis of General and Specific Bias Types. *Journal of Interpersonal Violence, 32*(5), 703–729.

Pulitanò, D. (2015). Offensività del Reato (Principio di). In *Enciclopedia del Diritto*, IX: 665–685. : Giuffrè.

Riccardi, G. (2013). Omofobia e Legge Penale. Possibilità e Limiti dell'Intervento Penale. *Diritto Penale Contemporaneo*. Retrieved July 25, 2022, from http://www.penalecontemporaneo.it/upload/1380446460RICCARDI%20 2013a.pdf.

Schonsheck, J. (1994). *On Criminalization: An Essay in the Philosophy of the Criminal Law*. Kluwer.

Schweppe, J., & Walters, M. A. (2015). Hate Crimes: Legislating to Enhance Punishment. In *Oxford Handbooks Online. Criminology and Criminal Justice*. : Oxford University Press.

Sharrock, S., Pullerits, M., Piggot, H., Edwards, S., & DeMarco, J. (2018). *The Experiences of Victims of Hate Crime—Final Report*. NatCen Social Research.

Simester, A. P., & von Hirsch, A. (2011). *Crimes, Harms, and Wrongs: On the Principles of Criminalisation*. Hart Publishing.

Smith, K., Lader, D., Hoare, J., & Lau, I. (2012). Hate Crime, Cyber Security and the Experience of Crime among Children: Findings from the 2010/11 British Crime Survey. *Home Office*. Retrieved July 25, 2022, from https://www.report-it.org.uk/files/hosb0612-2.pdf.

Smith, S. D. (2006). Is the Harm Principle Illiberal? *The American Journal of Jurisprudence, 51*(1), 1–42.

Strom, K. J. (2001). *Hate Crimes Reported in NIBRS, 1997-99*. U.S. Department of Justice.

Tay, L., & Diener, E. (2011). Needs and Subjective Well-Being Around the World. *Journal of Personality and Social Psychology, 101*(2), 354–365.

Tesauro, A. (2012). Spunti Problematici in Tema di Dignità Umana come Bene Penalmente Rilevante. *Diritto e Questioni Pubbliche*. Retrieved July 25, 2022, from http://www.dirittoequestionipubbliche.org/page/2011_n11/29_studi%20-%20Tesauro.pdf.

The National Coalition for the Homeless. (2012). *Hate Crimes against the Homeless: The Brutality of Violence Unveiled.* Retrieved July 25, 2022, from http://nationalhomeless.org/wp-content/uploads/2013/01/hate-crimes2011.pdf.

Tiby, E. (2009). Homophobic Hate Crimes in Sweden: Questions and Consequences. In B. Perry & P. Iganski (Eds.), *Hate Crimes. The Consequences of Hate Crime, 2* (pp. 31–48). Praeger.

United Nations. (2020). *Impact of the Coronavirus Disease (COVID-19) on the Enjoyment of All Human Rights by Older Persons.* Retrieved July 25, 2022, from https://undocs.org/A/75/205.

Vedaschi, A. (2011). Il Principio Personalista. In L. Mezzetti (Ed.), *Principi Costituzionali* (pp. 274–290). Giappichelli.

Verdun-Jones, S. N., & Rossiter, K. R. (2010). The Psychological Impact of Victimization: Mental Health Outcomes and Psychological, Legal, and Restorative Interventions. In S. G. Shoham, P. Knepper, & M. Kett (Eds.), *International Handbook of Victimology* (pp. 611–637). CRC Press.

Von Hirsch, A. (2014). Harm and Wrongdoing in Criminalisation Theory. *Criminal Law and Philosophy, 8*, 245–256.

Von Hirsch, A., & Jareborg, N. (2005). Gauging Crime Seriousness: A 'Living Standard' Conception of Criminal Harm. In A. von Hirsch & A. Ashworth (Eds.), *Proportionate Sentencing* (pp. 186–219). Oxford University Press.

Von Liszt, F. (1883). Der Zweckgedanke im Strafrecht. In *Zeitschrift für die Gesamte Strafrechtswissenschaft*, Vol. 3 (pp. 1–47). Berlin; Leipzig: Buttentag.

Von Schulthess, B. (1992). Violence in the Streets: Anti-Lesbian Assault and Harassment in San Francisco. In G. M. Herek & K. T. Berril (Eds.), *Hate Crimes: Confronting Violence against Lesbians and Gay Men* (pp. 65–75). SAGE.

Weinstein, J. (1992). First Amendment Challenges to Hate Crime Legislation: Where's the Speech? *Criminal Justice Ethics, 11*(2), 6–20.

Williams, M. L., & Tregidga, J. (2014). Hate Crime Victimization in Wales: Psychological and Physical Impacts across Seven Hate Crime Victim Types. *British Journal of Criminology, 54*(5), 946–967.

Wilson, J. K. (Ed.). (2009). *The Praeger Handbook of Victimology.* Praeger.

World Health Organization. (2004). *Promoting Mental Health: Concepts, Emerging Evidence, Practice (Summary Report).* World Health Organization.

Zempi, I., & Smith, J. (Eds.). (2021). *Misogyny as Hate Crime.* Routledge.

4

Analysis of Italian Hate Crime Law

1 Introduction

In the previous chapters, we have developed a four-tier framework to identify and examine different theoretical models of hate crime law, which have then been analysed through the Integrated Legitimacy Test (ILT) to determine their *prima facie* legitimacy. In this chapter, we will apply the ILT to Italian hate crime law. This exercise pursues two aims. First, it will allow us to analyse Italian law through a novel approach to feed the current debate with sound and evidence-based arguments, while at the same time discharge unfounded and biased claims. Second, it will constitute a useful demonstration of how the ILT can be applied to a concrete legislation.

In Italy, hate crimes have been at the centre of a heated debate for some years now, not only in academia but also within civil society and at the legislative level. For its part, legal research has recently started looking at other scientific areas, such as psychology, sociology, criminology and victimology, as well as engaging in comparative studies, to better

L. Micheletto, *Assessing Hate Crime Laws*, Palgrave Hate Studies,
https://doi.org/10.1007/978-3-031-19020-9_4

understand how to address this criminal phenomenon.[1] On the other hand, the response of the Italian legal system to hate crime has chiefly focused on the enactment of hate crime and hate speech law that cover only a limited number of grounds: race, ethnic origins, national origins, religion and linguistic minorities.

The extension of the existing provisions to protect other social groups—LGBTI people, women, and persons with disabilities—has been discussed for many years without success. Just to have an idea, since 1996 more than 20 bills have been put forward to include sexual orientation and gender identity in the law. The last, and more promising one, was eventually rejected by the Italian Senate in October 2021 after having already been approved by the lower chamber. The bill (named "Zan Bill" from the surname of one of its proponents) would have extended hate crime and hate speech provisions to sex, gender, sexual orientation, gender identity and disability. The legislative proposal received transversal support on the part of civil society, hate crime experts, academics, legal professionals and politicians. However, that was not sufficient. To reject the legal reform, opponents to the bill made use of a number of political manoeuvres that had little to do with an evidence- and principled-based analysis of the criminal phenomenon at issue.[2] Even the Vatican felt the urge to intervene. In June 2021 the Holy See made an official call to the Italian Government to modify the bill in the part concerning hate speech, claiming that it would intrude upon the Catholic church's "freedom of organisation" and "freedom of thought" (Giuffrida, 2021). In May 2022, members of the Democratic Party announced that they had presented another legislative proposal to the Senate having the same content as the previous Zan Bill (Il Post, 2022). However, in July 2022 the Government collapsed and Parliament was dissolved. As a result, pending bills were dropped.

In this chapter, we will examine the most important provisions that can be framed as hate crime law in Italy. Therefore, we will analyse art.

[1] See, for example, Luciana Goisis' thorough research on this topic (e.g. Goisis, 2019, 2020 and her previous works cited therein).

[2] For a thorough review of the Bill's legislative procedure, and of the reasons why it was rejected, see Lim (2021) and Curreri (2022).

604-ter of the Penal Code on race, ethnic origins, nationality, religion and linguistic minorities, art. 36 of Act 104/1992 on disability, art. 628(3)(3quinques) and art. 61(5) of the Penal Code on age, as well as the legislative proposals aiming at including sex, gender, sexual orientation and gender identity in hate crime legislation. These statutes have been identified by applying a wide definition of hate crime law. This includes all those provisions that foresee a penalty enhancement when a conduct that is already criminalised is committed in connection with a characteristic of the victim that the legal system considers of particular importance, regardless of their official labelling. This means that this chapter addresses not only the provisions that are officially considered as hate crime law, but also other provisions whose rationale lies in the protection of certain types of victims' presumed vulnerability. Along with "official" hate crime law, in fact, Italian criminal law foresees penalty enhancements when crime victims belong to social groups that are considered particularly vulnerable and in need of special protection. This includes specific provisions covering people with disability and the elderly. The concept of vulnerability these provisions adopt is an *objective* one: the sentence increase applies anytime the victim falls under a certain category (e.g. persons with disabilities or the elderly). This is so even though the offender does not harbour or express negative prejudices against their victims, nor does the victim's condition play any roles in facilitating the commission of the offence.

This conception of vulnerability leaves no room to consider the victim's agency and the complexity of certain personal situations; victims are seen as passive subjects regardless of more nuanced considerations. This approach has been criticised. In particular, Chakraborti and Garland (2012) have developed a different notion of vulnerability that may better explain why some personal features, under certain circumstances, may be considered among the protected grounds of hate crime legislation. Vulnerability, under their conception, is not considered in absolute terms. A certain personal feature such as age and disability does not render a person vulnerable *per se*; what counts instead is how offenders perceive certain features, alone or together, as particularly vulnerable in certain circumstances (Chakraborti & Garland, 2012, 510). This approach thus moves away from the assessment of the perpetrator' motives and focuses instead on the victims' characteristics.

On the other hand, this work does not deal with a large number of other laws that, albeit being labelled as hate crime legislation in research or by their political proponents, cover instead hate speech, hate incidents, or other kinds of hate/prejudice-related conducts.

The application of the Integrated Legitimacy Test to a concrete legislation requires analysing the proscribed conduct's harmfulness and wrongfulness. Since we have already carried out a general assessment of the added harmfulness and wrongfulness of hate crime law in Chap. 3, we will now examine Italian legislation in light of the results previously obtained. We will thus analyse each tier of Italian provisions by contrasting the elements that are specific to the Italian context with the more general remarks concerning hate crime law and its legitimacy highlighted in Chaps. 2 and 3.

Furthermore, while Italian case law and doctrine will be taken into account in the assessment of these provisions under the ILT, the main purpose of this chapter is to provide a general example of the application of the legitimacy test to a concrete legislation that remains accessible to a wide, international audience. Therefore, it will not be possible to examine these factors in depth.

2 Race, Ethnicity, Nationality, Religion and Linguistic Minorities

2.1 Overview of Art. 604-ter

Along with art. 604-bis, that covers certain forms of violent behaviour and hate speech, art. 604-ter of the Penal Code is the only criminal law provision that is explicitly and officially referred to as hate crime law in Italy.[3] It foresees two aggravating circumstances for offences committed

[3] The legal norms contained in arts. 604-bis and 604-ter were originally included in art. 3 of Act 654/1975 and art. 3 of Act 205/1993, respectively. These acts are referred to as Reale-Mancino Act from the surname of their proponents, and contain a framework of provisions addressing hate speech, hate crimes, and other hate-related conducts.

out of bias. It covers race, ethnic origins, nationality, religion and belonging to a national linguistic minority.[4]

Apart from arts. 604-bis and 604-ter, there are a number of other provisions that, in one way or another, address discrimination and hate on the grounds of race, ethnicity, religion or nationality from a criminal law viewpoint. Italian doctrine or authorities sometimes refer to them as "hate crime law". However, these provisions do not provide for a penalty enhancement of a conduct that already constitutes an offence in the Italian legal system. Therefore, the present work will not consider them.

Art. 604-ter of the Penal Code reads as follows:

> [t]he sentence shall be increased up to a half for those offences, punishable with a penalty other than life imprisonment, that are committed with an ethnic, national, racial, religious discriminatory or hate purpose, or in order to facilitate the activity of organisations, associations, movements or groups pursuing the same aims …

The second part of the article foresees that this aggravating circumstance prevails when balanced with other mitigating circumstances.

Thus, this provision includes two aggravating circumstances. The first applies to crimes committed with a hate or discriminatory purpose; the second applies to offences committed in order to facilitate the activity of organisations that pursue discriminatory or hateful aims.

Italian lawmakers have taken a severe approach as regards the amount of sentence increase for hate crime offenders. First, art. 604 provides that the base sentence shall be enhanced up to a half, while the common penalty enhancement is up to a third (art. 64 of the Penal Code). Second, Italian criminal law, as with other legal systems, allows courts to have a certain margin of discretion when balancing aggravating circumstances with concurring mitigating circumstances (art. 69 of the Penal Code). This enables judges to adapt criminal law provisions—which are by definition general and abstract—to the specific and concrete circumstances of a given case. If mitigating circumstances are found to prevail on

[4] Linguistic minorities were included in hate crime law by art. 18-bis of Act 482/1999, on the protection of certain languages and cultures belonging to a number of historical minority ethnic groups living on the Italian territory.

aggravating factors, the latter's penalty enhancement will not be applied and the aggravating circumstance will thus disappear.[5] In order to avoid the important drawbacks following the application of this general rule in the context of hate crimes (see Chap. 2, Sect. 3.2.1), art. 604-ter provides that concurrent mitigating circumstances cannot be considered as equivalent or prevailing on the bias element, except when the mitigating factor consists of the offender being a minor. While this approach prevents the consideration of the bias element from disappearing *vis-à-vis* possible concurring mitigating factors, it may be criticised as being disproportionate and in possible violation of the principle of equality.

2.2 Legitimacy Assessment under the ILT

2.2.1 Tier I: Drafting Method

Art. 604-ter foresees two general aggravating circumstances that are in principle applicable to all offences except for those punishable with life imprisonment. This exception appears logical as it is not possible to further increase a life imprisonment's sentence. However, it may be doubtful from the point of view of data collection and correct labelling of the offence, as it excludes some serious crimes from being framed as hate crimes (particularly, the offences of mass murder ("*strage*"—art. 422 of the Penal Code), aggravated murder (arts. 576 and 577), or murder following the torture of the victim (art. 613-bis(2)).

This provision thus adopts a wide conception of hate crime, as it is applicable to any conducts that are already considered as an offence and are committed for racist purposes. However, while convenient and reasonable from a conceptual and systematic point of view, this drafting method presents legitimacy issues. As we saw in Chap. 3 (Sect. 4.1.1), general aggravating circumstances foresee a penalty enhancement for conducts that cannot be possibly committed out of bias and for other conducts the added harmfulness and wrongfulness of which has not been

[5] In case of substantive offences, nonetheless, this does not happen—an element that is considered as a constitutive element of an offence, if proved to exist, cannot be balanced and be overcome by mitigating factors external to the offence definition.

proved empirically. The first argument can be overcome *in concreto*, by considering that it is commonly accepted among Italian scholars that general aggravating circumstances can be applied only to those offences they are not incompatible with (Mantovani, 2015, 402). Moreover, it has been argued that the second circumstance can be applied only to those offences that aim to assist the organisations forbidden by the same article, such as the commission of the crimes that constitute the purpose of those groups, as well as those criminal conducts aiming at aiding the association through the reinforcement of its structure (De Francesco, 1994b, 212; Licastro, 2019, 106).

However, there remains the issue of providing empirical evidence as to which base conducts present a higher degree of harmfulness and wrongfulness when committed out of bias. In Italy, data collection shows that a wide range of base offences are sometimes committed out of a racist, religious, etc., motive. These are, in particular, personal violent offences such as murder, simple and aggravated assault, threats, defamation, incitement to violence, and property offences such as property damage, vandalism or theft/robbery (Lunaria, 2020, 70).[6] Thus, a penalty enhancement is justified under a legitimacy point of view at least as regards these base offences as the analysis conducted in Chap. 3 has shown that these crimes are usually more harmful and wrongful when committed out of bias.

As it stands, the approach chosen to draft art. 604-ter does not pass the ILT, unless it is interpreted as applying only to these base crimes. In any event, it would be advisable to restructure it as a specific aggravating circumstance that applies only to certain crimes for which it is very likely that victims suffer more harm, and are more wrongful, when they are committed out of bias.

2.2.2 Tier II: Protected Grounds

The two aggravating circumstances provided for in art. 604-ter of the Penal Code explicitly cover the strands *ethnicity*, *nationality*, *race* and

[6] See also https://hatecrime.osce.org/index.php/italy?year=2020 (accessed 25 July 2022).

religion. Moreover, art. 18-bis of Act 482/1999 also applies this article to members of *linguistic minorities*.

Art. 604-ter refers only indirectly to the personal characteristics it covers; in fact, the wording of the article focuses on a characteristic of the *offender's aim*, which is defined as "ethnic, national, racial or religious discrimination or hate *purpose*." Three consequences follow. First, the aggravating circumstances are applicable also to hate crimes *by association*, i.e. when the victim does not belong to one of the protected groups but is somehow associated to them. In judgment no. 563/2011, for example, the Court of Cassation considered that anti-Semitic threats addressed to a university professor specialised in the persecution of Jews in Italy during the fascist era constituted a hate crime on the grounds of race and religion even though the victim was not Jewish (Pavich & Bonomi, 2014, 6–7; Miraglia, 2019, 49). Second, this line of reasoning is applicable also when there is a mistake in the offenders' perception of their victims' salient feature. By focussing on the offender's aim, and not on the victim's characteristic/group belonging, this provision appears to be applicable also to *mistakes in perception*, as what counts is offenders' purpose and not their victims' actual feature. Third, it has also been argued that, as a consequence of art. 604-ter's focus on the offender's animus, victim and perpetrator can belong to the *same* racial, ethnic, national, religious or linguistic group (Trapasso, 2010, 3837).

Art. 604-ter adopts a *narrow conception* of hate crimes, as the protected grounds are those traditionally included in hate crime legislations. More specifically, the ground-selection criteria that lawmakers have followed are those concerning the protected groups' *previous history of oppression and/or discrimination*, and the *high risk of current hate crime victimisation*. As to the first criterion, it is sufficient to recall Italian racist law during the Fascist era, as well as the country's colonial past. On the other hand, research shows that racist violence is widespread in Italy, particularly with regard to certain specific ethnic groups or religious minorities (people of African or Arab descent, Roma, Muslims and Jews) (Lunaria, 2020; Perry, 2019). Thus, the criteria regarding the *high risk* of hate crime victimisation, and current *discrimination and oppression* are certainly applicable. More in general, all ground-selection criteria seem to apply as well in the Italian context. These social groups find themselves in a position of vulnerability and overall disadvantage; moreover, they also face hostility from a part of the population and also from certain representatives of official institutions.[7]

Art. 604-ter does not specify which racial, ethnic, religious or national groups are protected. Courts seem to prefer an interpretation that takes into account the relationship between minority and majority groups, and the fact that certain groups are more disadvantaged than others (also considering the public opinion in a given time and space). For example, when insult was still a criminal offence, the Court of Cassation explained that the aggravating circumstance could not be applied to those cases in which a foreigner insults an Italian (judgment no. 11590/2010; see also Spena, 2017, 601–602).

From the above considerations, we can conclude that this aspect of art. 604-ter passes the ILT and is thus legitimate.

2.2.3 Tier III: Amount of Hate

Art. 604-ter does not specify whether the base offence shall be committed only, predominantly or partially out of bias. It merely provides that "those offences … committed with a discrimination or hate purpose" shall be punished more harshly. By analysing the way this article has been interpreted by courts and doctrine, however, it can be inferred that hate/prejudice must be at least the *predominant* factor behind the commission of the crime. The coexistence of other motives behind the commission of the base offence is, in fact, not excluded. The interpretation of the terms discrimination and hate, which are the conduct's aims that express the bias connected with the crime, has been controversial. Doctrine and courts however agree that to make the aggravating circumstances applicable, the prejudice expressed by the conduct cannot simply be an incidental factor that concurs with other motives. It must be instead a fundamental element that is clearly identifiable by the way the conduct

[7] See, for example, the Maps of Intolerance developed by Vox (2022a) after monitoring on-line hate speech against Muslims, Jews and foreigners in Italy in the year 2021.

at stake is performed.[8] Furthermore, due to the particular drafting of the provision (hate and discrimination are the *purposes*, not the motives of the conduct), the Court of Cassation has interpreted it as compatible with other motives behind the offender's conduct (see judgments nos. 42258/06, 43488/2015, and 27462/2018).

In short, the approach taken by the hate crime provision at hand as regards the required amount of hate is that of an *intermediate* conception of hate crime and hate crime law, which is legitimate according to the results obtained in Chap. 3.

2.2.4 Tier IV: Nexus Between Bias and Offence

Art. 604-ter's focus on the offender's purpose to discriminate or generate hate has been interpreted in two main ways as regards the kind of evidence necessary to apply the aggravating circumstances (Micheletto, 2021, 211–213). In both cases, however, the expression *purpose* is understood literally, meaning that there is no need to prove the offenders' hateful or discriminatory motives. What is required is the proof that they intended to spread hate through the commission of the base offence.[9]

Many authors have criticised art. 604-ter's choice of focussing on the conduct's purpose. They stress that hate and prejudice are emotions or mental attitudes and should thus be framed as *motives* instead (De Francesco, 1994a, 182–183; D'Amato, 2006, 387–388; Pagliarulo, 2014, 20).[10] Hate crimes are worse than parallel crimes because the offender's conduct has been triggered by discriminatory reasons and not because the offence has been committed with the aim to discriminate. In particular, what justifies the penalty enhancement is that the crime has

[8] For a detailed analysis of Italian case law and doctrine on these issues see Micheletto (2021), 210–211.

[9] In the Italian criminal law system, motives are taken into account as aggravating or mitigating circumstances, as well as constitutive parts of certain offences (Mantovani, 2015, 636). In its judgment no. 44295/2005 the Court of Cassation points out that, according to the literal meaning of art. 604-ter, the legislator has explicitly chosen to address the offenders' purpose, and not their motives. This is the interpretation to take into account "out of respect for the legislator," unless we want to argue that the term *purpose* has been randomly chosen.

[10] In the context of the numerous attempts to widen the number of grounds protected by arts. 604-bis and 604-ter, bills A.C. 2807 and A.C. 245 also suggested the replacement of the term *purpose* with *motives*.

been committed because of one or more protected characteristics of the victim and thus violates the principle of equality. What we should ask ourselves, in sum, is whether the crime would have been committed anyway if the particular characteristic had not been there (Pagliarulo, 2014, 20).

Supporters of the use of the term *purpose* focus instead on the severe penalty enhancement brought about by art. 604-ter. Only the focus on the offender's purpose—which consists of instigating hate, and is much worse than a mere hateful motive—could justify such a high sentence increase. However, the studies examined in Chap. 3 show that hate crimes cause direct and indirect harm not only because of offenders' hostility but also because of the high rate of victimisation certain groups show, which is also the consequence of a mere discriminatory selection of the offenders' targets. Moreover, if *hate* is considered as the conduct's motive, what a hate crime law punishes is the *direct harm* caused by the base conduct plus the added harm caused by the bias element; if the focus is on the conduct's purpose instead, the penalty enhancement addresses the *risk* that the hateful purpose can cause *indirect harm* through the commission of discriminatory violence by other people that might be instigated to do so by the first offender's conduct (see also Spena, 2017, 593–594; 596). Another argument put forward by supporters of the term *purpose* is that a focus on the offender' motives would end up being a focus on the perpetrator's character, as motives are psychic elements that are very difficult to prove (see Licastro, 2019, 126). However, other aggravating circumstances already focus on the perpetrator's motives (e.g. art. 61(1) on trivial and hideous motives); thus, this kind of exercise is not new to judges and prosecution authorities. Moreover, given that it is impossible to read one's mind, the offender's motives can be deducted from the same elements that describe their intentions, such as the uttering of racist insults or the performing of similar gestures before, during or after the attack, the offender's belonging to racist groups, or their previous history of racist violence.

Under the concepts of hate crimes analysed in Chap. 2, both hate crime provisions focusing on the offender's motives and those addressing their purposes fall under the Hostility Animus model (Brax & Munthe, 2013, 20) and thus reflect a *narrow* understanding of hate crimes. This stance is supported by the fact that hate and discrimination are expressly mentioned in art. 604-ter, and that courts require in any event the proof that the offender's conduct intended to express. Thus, the way this part of the provision is drafted passes the ILT.

2.3 Conclusions

This section has analysed art. 604-ter under the four-tier framework and the ILT. This article foresees two aggravating circumstances when certain offences are committed with a racial, national, ethnic, religious, or linguistic minority-related hate or discriminatory purpose, or to assist organisations pursuing the same aims.

This assessment shows that, in general, this provision's approach adopts a narrow conception of hate crimes and hate crime law. It covers a limited number of *traditionally* protected grounds and requires hate and prejudice to play a decisive role in the selection of the crime victim. Thus, these aspects of the law can be considered legitimate. However, the *method* adopted to draft the provision presents some legitimacy issues. Art. 604-ter is a general aggravating circumstance applicable to any existing offences. As it was argued in Chap. 3, this drafting method is not legitimate under the ILT if considered *in abstracto*. The penalty increase is applicable also to base conducts that cannot be possibly committed out of bias, as well as to other conducts for which there is no proof that the bias element causes extra harm and wrongfulness. However, these legitimacy issues are not unsurmountable. As to the first aspect, it is generally understood in Italy that general aggravating circumstances are applicable only to those offences they are not incompatible with. As to the second issue, courts can play a key role in limiting the actual application of the circumstance only to those base offences for which there is empirical data available. Therefore, we can conclude that art. 604-ter is legitimate.

3 Disability

"Official" hate crime law in Italy does not include disability among the protected grounds. Legislative proposals to introduce disability in the existing law have been put forward a few times, but they were eventually unsuccessful.[11] However, the Italian criminal law system foresees a number of provisions that specifically take disability into account. Some of them provide for a penalty enhancement when the victim of certain crimes has a disability. The rationale of these provisions is that people with disabilities are objectively more vulnerable than non-disabled persons, at least as regards certain offences.

Not all these provisions, however, can be framed as hate crime law. Those which are excluded are of two kinds. Under the first category, there are those provisions that criminalise conducts that would not be a crime but for the victim's disability (or other vulnerable condition, such as being a child). The second type concerns those cases in which the lack of the victim's valid consent to the conduct of the perpetrator is a necessary condition for the criminalisation of a conduct that would be otherwise legal, or for a less serious offence or for a mitigating circumstance to apply. Under these provisions, when victims have some forms of serious mental disabilities the law presumes that their consent to the conduct is not valid and thus the offender's conduct is criminalised or punished more seriously.

The provisions that can be framed as hate crime law are art. 36(1) of Act 104/1992, and arts. 61(5), 572(2), 612-bis(3), 612-ter(4), and 602-ter(6) of the Penal Code. However, taking into consideration their relevance and practical application, we will examine only the first one under the ILT.

---

[11] Bills A.C. 280 (15 March 2013), A.C. 2802-bis-A (disability was introduced in the original text on 18 May 2011), A.C. 1071 (28 May 2013), and A.S. 2005 (Zan Bill) (5 November 2020).

3.1 Overview of Art. 36(1) of Act 104/1992

Act 104/1992 contains a legal framework that covers different areas concerning the assistance, social integration and rights of persons with disability. Its art. 36(1) foresees that

> [w]here the offences referred to in Article 527 of the Penal Code [gross indecency], the intentional offences referred to in chapter XII and XIII of Book II of the Penal Code [crimes against persons and property], as well as the offences referred to in Act no. 75 of 20 February 1958 [pandering], are committed toward a person having a physical, psychic or sensory impairment, the punishment shall be increased by a third up to a half.

3.2 Legitimacy Assessment

3.2.1 Tier I: Drafting Methods

Art. 36 of Act 104/1992 is a specific aggravating circumstance that applies only to certain offences. In fact, art. 36 of Act 104/1992 covers both personal and property crimes (thus including offences against freedom and autonomy, physical integrity, sexual integrity, personal property, and so on).

Lawmakers' choice as to which kinds of base offences to cover seems reasonable and legitimate. These are all offences that can be committed out of bias against a person with a disability, and for which there is evidence on their added harmfulness (see Chap. 3). They thus fulfil the empirical requirements of the ILT.

3.2.2 Tier II: Protected Grounds

According to the Convention of the Rights of Persons with Disabilities (CRPD),

> [p]ersons with disabilities include those who have long-term physical, mental, intellectual or sensory impairments which in interaction with

> various barriers may hinder their full and effective participation in society on an equal basis with others (art. 1(2)).

Until recently, medical and social sciences considered disability as an individual issue caused by a physical or mental impairment. As a result, people with disabilities had objective difficulties to carry out "normal" activities and, as a consequence, were prevented from fulfilling "normal" social roles. Thus, the more appropriate social response to these persons' situation was to try to fix the impairment or to help the individual to cope with it by accepting "a less valuable" social role (Marra, 2013, 467). The current approach, also reflected by the CRPD, has shifted the focus onto the *social barriers* that play a fundamental role in shaping the seriousness of the disability. An impairment that causes someone to have a disability can, under other circumstances, be just a personal characteristic among others. Thus, according to this approach, what causes the disability "is not the physical or sensory impairment *per se* … but society's failure to integrate natural aspects of human diversity" (Marra, 2013, 467).

The overall approach to disability in criminal law reflects an old-fashioned conception of this personal condition according to which people with disabilities would inevitably be objectively vulnerable. However, as it has been pointed out by anti-ableism activists and specialised research, likewise other personal characteristics a disability renders a person vulnerable only in certain situations and depending on the overall circumstances—in particular, it would depend on the offender's hostility towards that particular condition (see, e.g., Burch, 2021, 52–54; Paolini & Paolini, 2022).

Art. 36(1) of Act 104/1992 applies to victims with a "physical, psychic or sensory impairment." It shall be read together with art. 3(1) of the same Act, which provides a more detailed definition of 'handicap' (as the Act refers to disability). This article states that

> [a] person is handicapped [*sic*] if he has a physical, mental or sensory impairment, stable or progressive, which causes him learning difficulties, hardship in relating with other people or in integrating in the work environment, and results in a process of social disadvantage or marginalisation.

Along with the use of a terminology that is nowadays considered not appropriate and even offensive, this definition reflects a traditional take on disability. In fact, although it mentions social disadvantage, this is seen as the result of a process that finds its causes in the impairment itself, and not in social institutions' lack of proper response to it.

Nonetheless, in recent years it seems that, if not the approach, at least the terminology of the CRPD has started to penetrate Italian criminal law language. In fact, arts. 612-bis(3) and 572(2) of the Penal Code, introduced in 2009 and 2019, respectively, state that they are applicable when the victim of the offences of stalking or domestic abuse have a "*disability* as it is defined by art. 3 of Act 104/1992." They thus seem to suggest that what, in 1992, was called *handicap*, nowadays is better referred to as *disability*. In any event, they try at least to link the particular condition the victims of these offences find themselves in with a specific definition.

Art. 36's objective focus on victims' disabilities and the lack of further specification render it not applicable to hate crime by association (unlike art. 604-ter, for example). On the other hand, when offenders target someone because they mistakenly think that the victim has a disability, the aggravating circumstance seems to be applicable. Art. 60 of the Penal Code foresees that, generally speaking, aggravating circumstances concerning the victim's conditions or characteristics do not apply when the offender makes a mistake as regard the victim's identity. However, section 3 of the article excludes the application of this provision if the aggravating circumstances in question concern, among others, the victim's physical or psychic conditions or characteristics. Thus, it can be argued that disability can be included among these conditions or characteristics.

The ground-selecting criterion adopted by lawmakers is explicitly that of objective vulnerability, meaning that a disability makes individuals vulnerable anytime and under all circumstances. This approach is outdated and does not reflect the fact that a given disability can render someone more vulnerable in certain situations but not in others. Along with vulnerability, other ground-selection criteria appear to also be applicable, as people with disabilities still find themselves in a situation of disadvantage, are often targets of hate speech, hate incidents and discrimination, and they present an historical background of social exclusion, institutionalisation and forced medicalisation (see, for example, Paolini & Paolini, 2022).

In Italy, the police and other civil society organisations collect data on disability hate crime. According to the figures published on the OSCE's website, this kind of bias-motivated offences actually constitutes a significant part of all hate crimes reported to the police. In 2020, 192 cases were reported to the police, which corresponded to 17% of all hate crimes. In 2019 there were 207 (18%), in 2018 210 (19%), in 2017 157 (15%), in 2016 204 (28%), and in 2015 141 (25%).[12] Civil society organisations and official authorities have started raising awareness on the phenomenon of disability hate crime.[13] However, specific studies on the psychological impact of disability hate crimes in Italy have not been found. Still, research carried out in other countries, analysed in Chap. 3, has shown that bias offences against people with disabilities are similar to other hate crimes in terms of harm caused and added wrongfulness.

We can thus conclude that, as regards its second tier, art. 36 of Act 104/1992 can be considered legitimate. However, it would be appropriate, as well as convenient for clarity purposes, to update its terminology.

3.2.3 Tiers III and IV: Amount of Hate and Nexus Between Bias and Offence

The aggravating circumstance analysed in the present section is applicable objectively, i.e. every time the victim fulfils one of the conditions related to disability foreseen by art. 36. This provision is not framed as hate crime law, and therefore does not require the proof of any kind of prejudiced bias or hostile animus on the part of the offender. It falls therefore under the Discriminatory Selection model and can be committed out of different motives. As it was observed in Chap. 3, these models can be considered legitimate only when the law requires the resulting

[12] See https://hatecrime.osce.org/italy (accessed 25 July 2022).

[13] See, for example, OSCAD's work on this issue at https://www.interno.gov.it/it/ministero/osservatori-commissioni-e-centri-coordinamento/osservatorio-sicurezza-contro-atti-discriminatori-oscad (accessed 25 July 2022). See also Chirico and Buscarino (2020).

harm to be particularly serious. This can be the case, for example, when the targeted group is seen as very vulnerable.

As regards disability hate crimes, the application of the objective vulnerability criterion is not fully convincing from a legitimacy point of view, at least with regard to the less serious forms of disabilities. However, all things considered we can regard the provisions at stake as exceptionally legitimate.

3.3 Conclusions

This section has analysed art. 36 of Act 104/1992, which foresees a penalty enhancement when the victim of certain crimes has a disability. This offence is considered as hate crime law, at least implicitly, because it increases the base sentence when certain crimes target a victim being in a particularly vulnerable condition and are thus more harmful and wrongful than parallel offences.

As to its structure, art. 36 has been considered legitimate as it is drafted in the form of special aggravating circumstance.

As regards the protected grounds, it refers to disability, albeit in vague and ambiguous terms. The Italian legal system (including the criminal law) still regards people with disabilities as passive subjects with little agency. This situation is probably the consequence of an inadequate response by social institutions to the needs of persons with disabilities, which results in turn in a situation of disadvantage and discrimination. This is reflected also in the criminal law that has been examined. In the first place, the article identifies the victim's disability with old-fashioned (and possibly offensive) expressions. Moreover, this provision applies objectively, any time the victim has a certified disability. It is irrelevant whether the disability has played a role in the offender's decision to target that particular victim, or whether it has somehow facilitated the commission of the crime.

This aspect raises some legitimacy problems as regards the third and the fourth tiers. Bias does not need to be the predominant motive of the offence, and the nexus between the mental attitude and the offence is explained by the Discriminatory Selection model. However, in the current state of things it can be accepted that the seriousness of the harm and wrongfulness caused by crimes committed against persons with disabilities may in principle render art. 36 legitimate.

Taking into account both the criminological and the legitimacy outcomes of the present research, the better approach against disability crimes is considered to be a combination of a hate crime provision proper, which addresses the offender's bias, and a provision (perhaps narrowed down to apply only to certain categories of crimes), that focuses on the fact that perpetrators have actually taken advantage of their victims' disability to commit the offence (see art. 61(5) of the Penal Code, examined in Sect. 4 below). In the OSCE region, a growing number of hate crime legislations include disability among the protected grounds.[14] The Zan Bill, eventually rejected by Italian Parliament in 2021, included disability among the protected grounds that it aimed to add to existing hate crime law. Considering the results of the present analysis, its dismissal was unfortunate, since it has left a legislative gap that cannot be properly covered by existing legislation.

4 (Old) Age

In Italy, old age is not covered by official hate crime law. In the past, two bills proposed its inclusion in hate crime legislation, but were both unsuccessful.[15] The more recent legislative proposal before the Parliament did

---

[14] Albania (Article 50 of the Penal Code); Andorra (art. 30 of the Penal Code); Austria (art. 283(1) of the Penal Code); Belgium (arts. 377-bis, 422-quater, 438-bis, 453-bis, 514-bis, and 532-bis of the Penal Code); Bosnia and Herzegovina (art. 2 of the Penal Code); Canada (Section 718.2 of the Criminal Code); Croatia (art. 87(21) of the Penal Code); Finland (Section 5 of the Penal Code); Georgia (art. 53 of the Penal Code); Greece (art. 81A of the Penal Code); Hungary (Section 216 of the Penal Code); Lithuania (art. 60 of the Penal Code); Montenegro (art. 42a of the Penal Code); North Macedonia (arts. 39 and 122 of the Penal Code); Norway (Section 77 of the Penal Code); Romania (art. 77 of the Penal Code); Spain (art. 22(4) of the Penal Code); United Kingdom (Section 66 of the Sentencing Act 2020); and most US states (United States' Department of Justice, *Federal Bias Categories Included by State Laws*, updated May 9, 2022, and accessed 29 June 2022 https://www.justice.gov/hatecrimes/laws-and-policies).

[15] Bills A.C. 1071 (28 May 2013) and A.C. 2802-bis-A (age was introduced in the original text on 18 May 2011).

not include age among the protected grounds; the issue was not even debated.

On the other hand, the Penal Code includes several provisions in which the age of the victim plays a decisive role in supporting the rationale of either the criminalisation of a particular conduct, or the increase of the base sentencing range. In all these cases, the legal system regards certain age ranges as particularly vulnerable to crime, either because offenders can take advantage of their victims more easily, and/or because the harm caused to them is bigger when they are very young or very old. However, only few of these provisions can be considered as hate crime law proper and will thus be analysed under a legitimacy perspective. Most of the articles taking age into account that are excluded from our analysis concern children. Some of them may be formally considered as hate crime law because they fulfil the requirements of foreseeing a penalty enhancement when the victims of an already existing offence belong to a certain vulnerable social group. However, crimes against children are very difficult to frame as hate crimes proper, even under a wide definition of bias offences. So far there is neither data nor a proper discussion on crimes motivated by hostility or prejudice against children. On the other hand, another provision excluded from our analysis addresses the issue of age only indirectly, by introducing an aggravating circumstance when certain crimes are committed towards persons who are hospitalised in public or private structures or reside in socio-educational establishments and can thus include old persons in residential care centres (art. 61(11–sexies)).

Only three criminal law provisions concerning the elderly fall more clearly under the definition of hate crime law and will thus be examined in the following sections. Since they share many common features, they will be analysed together.

4.1 Overview of Arts. 61(5), 628(3)(3quinques), and 640(2) of the Penal Code

Art. 61(5) of the Penal Code considers as a general aggravating circumstance the fact that the offender has taken advantage of temporal, spatial or personal circumstances that impaired victims' defence. It includes the victim's age among the elements that could be taken into account, without specifying to which age ranges it refers. In turn, art. 640(2) on fraud provides for a specific aggravating circumstance when the conditions foreseen in art. 61(5) are met.

Furthermore, art. 628(3)(3quinques) foresees a specific aggravating circumstance when the offence of robbery is committed against a person who is 65 or older.

4.2 Legitimacy Assessment

4.2.1 Tier I: Drafting Methods

Art. 61(5) is a general aggravating circumstance that can virtually apply to any base offences. While it may be practical from a systematic point of view, as with other general aggravating circumstances, this kind of provision falls foul of the empirical verifiability requirement of the ILT. Even if we admit the current interpretation according to which general aggravating circumstances are applicable only to those base offences they are not incompatible with (Mantovani, 2015, 402), there still remains the problem of verifying whether the compatible base offences do cause more harm and wrong when committed under the circumstances included in the provision at stake. In the case of art. 61(5), however, the way the provision is drafted actually requires the proof that the offender has *taken advantage* of a particular feature of the victim (age, in this case), which would in turn make the base conduct more wrongful in comparison with a parallel offence.

All the other provisions are drafted in the form of specific aggravating circumstances that apply only to specific, property crimes: robbery (art. 628(3)(3quinques)) and fraud (art. 640(2)). In these cases, the legislator has made a very specific choice as to which crimes to address, also on the basis of the relevance, frequency, and particular seriousness of these offences when committed against an old person. Hence, the way they are drafted is legitimate from a criminalisation perspective.

4.2.2 Tier II: Protected Grounds

The offence of robbery (art. 628(3)(3quinques) foresees a specific age limit for the application of the aggravating circumstance based on the age of the victims (they must be at least 65 years old). The other provisions applicable to this age group require instead a verification case-by-case on how the victim's age has played a role in the offender's commission of the crime (in particular, art. 61(5) as regards any base crime and art. 640(2) in relation to fraud).

Since these provisions do not focus on the offender's motives or aim, but on the victim's feature instead, they are not applicable to ageist crimes committed because of the victim's association with a person of a certain age. As a general rule, mistakes as to the age of the victim cannot be taken into account for the non-application of the aggravating circumstances, even when the offender acts with negligence or recklessness (arts. 59 and 60 of the Penal Code).

It is very difficult to gather consistent and accurate data on the extent of ageist crimes, not only in Italy but also in those countries with a better structured data collection system. This is particularly so because these types of crimes, like disability crimes, tend "to take place in 'hidden' environments such as the home or institutional settings" (Chakraborti & Garland, 2009, 98). Moreover, they are usually understood in terms of elderly abuse or as crimes in which the victim's old age is merely instrumental to the perpetrator's conduct, thus overlooking the possible hate motivation of the offender. In Italy, neither the police nor civil society organisations collect data on ageist hate crime and speech.

The inclusion of age among the grounds protected by hate crime law is still controversial in hate crime studies. This depends on the different ways in which violence is conceptualised and understood in research and practice according to the kind of victim involved, as well as how victims frame their claims in advocating for a better protection (see Mason-Bish, 2013).[16] Unlike racist or religious-based hate crimes, and like gender-motivated and disability offences, crimes against the elderly have been framed as "private and interpersonal incidents" (Mason-Bish, 2013, 298).

[16] See also Chapter 3, Section 4.2.

Studies on the concept and dynamics of bias offences, however, have stressed important factors that are also common to those crimes that target groups that do not belong to the traditional protected characteristics (for example, homeless people, or persons belonging to a subculture), including age (Chakraborti & Garland, 2009; Mason-Bish, 2013; Schweppe, 2012). In particular, the ground-selection criterion based on the concept of vulnerability as developed by Chakraborti and Garland (2012) well captures the reasons why age could be covered by hate crime law. It is important to stress, however, that in their perspective, vulnerability is not an objective element of certain personal features (as it is understood by the criminal provisions we have analysed). In this regard, the age limit foreseen by art. 628(3)(3quinques) on robbery might be considered arbitrary. However, official age-related studies usually take this age into account as the "beginning of old age", so to say (see, for example, the European-wide research of Eurostat, 2019a, 2019b). Thus, the Italian legislator's choice seems reasonable. In any event, the approach used by art. 61(5) (and thus, by art. 640) appears to be better suited to comply with the ILT as it requires to prove that the offender has actually taken advantage of the age of the victim to commit the base offence.

4.2.3 Tiers III and IV: Amount of Hate and Nexus Between Bias and Offence

The aggravating circumstance foreseen by art. 628(3)(3quinques) applies whenever a robbery is committed against a person who is 65 years old or older; on the other hand, art. 61(5) (and thus art. 640) focuses on the perpetrator's taking advantage of the victim age to commit a crime. In both cases, the offender's motive is irrelevant for the application of the aggravating circumstances. Thus, the nexus between the perpetrator's mental attitude and the offence is expressed by the Discriminatory Selection model.

However, while the former aggravating circumstance applies objectively, the latter requires proof that the victims' age has played some role in the offender's decision. The situation of the elderly is similar to that of persons with disabilities. Both conditions are indirect proxy to vulnerability—it is not age *per se* that makes a person vulnerable, but the medical and situational consequence of having a certain age. In these cases, the provision of art. 61(5) seems more respectful of the requirements of the ILT. However, age may also be a direct proxy of vulnerability when the offender is actually motivated by, or expresses, bias or hate against someone because of their particular age.

Mixed-motives hate crime law models, and those adopting a Discriminatory Selection model have been considered legitimate only if the protected group they address is in a severe condition of vulnerability or disadvantage in the jurisdiction under exam. People aged 65 or more constitute almost one fifth of the European population, with Italy as the country with the highest percentage (22.6% in 2018) (Eurostat, 2019a, 22). An increasing share of these persons is living alone, and they are at higher risk of poverty and social exclusion (Eurostat, 2019a, 32). Moreover, the median age is increasing both in Europe and in Italy, and so is the old age dependency ratio—meaning that in the next decades there will be more old people that will need assistance in their daily life (Eurostat, 2019a, 18–20; , 2019b). All these factors contribute to position people over 65 in a situation of disadvantage that is very likely to exacerbate the harm caused by base offences in comparison with younger victims. Thus, the very narrow exception to the legitimacy requirements of hate crime law as regards its third and fourth tiers can apply here as regards art. 628(3)(3quinques).

Arts. 61(5) and 640 are less troublesome from this point of view, because their application is conditioned to the proof that the offender has somehow taken advantage of the victim's age to commit the crime. Thus, they cannot automatically apply.

4.3 Conclusions

Although age is not included among hate crime law's protected grounds, Italian criminal law foresees three aggravating circumstances that apply when a crime is committed against a person of a certain age. Art. 628(3)(3quinques) of the Penal Code explicitly addresses old people, while art.

61(5) and 640(2) do not specify the age range but require instead the crime to be committed by taking advantage of the victim's age (implying that young or old persons might be more vulnerable than others, at least in certain situations).

The three provisions analysed in this section pass the ILT, although some specific legitimacy problems have been discussed.

As to their structure, arts. 628(3)(3quinques) and 640(2) are framed as specific aggravating circumstances that apply only to certain crimes, and thus do not present particular issues. Art. 61(5) is a general aggravating circumstance that applies, however, only when it can be proved that the offender has taken advantage of their victim's old age to commit the crime.

Age is one of the protected grounds belonging to the third wave of hate crime law. Only some countries cover it in their hate crimes provisions.[17] In hate crime studies, it is currently debated whether ageist crimes can be framed as hate crime proper. However, growing research on non-traditional protected groups (e.g. the homeless, or members of subcultures) shows that the harm inflicted to these victims has a similar impact and causes as when more traditional grounds are concerned. The same can be probably argued as regards ageist crimes, albeit more research on this topic is needed.

Moreover, the examined provisions belong to the Discriminatory Selection model and do not require proof of prejudice or hate on the part of the offender. However, old people's particular vulnerability and the seriousness of the harm that may result from the offences concerned allow for an exception to the general legitimacy rule according to which bias has to be the predominant motive. In any event, it has also been observed that the way art. 61(5) is drafted allows partially overcoming this issue as it requires evidence that the victim's age has actually played a role in facilitating the offender's commission of the crime.

[17] E.g. Andorra (art. 30 of the Penal Code); Belgium (arts. 377-bis, 405-quater, 422-quater, 438-bis, 453-bis, 514-bis, 532-bis of the Penal Code); Lithuania (arts. 60, 129, 135, and 138 of the Penal Code); and Romania (art. 77 of the Penal Code).

In sum, all the aggravating circumstances can be considered legitimate. However, the inclusion of age in "official" hate crime law along with the use of art. 61(5) would be beneficial in order to separate ageist crimes proper (i.e. those crimes committed out of some form of hostility against the elderly) and those offences addressing older people that are better explained through lifestyle/routine activity and rational choice theories. In doing so, art. 628(3)(3quinques)—the legitimacy of which has been confirmed only by applying a narrow exception—would be superfluous as hate crime provisions or art. 61(5) could be applied when the victim's age is somehow relevant in the commission of the crime.

5 Grounds Not Covered: Sex, Gender, Sexual Orientation and Gender Identity

As we have seen, Italian hate crime legislation is quite conservative, as it covers only a very limited set of traditional grounds. However, an important number of legislative proposals to extend existing legislation to sex, gender, sexual orientation and gender identity have been discussed and eventually dismissed by the Parliament.

This section examines under the ILT the different options that have been put forward over the years to try to extend the scope of hate crime law to the strands sex, gender, sexual orientation and gender identity. We will focus only on the analysis of the second tier, namely whether the inclusion of these grounds in Italian hate crime law would be legitimate under the ILT. In fact, the legislative proposals put forward so far did not raise particular legitimacy issues under the other three variables (drafting method adopted; amount of bias required; and nexus between bias and offence).

In the discussion accompanying the legislative proposals, and in the structure of the bills, the grounds sex and gender have been practically considered as synonymous, and have been conceptually separated from the strands sexual orientation and gender identity. While this approach is not entirely correct from a theoretical viewpoint, it reflects a more general differentiation between the social groups the legislative proposals wanted to cover. In fact, with the terms "sex" and "gender" the proponents aimed to address cisgender women, whilst the expressions "sexual orientation" and "gender identity" referred to LGBTI people more in general. This research will also follow this distinction. However, the conceptual and practical differences between these four grounds will be identified and taken into account.

5.1 Tier II: Sex and Gender

5.1.1 The Criminal Law Response to Gender-Based Crime in Italy

Italian society's awareness of gender-based violence and research in this field have increased notably in the past decades (see Toffanin, 2019). They have been followed by some legislative attempts to respond to the phenomenon. Nonetheless, in Italy, like elsewhere, gender-based violence has been traditionally framed as an interpersonal and private issue. Criminal law's response to this problem has taken a separate path than that of hate crime law. A number of criminal law reforms have been implemented, both of procedural and substantial nature (see Viggiani, 2020). However, the criminal law provisions currently in force addressing gender-related crimes cannot be considered as hate crime law proper under the definition adopted in this work. Most of them do not explicitly provide for the penalty enhancement of an already existing criminal offence when the crime is motivated by the victim's gender. They concern instead a number of offences that are somehow typical of gender-based violence (and, in particular, of men's violence against women). On the other hand, a number of other provisions increasing the base sentence when the victim is a pregnant woman could formally be labelled as hate crime law. However, they apply objectively, i.e. whenever the victim is pregnant, and no proof of bias on the part of the offender is required. This, compounded with the lack of empirical data and the absence of an actual debate on the existence and impact of hate crimes against pregnant women in Italy or elsewhere, runs against the conceptualisation of these provisions as hate crime law.

In the OSCE region, 22 Participant States foresee sex or gender as a protected ground in hate crime law.[18] In Italy, in past years there were two timid, unsuccessful attempts to introduce gender (or, better, sex) among the other grounds protected by hate crime law.[19] In both cases, the inclusion of these strands in the bills was not given much space in the overall discussion surrounding the legislative proposals, since the debate focused more narrowly on sexual orientation and gender identity. With the more recent Zan Bill, proponents adopted a more energetic approach. The possible inclusion of sex and gender in hate crime law was openly discussed, and the final version of the bill included both terms.

5.1.2 Conceptual Issues

Including sex and gender in hate crime law has been a controversial issue, not only in Italy but also in other geographical contexts, such as the United States (see McPhail, 2002; Weisburd & Levin, 1994) and in the United Kingdom (see Mason-Bish, 2013; Zempi & Smith, 2021).

The argument typically raised against this inclusion maintains that gender-based crimes are mostly due to interpersonal issues that happen in the context of a relationship where offender and victim are not strangers to each other. Thus, in comparison with bias-motivated crimes, they would lack the element of "interchangeability", i.e. the fact that the target of hate crime offenders can be any person that is perceived to possess a given trait or belong to a specific social group (see Pezzella, 2017, 7). However, whilst the interchangeability of victims is a recurrent factor in

[18] Albania (art. 50 of the Penal Code); Andorra (art. 30 of the Penal Code); Austria (art. 283 of the Penal Code); Belgium (arts. 377-bis, 405-quarter, 422-quater, 438-bis, 453-bis, 514-bis, 532-bis of the Penal Code); Bosnia and Herzegovina (art. 2 of the Penal Code); Canada (Section 718.2 of the Criminal Code); Croatia (art. 87(21) of the Penal Code); France (arts. 132-77 and 222-13 of the Penal Code); Georgia (art. 53 of the Penal Code); Greece (art. 81A of the Penal Code); Latvia (art. 150 of the Penal Code); Lithuania (art. 60 of the Penal Code); Luxembourg (arts. 454 and 457-1 of the Penal Code); Malta (art. 83B of the Criminal Code); Mongolia (art. 10.1 of the Penal Code); Montenegro (art. 42a of the Penal Code); North Macedonia (arts. 39 and 122 of the Penal Code); Portugal (art. 132 of the Penal Code); Romania (art. 77 of the Penal Code); Serbia (art. 54A of the Penal Code); Spain (art. 22(4) of the Penal Code); and 35 US States.

[19] By bills no. A.C. 1071 and no. A.C. 2802-bis-A (sex was introduced in the original text on 18 May 2011).

hate crimes, it is by no means a necessary element to frame a crime as a hate crime (Weisburd & Levin, 1994, 37; see Chap. 2, Sect. 2.2.2). Previous knowledge between victim and offender is often observed even in the most "traditional" types of hate crimes involving racism and xenophobia (see, e.g. Hardy & Chakraborti, 2020, 102).[20]

Another argument that is often raised concerns the motivation behind the crime. Opponents to the inclusion of gender in hate crime law claim that "those who perpetrate gender crimes do not 'hate' all women in the same sense that a white supremacist hates all African-Americans or an anti-Semite hates all Jews" (Weisburd & Levin, 1994, 35). However, this argument fails to consider that in some cases hate crime offenders target women because they actually hate all women (Weisburd & Levin, 1994, 35). Secondly, and more importantly, hate crimes can be motivated not only by the emotion "hate" in the stricter sense, but rather by a more general prejudice towards the social group the victim belongs to. Putting too much emphasis on hate leads us to disregard the profound social roots of gender-motivated crimes and of hate crimes more in general. In this regard, Weisburd and Levin observe that "[w]hether or not the attacker's 'primary motivation' is hatred toward all women, the offense may still be a bias crime because it directly reinforces the subjugated status of women and has the effect of terrorizing the entire community." In this sense, "gender-related crimes of violence can be used as a way to keep women 'in their place' and to send a message to all women, reinforcing and reifying their subordinated status" (Weisburd & Levin, 1994, 36; Viggiani, 2020, 19).

In certain cases, though, it is not easy to frame a gender-based crime as a hate crime, particularly when the dynamics resulting from the relationship between victim and perpetrator can have somehow contributed to the victimisation (Weisburd & Levin, 1994, 38). In this respect, "[p]erhaps it [is] felt that gender violence, which is mostly made up by

[20] A well-known case of this kind in Italy concerns former senator Roberto Calderoli. In 2019 he was convicted of racially aggravated slander for having insulted the then Minister for Integration Cécile Kyenge Kashetu, a black woman of Congolese origins. During a public assembly of his party, the North League, Calderoli referred to Kyenge by saying that "she looks like an orangutan". The fact that the two politicians clearly knew each other did not prevent this offence to be considered as a hate crime by the court as well as by the general public.

men's violence against women, will be difficult to distinguish in a legally secure way from violence between, e.g., spouse that comes out of individual conflicts and feelings of animosity, albeit partly dependent on existing gender or sexual identity structures or 'roles' or domination patterns, and the expectations and conflicts they create" (Brax & Munthe, 2013, 40). Nonetheless, "even if there is an individual component to these gender-related crimes, that should not preclude bias crime classification when there is also a significant group component" (Weisburd & Levin, 1994, 38). In fact, hate crime statutes can legitimately foresee that hate or bias be one among other motives behind the crime, provided that it is at least the predominant motivation. Moreover, it has been argued that even in those cases where a more general misogynist motivation of the crime is not so clear (e.g. acquaintance rape or partner abuse), offenders "tend to define their victims as legitimate targets of aggression or domination on the basis of group status. The man who beats his wife or commits a date rape regards his victim as properly dominatable. Like bias offenders, gender-motivated offenders tend to commit habitual victimizations, often against the same target" (Weisburd & Levin, 1994, 35).

5.1.3 Legitimacy Assessment

Research indicates that gender-motivated crimes cause more harm and are more wrongful than non-bias crimes. It has been shown that they cause more *psychological* harm in comparison with parallel offences, both to direct (Mellgren et al., 2017) and vicarious victims (see McPhail, 2002, 136). Moreover, they also cause more *normative* harm by severely intruding upon victims' interest to *equal dignity and respect*, since they are attacks to the victim's social identity, which have the explicit or implicit effect of debasing them (Viggiani, 2020, 19); upon their interest to *autonomy*, since "these types of violations clearly reflect a total disregard of the other's right to exercise the most fundamental aspects of personal autonomy—the right to control one's body and to be free from forceful, violent victimization by virtue of one's gender" (Weisburd & Levin,

1994, 36); and upon their interest to *individuality*, because even when victim and perpetrator know each other, the offence is committed because of the victim's gender: the offender would not have committed the crime if the victim was not a woman. The discriminatory element of these crimes makes them more wrongful, too.

All the ground-selecting criteria thus apply in this context. In Italy, women have been historically subjected to discrimination and oppression, including in some fields of law such as Family Law and Criminal Law.[21] Albeit nowadays women and men are formally equal before the law, women still suffer widespread discrimination in several areas of life, such as employment, politics, access to reproductive healthcare,[22] disproportionate burden in the care of children and the elderly, and so on. Moreover, gender-related crime and hate speech in Italy is widespread, and strongly enrooted in the Italian heterosexist culture and history (Toffanin, 2019; Viggiani, 2020). In particular, data on online hate speech against women reflects an increasing hostility against women, especially when they perform certain roles that are not the traditionally accepted ones (Vox, 2022b). Furthermore, according to the more recent national-wide survey conducted in Italy, approximately 7 million women have been the target of some form of physical or sexual violence during their lifetime. This means 31.5% of women aged 16 to 70. Of them, 20.2% reported having suffered physical violence and 21% sexual violence (ISTAT, 2015, 1). The types of criminal conducts identified in the survey cover a wide range of violent offences: pushing, hair pulling,

[21] Until the 1975 Family Law reform (Act 151/1975) women and men did not have the same rights and obligations as regards the family unit, their children, and their common properties, among other things. Moreover, until the Constitutional Courts' judgment nos. 126/1968 and 147/1969, criminal law punished more harshly adultery committed by a wife than that of a husband. Furthermore, until 1981, the Penal Code foresaw a mitigating circumstance for the so-called honour killing, i.e. when offenders (usually the husband, brother or father) murdered their spouse, daughter or sister if that happened while, or right after, finding out that they were having an illegitimate sexual relationship (former art. 587 of the Penal Code).

[22] For example, although abortion was already decriminalised in 1978, the right to access to a safe abortion procedure is severely impaired in Italy due to the extremely high number of health professionals that are exempted from performing such procedures for religious or moral beliefs (Autorino et al., 2020).

punching or hitting with an object, a knife, a gun, or other weapons; attempting to strangle, choke, or burn them; threats to their life or physical safety; unwanted sexual relationships, including rape and attempted rape. The survey results show that the most serious forms of violence are caused by persons known to the victim (partners, relatives, friends or acquaintances). For example, rapes were committed by partners in 62.7% of cases, by relatives 3.6% of cases and by friends 9.4%. As to crimes committed outside a previous or current relationship, 24.7% of violent acts were committed by non-partner men: strangers (13.2%), acquaintances (6.3%), friends (3%), relatives (2.6%) and work colleagues (2.5%). With regard to the emotional and psychological consequences of the violence inflicted by current or former partners, victims reported "loss of trust and self-esteem (52.75%) … anxiety, phobia and panic attacks (46.8%), despair and feeling of helplessness (46.4%), sleep and food disorders (46.3%), depression (40.3%), as well as difficult focusing and loss of memory (24.9%), recurrent pain in the body (21.8%), difficulties with children (14.8%) and finally self-harm and suicidal ideas (12.1%)" (ISTAT, 2015, 5).

From these considerations, and particularly in light of the added wrongfulness and harmfulness of gender-motivated hate crimes, we can conclude that the inclusion of sex and gender in hate crime law would be legitimate.

5.2 Tier II: Sexual Orientation and Gender Identity

5.2.1 The Criminal Law Response to Anti-LGBTI Crime in Italy

So far, almost 20 bills have been presented to extend Italian hate crime legislation to LGBTI persons. However, none of them succeeded. The comparison with other OSCE States is striking. Out of the 57 OSCE participating States in North America, Europe and Asia, 21 include both sexual orientation and gender identity,[23] and 10 cover at least sexual orientation.[24]

Overall considered, the legislative proposals did not succeed for two main reasons. Some of them were rejected on constitutional grounds since the new provisions were said to encroach upon the Italian Constitution. The vast majority of them—including the Zan Bill—were however dismissed, or simply dropped, for political reasons. It is important to note that the proposed bills did not exclusively focus on hate crime law. They also aimed to extend existing hate speech and non-discrimination legislation to LGBTI persons. An important part of the arguments against these bills thus concerned the possible encroachment of hate speech law upon freedom of expression principles. Given the limited scope of this work, we will however limit our analysis to the arguments addressing hate crime law proper.

5.2.2 Legal and Constitutional Issues

Opponents to the inclusion of sexual orientation and gender identity in hate crime law have put forward a number of legal and constitutional arguments (for a thorough overview see, for example, Dolcini, 2014; Goisis, 2019, 2020).

From a strictly legal viewpoint, some authors (and courts) have suggested that new hate crime provisions are not necessary. Existing criminal

[23] Albania (art. 50 of the Penal Code); Andorra (art. 30 of the Penal Code); Belgium (arts. 377-bis, 405-quater, 422-quater, 438-bis, 453-bis, 514-bis, 532-bis of the Penal Code); Bosnia and Herzegovina (art. 2 of the Penal Code); Canada (Section 718.2 of the Criminal Code); Croatia (art. 87(21) of the Penal Code); Cyprus (art. 35A of the Penal Code); France (arts. 132-77 and 222-13 of the Penal Code); Georgia (art. 53 of the Penal Code); Greece (art. 81A of the Penal Code); Hungary (art. 216 of the Penal Code); Malta (art. 83B of the Criminal Code); Montenegro (art. 42a of the Penal Code); North Macedonia (arts. 39 and 122 of the Penal Code); Norway (art. 77 of the Penal Code); Portugal (art. 132 of the Penal Code); Serbia (art. 54A of the Penal Code); Spain (art. 22(4) of the Penal Code); Sweden (Chapter 29(2) of the Penal Code); United Kingdom (Section 66 of the Sentencing Act 2020); and 16 US states (United States' Department of Justice, *Federal Bias Categories Included by State Laws*, updated May 9, 2022, https://www.justice.gov/hate-crimes/laws-and-policies, accessed 25 July 2022).

[24] Austria (art. 283 of the Penal Code); Denmark (art. 81(6) of the Penal Code); Finland (art. 5 of the Penal Code); Latvia (art. 150 of the Penal Code); Lithuania (art. 60 of the Penal Code); Luxembourg (arts. 454 and 457-1 of the Penal Code); Mongolia (art. 10.1 of the Penal Code); Romania (art. 77 of the Penal Code); San Marino (art. 90(1) of the Penal Code); and 18 US states.

law (arts. 61(1) and 604-ter of the Penal Code) would already cover homophobic and transphobic hate crimes. However, these arguments have easily been rebutted by criminal law doctrine (see, e.g., Dolcini, 2014, 12; Pellissero 2015, 21; Gentile, 2016, 203–205).

On their part, constitutional-based arguments have focused on the alleged violation of the principles of equality and of legal certainty resulting from the terms chosen to express the protected characteristics to include.[25] Most bills proposed the adoption of the expressions *sexual orientation* and *gender identity*, including the Zan Bill.[26] Fewer proposals suggested instead focusing on the perpetrator's *homophobic* or *transphobic* motives or aims.[27]

The claim that these expressions would violate the *equality principle* has been based on three arguments. First, extending hate crime law to LGBTI people would leave outside, and thus discriminate against, other vulnerable groups (e.g. people with disabilities and the elderly). Second, the expressions *homophobia* and *transphobia* refer only to a specific sexual orientation and gender identity, thus discriminating against heterosexual and cisgender persons. Third, these expressions focus on the offender's motives and aims, and not on the victim's characteristic, thus risking the criminalisation of the offender's thought. All these arguments can be easily rebutted. As to the first issue, Italian criminal law already provides for enhanced sentences when certain crimes are committed against persons that are considered vulnerable because of their age or because of a disability. Moreover, the more recent proposal also included disability among the other protected grounds, and age could be also included in hate crime law proper. As regards the second argument, research shows that hate crimes directed against LGBTI people cause more harm and are more wrongful than non-bias crimes. The same cannot be shown as regards crimes committed because the victim is cisgender and/or heterosexual. This is because heterosexual and cisgender persons do not have a

[25] The older bills that managed to be eventually discussed by the Parliament (A.C. 1658-1882-A and A.C. 2802) were dismissed on these very grounds by the Chamber of Deputies' Commission for Constitutional Affairs.

[26] Bill no. 2551; A.S. 2147; A.C. 606; Bill no. 1639; A.C. 1658; A.C. 1882; A.C. 1658-1882-A; A.C. 2802-bis; A.C. 4631; A.C. 245; A.C. 280; A.C. 1071; A.S. 2005.

[27] A.C. 2802; A.C. 2807; Bill no. 245-280-1071-A; A.S. 1052.

history of oppression or discrimination, are not currently victims of discrimination, prejudice or hostility, and neither can they be considered as disadvantaged or vulnerable groups because of their sexual orientation or gender identity (even if they can be so for other reasons, of course). Thus, the use of the terms *transphobia* and *homophobia* allows a very specific protection that does not overstep the boundaries of a legitimate criminalisation.[28] Anyway, some authors suggest the use of *sexual orientation* and *gender identity* (or the umbrella term *sexual identity*) to overcome this problem (e.g. Pugiotto, 2015, 10–11; Gentile, 2016, 184–185; Goisis, 2020). The third criticism, concerning the risk of criminalising offenders' thoughts, may appear to be more grounded. However, arts. 604-bis and 604-ter already refer to the offender's racist, religious-based, etc., motives and aims. Thus, the best option would be that of redrafting the whole articles to focus on the victim's characteristics instead. However, this could cause another problem, because it would leave outside those persons that are victimised because the offender mistakenly perceives them as being LGBTI (hate crimes by *erroneous perception*) or are merely associated with LGBTI people (hate crimes *by association*). The simplest way to overcome this issue, however, is to explicitly include these circumstances in the law.

With regard to the possible violation of the *legal certainty* principle, it has been argued that homophobia, transphobia, sexual orientation and gender identity are ambiguous concepts that are not defined by Italian law. This line of reasoning, however, is not very convincing. First, social and psychological research on gender and sexuality has produced evolving, but quite clear descriptions of these concepts, also in Italy (see, for example, Ferrari et al., 2017). Second, both the Italian and the European legal systems already provide definitions of these terms (Goisis, 2020, 17–18).[29]

[28] From a different point of view, it might not be the best option, though, as it leaves out other kinds of prejudice based on victim's bisexuality or intersexuality, or for them being agender, genderfluid or non-binary, for example.

[29] As to Italian legislation, Legislative Decree n. 273 of 10 September 2003 transposing the Council Directive 2000/78/EC of 27 November 2000 establishing a general framework for equal treatment in employment and occupation forbids discrimination in the workplace on the grounds of "sexual orientation". Moreover, Legislative Decrees nos. 123 and 124 of 2 October 2018 forbid any discriminatory treatments on the grounds of sexual orientation and gender identity towards inmates.

5.2.3 Conceptual Issues

In the past few years, most of the legal and constitutional arguments discussed above have lost weight. The Zan Bill actually passed the constitutional scrutiny of the Chamber of Deputies' Commission for Constitutional Affairs without much trouble.

However, the inclusion of the expression "gender identity" in hate crime law is still debated by different sectors of public opinion. Far-right politicians, conservative Catholics, anti-abortion groups, and also minority parts of the feminist movement (see Fanlo Cortés, 2022, 5) have opposed the inclusion of this term in the law. Their motivations differ, however. Far-right and Catholic parties oppose the inclusion of LGBTI people in hate crime law *tout court*. They are worried that such inclusion would be a slippery slope that would inevitably lead to the recognition of other rights (such as same-sex marriage and adoption), and the obligation to teach gender studies (or, as they call it, "gender ideology") in schools. Radical feminists, on the other hand, maintain that the concept of "gender identity" is far-fetched and subjective, as it would be based on the individual's will and not on objective factors (contrary to sex, which would be an objective characteristic). As such, it could open the doors to another kind of slippery slope: gender self-identification, i.e. the possibility to officially modify the gender assigned at birth without having to undergo any kind of psychological, medical and judicial procedure. They are concerned that ill-motivated cisgender men could use this possibility to self-certify themselves as women and take advantage of their position.

If closely scrutinised, both kinds of arguments can be easily rebutted. The first one is clearly based on homophobic, transphobic, and more generally misogynist and sexphobic premises that run against a plural and diverse conception of society and respect for diversity. They are grounded on non-scientific and discriminatory assumptions, and have been often accompanied by other insulting and far-fetched claims, such as that the concept of *sexual orientation* would include also paraphilias such as paedophilia, necrophilia, bestiality, and so on (and that, generally speaking, homosexuals would be paedophiles).[30]

[30] See Morassutto (2013) for a thorough reference to, and analysis of these kinds of political interventions.

As to the concerns raised by some, radical feminists, they are problematic in three regards. First, they do not seem to take in due account the actual life experiences of trans persons. Claiming that gender identity is a subjective construct that has no basis in reality simply disregards and trivialises the lives and identities of non-cisgender people.[31] Second, they seem, in some respects, "out of touch with reality" (TGEU, 2017, 1). The fact that a cisgender man could recur to self-recognition to be protected by specific legislation addressing women does not seem to be realistic. But even admitting that some cis men would actually do that, how many would they be in comparison with the actual trans people that could find protection in the law? Third, they overestimate the potential impact of the inclusion of gender identity in hate crime law. Simplifying the legal gender recognition (LGR) process in Italy would actually be an important step in protecting the rights of trans people, whose lives are still paved with incredible difficulties. Including gender identity in hate crime law would certainly be an improvement of trans rights overall considered, but it can hardly be seen as a step towards a legal reform of the LGR law.

5.2.4 Legitimacy Assessment

The legitimacy assessment of the extension of hate crime law to sexual orientation and gender identity can help in dismissing most of the arguments analysed so far against such inclusion. In fact, to consider hate crime law legitimate, the ILT requires the existence of principle- and evidence-based arguments showing that the conduct is more harmful and more wrongful than in parallel crimes.

In Chap. 3, a number of studies have shown that anti-LGBTI crimes cause *more harm* and are *more wrongful* than non-bias crimes. With regard to the Italian context, criminal law research and civil society organisations have focused chiefly on LGBTI people's alleged condition of *vulnerability* to justify their inclusion in the law (see, for example, Dolcini,

[31] See Fanlo Cortés (2022) for an analysis of the definitions of "sex", "gender", "sexual orientation" and "gender identity" proposed by the Zan Bill in light of the debate on the relationship between "sex" and "gender" in feminist studies. In the British context, see Zanghellini (2020) for a thorough reply to gender-critical feminist arguments against trans inclusion.

2014, 17; Goisis, 2020, 3, 17–18). However, all the selection criteria identified in Chap. 2 apply as well. Violence and discrimination against non-heterosexual and gender variant people in Italy has been recurrent in this country's history. Although same-sex relationships were already decriminalised in 1889, a number of criminal and administrative provisions have been used to punish and deter homosexual and trans persons to express themselves up to recent years (Winkler & Strazio, 2011). Although there has been a significant advancement of LGBTI people's rights in the past decade, this has often been the result of the implementation of International and European law. Moreover, institutional discriminations are still in place as marriage, step-child adoption and general adoption are not allowed to same-sex couples. The legal gender recognition process is based on a law enacted in 1982, and is extremely burdensome: trans persons have to pass through a long judicial procedure and have to meet intrusive medical requirements. As to intersex people, a legal vacuum still allows health professionals to undergo surgical interventions and other medical therapies on newborns and children to align their sexual morphology to one of the two sexes. These arbitrary procedures completely disregard the psychological and social consequences of these surgeries, and seriously impair intersex people's right to self-determination (see Balocchi, 2019).

On the other hand, there is increasing data on the recurrence of hate crimes and incidents against LGBTI people. As with gender-based hate crimes, Italy provides the OSCE with data on hate crime committed against LGBTI persons.[32] According to the OSCE, the overall number of reported cases of homophobic and transphobic hate crime was 42 in the year 2016, 68 in 2017, 113 in 2018, 158 in 2019, and 100 in 2020. However, the overall data-collection system on hate crimes in Italy presents several shortcomings and these numbers should be considered with caution. Generally speaking, the lack of an official definition of hate crime affects the overall quality of the data collected by official authorities and CSOs (Perry, 2019, 19; see also Godzisz & Viggiani, 2018). Moreover, since hate crime law does not include the strands sexual orientation and gender identity courts cannot frame these offences as hate crimes. This

[32] See https://hatecrime.osce.org/italy (accessed 25 July 2022).

has two consequences: first, there exist no data relating to the outcomes of prosecutions and sentencing and official data only concern cases of *reported* homophobic and transphobic hate crimes; and second, given that the bias component these types of crimes will not be taken into account by official authorities, victims are further prevented from reporting them.

The EU Fundamental Rights Agency (FRA)'s second large study on LGBTI people's perception of victimisation across Europe has given important insights about the situation of LGBTI people in Italy (FRA, 2020). For example, 8% of the overall Italian respondents reported having been victims of physical or sexual attacks due to being LGBTI in the past 5 years. However, the percentage is higher as regards trans people (12%) and intersex individuals (19%). Most respondents (76%) did not report the incident to the authorities. As to the way the last hate-motivated violent incident has affected the respondents' health and well-being, overall 7% has needed medical assistance or hospitalisation (but 16% of trans respondents); overall 44% has reported psychological problems (but 71% and 49% as regards trans and intersex respondents, respectively). Moreover, 33% of all respondents reported being afraid of going out or visiting places as a consequence of their most recent hate incident. This is reflected also by the general reply to the question of whether they avoid certain places or locations for fear of being assaulted, threatened or harassed due to being LGBTI: only one third of respondents replied *never* to this question. Quite alarmingly, among the places where the respondents do not feel safe enough to come out as LGBTI there are their homes (18%), their families (33%), school (18%) and the workplace (37%). These data also show the higher severity of the victimisation trans and intersex individuals suffer vis-à-vis LGB persons. Intersexuality has never been discussed as a possible candidate for its inclusion in Italian hate crime law. Nevertheless, the inclusion of both *sex* and *gender* in the legislation can actually be beneficial in order to extend the protection of hate crime law to intersex people, too. In fact, the wording used by the legislative proposal ("sex" refers to a person's biological *or* officially recorded sex) seems to indicate that lawmakers have accepted a wider concept of sex that is not limited to the sex that was attributed to the child at birth (Fanlo Cortés, 2022, 7).

From this data, compounded with the conclusions reached in Chap. 3 on the added harmfulness and wrongfulness of anti-LGBTI crime, it can be concluded that the inclusion of sexual orientation and gender identity in hate crime law would be legitimate.

5.3 Conclusions

This section has examined the possible inclusion of the grounds sex, gender, sexual orientation and gender identity in Italian hate crime legislation. A number of legal, constitutional and conceptual arguments against this inclusion have been discussed and, we believe, convincingly rebutted. More importantly from a legitimacy point of view, it has been shown that hate crimes motivated by sex, gender, sexual orientation or gender identity are more harmful and more wrongful than their parallel counterparts. Thus, it can be concluded that the inclusion of these strands in hate crime law would be legitimate.

6 Conclusions

This chapter has examined Italian hate crime law under the ILT, with the two-fold purpose of determining whether the identified provisions are prima *facie legitimate* under an interdisciplinary perspective,[33] and to provide an example of how the ILT can be applied in practice.

To identify which provisions to examine, this work has adopted a wide definition of hate crime law. We have considered all those criminal provisions that foresee a penalty increase either when offenders are motivated by bias or hate, or when the victims are in a particularly vulnerable condition. Thus, the legitimacy assessment has considered both those provisions that are explicitly considered as hate crime, and a number of other provisions that, albeit framed differently, fall nevertheless under our definition.

[33] For a description of what is meant with "*prima facie* legitimacy", see Chap. 3, Sects. 1 and 2.

Section 2 focused on art. 604-ter of the Penal Code, which foresees a sentence increase when an offence is committed "with an ethnic, national, racial, religious discriminatory or hate purpose" or against someone belonging to a linguistic minority. This general aggravating circumstance is the most important hate crime provision in Italy. It has been considered legitimate only if courts apply it to offences that are shown to be more harmful and wrongful when they are committed out of bias.

Sections 3 and 4 examined a number of aggravating circumstances that apply when the victim has a certain characteristic that renders them very vulnerable to crimes.

First, we have examined art. 36 of Act 104/1992, which foresees a specific aggravating circumstance when certain crimes are committed against a person with a disability. This article has not been conceived as a hate crime law proper, but, instead, as a measure to protect individuals that are considered extremely vulnerable. Given that the "official" hate crime law provision does not include disability among the protected grounds, art. 36 plays an important role in the hate crime legal framework. This article however falls foul of the requirement according to which hate crime law is legitimate only when it foresees hate or bias at least as the predominant motive of the crime. Nonetheless, the serious level of harm victims of disability crime can suffer makes it reasonable to apply a narrow exception to the general rule. It has thus been considered legitimate.

Second, we have identified and analysed three penalty enhancement provisions regarding the victim's (old) *age*. They have all passed the ILT, but, as with those provisions addressing disability, some remarks have been necessary. In particular, art. 628(3)(3quinques), foreseeing an aggravating circumstance anytime the victim of robbery is 65 years old or older, has been considered legitimate only by applying a narrow exception to the general rule that bias has to constitute at least the main motive behind the crime. To do so, the age range at issue (people over 65), has been considered to be particularly vulnerable and at risk that the resulting harm be very serious. The approach of arts. 61(5) and 640(2) seems better suited to address crimes in which offenders target an old person because of their supposed vulnerability to that particular crime.

The final part of the chapter has assessed the legitimacy of the possible extension of hate crime law to the grounds *sex*, *gender*, *sexual orientation* and *gender identity*. Numerous legislative proposals foreseeing the inclusion of these grounds have been presented, and ultimately rejected, in the past three decades. The arguments raised by opponents to these bills have been examined through the lens of the ILT, and eventually rejected as unfounded, far-fetched or merely discriminatory. On the other hand, we have presented sound and growing evidence that gender-based and anti-LGBTI crime causes more harm and is more wrongful than non-bias offences. We have therefore concluded that the inclusion of these strands in hate crime law would be legitimate (Table 4.1).

The application of the ILT has allowed us to examine Italian hate crime law from a holistic perspective that has taken into account the different dimensions of criminal laws addressing hate crime. Overall, the analysis carried out in this chapter has provided a number of important insights.

The most evident aspect of the Italian hate crime legislation is that it is scattered in different legal provisions and lacks uniformity and consistency. There are significant differences in the way certain grounds are treated in comparison with others. What emerges is that lawmakers still lack a proper understanding of the phenomenon of hate crimes, despite the increasing awareness raised by civil society organisations, socio-legal research, and the proponents of the legislative reforms. For example, art. 604-ter focuses chiefly on the offender's aim and on the possible consequences of the *communicative* aspect of these kinds of offences. This narrow conception of hate crimes is not wrong, nor is it illegitimate; however, it is partial, as it ends up overlooking the psychological and normative harm that these kinds of crimes also cause to their direct victims. Focusing also, or instead, on the offender's motives could better reflect the different harm dimensions of these crimes.

The approach adopted to draft the provisions on disability, or age, is understandable. They aim to protect a situation that is considered particularly vulnerable, not to address crimes motivated by bias against the individuals concerned. However, this objective view of vulnerability is problematic because it does not fully grasp the interests at stake. There are two types of crimes that should be considered separately: first, those offences that are committed *out of prejudice* against a vulnerable group, in

Table 4.1 Legitimacy of Italian hate crime law

LEGITIMACY OF ITALIAN HATE CRIME LAW					
LAW	**TIER I Drafting method**	**TIER II Protected grounds**	**TIER III amount of hate/bias**	**TIER IV Nexus between bias and crime**	**Overall Conclusions**
604-ter	General aggravating circumstances *Not legitimate in abstracto* *Legitimate in concreto* if narrowly applied	Race, ethnicity, nationality, religion, linguistic minorities *Legitimate*	Hate/bias as main motive/aim *Legitimate*	Hostile Animus model *Legitimate*	***Legitimate* only if**, *in concreto*, applicability to base offences is **narrowly interpreted**
36(1) of Act 104/1992	Specific aggravating circumstance *Legitimate*	Disability *Legitimate*	Proof of hate/bias not required *Exceptionally legitimate:* seriousness of resulting harm	Discriminatory Selection model *Exceptionally legitimate:* seriousness of resulting harm	***Legitimate***
61(5) 640(2)	General aggravating circumstances *Legitimate*: requires proof of offender's taking advantage of victim's condition	Age *Legitimate*	Proof of hate/bias not required *Exceptionally legitimate*: it requires proof of offender's taking advantage of victim's condition	Discriminatory Selection model *Exceptionally legitimate*: it requires proof of offender's taking advantage of victim's condition	***Legitimate***
628(3)-3quinques	Specific aggravating circumstance *Legitimate*	Age, over 65 years' old *Legitimate*	Proof of hate/bias not required *Exceptionally legitimate*: seriousness of resulting harm	Discriminatory Selection model *Exceptionally legitimate*: seriousness of resulting harm	***Legitimate***

which the vulnerability is framed similarly to that of other groups targeted because of their ethnicity, sexual orientation, and so on. Second, those crimes in which the perpetrator *takes advantage* of a particular condition of the victim that make them more vulnerable to that crime in comparison with an individual who does not have that feature. In Italian law, these two scenarios are reflected by arts. 604-ter and 61(5) respectively. While the former focuses on the offender's biased mental attitude, the latter takes into account the offender's taking advantage of a particular characteristic of the victim. These two approaches are not in conflict; one complements the other. With regard to the grounds *disability* and *old age* the legislator should adopt a combined approach in which these characteristics are included in both hate crime law proper and in the provision of art. 61(5) of the Penal Code.

On a final note, it is important to recall that, whilst penalty enhancement law has proved to be legitimate (under certain criteria), and probably necessary, by no means can it be considered *sufficient* to address the phenomenon of hate crimes, in Italy or elsewhere. A wide assortment of legal and policy measures should accompany hate crime law proper, in order to combat prejudice and discrimination in different fields of social life. Moreover, specific measures should also be properly put in place and implemented to address both crime victims and offenders (see ODHIR, 2020). Furthermore, multidisciplinary research on hate crimes in Italy is still at a very early stage, and the official data collection and monitoring system should be improved following the recommendations of the ODHIR (2014) and the FRA (2018).

References

Autorino, T., Mattioli, F., & Mencarini, L. (2020). The Impact of Gynecologists' Conscientious Objection on Abortion Access. *Social Science Research, 87*, 1. https://doi.org/10.1016/j.ssresearch.2020.102403

Balocchi, M. (Ed.). (2019). *Intersex. Antologia Multidisciplinare*. Edizioni ETS.

Brax, D., & Munthe, C. (2013). *Introduction to the Philosophy of Hate Crime. When Law and Hate Collide*. University of Gothenburg. Retrieved July 25, 2022, from https://www.uclan.ac.uk/research/activity/perspectives-on-hate-crime

Burch, L. (2021). *Understanding Disability and Everyday Hate*. Palgrave Macmillan. https://doi.org/10.1007/978-3-030-86818-5
Chakraborti, N., & Garland, J. (2009). *Hate Crime: Impact, Causes and Responses*. SAGE.
Chakraborti, N., & Garland, J. (2012). Reconceptualizing Hate Crime Victimization through the Lens of Vulnerability and 'Difference'. *Theoretical Criminology, 16*(4), 499–514.
Chirico, S., & Buscarino, S. (2020). L'Odio contro le Persone Disabili, *Polizia Moderna*, Retrieved July 25, 2022, from https://poliziamoderna.poliziadistato.it/articolo/3535f8042a6b043e709449491.
Curreri, S. (2022). Il Travagliato Iter Parlamentare del C.D. Disegno di Legge Zan. *GenIUS, 2021*(2), 48–67.
D'Amato, S. (2006). Disorientamenti Giurisprudenziali in Tema di Finalità di Discriminazione o Odio Etnico, Nazionale, Razziale o Religioso. *Critica del Diritto*, 382–398.
De Francesco, G. (1994a). D.l. 26 Aprile 1993, n. 122, Convertito con Modificazioni dalla L. 25 Giugno 1993, n. 205—Misure Urgenti in Materia di Discriminazione Razziale, Etnica e Religiosa, Commento all'Art. 1. *La Legislazione Penale*, 173–200.
De Francesco, G. (1994b). D.l. 26 Aprile 1993, n. 122, Convertito con Modificazioni dalla L. 25 Giugno 1993, n. 205—Misure Urgenti in Materia di Discriminazione Razziale, Etnica e Religiosa, Commento all'Art. 3. *La Legislazione Penale*, 211–216.
Dolcini, E. (2014). Omofobi: Nuovi Martiri della Libertà di Manifestazione del Pensiero? *Rivista Italiana di Diritto e Procedura Penale, 57*(1), 7–31.
Eurostat. (2019a). *Ageing Europe: Looking at the Lives of Older People in the EU: 2019 Edition*. Publications Office of the European Union.
Eurostat. (2019b). *Population Structure and Ageing. August 2020*. Retrieved July 25, 2022, from https://ec.europa.eu/eurostat/statistics-explained/index.php?title=Population_structure_and_ageing#Median_age_is_highest_in_Italy.
Fanlo Cortés, I. (2022). Il DDL Zan e il Nodo dell'Identità di Genere. *GenIUS, 2021*(2), 37–47.
Ferrari, F., Ragaglia, E. M., & Rigliano, P. (2017). *Il 'Genere.' Una Guida Orientativa*. Società Italiana di Psicoterapia per lo Studio delle Identità Sessuali (SIPSIS). Retrieved July 25, 2022, from https://www.sipsis.it/wp-content/uploads/2020/09/IL_GENERE_UNA_GUIDA_ORIENTATIVA_2017.pdf

FRA (European Union Agency for Fundamental Rights). (2018). *Hate Crime Recording and Data Collection Practice Across the EU*. Publications Office of the European Union.

FRA (European Union Agency for Fundamental Rights). (2020). *A Long Way to Go for LGBTI Equality*. Publications Office of the European Union.

Gentile, G. (2016). La Tutela Penale dell'Identità Sessuale nelle «Disposizioni in Materia di Contrasto dell'Omofobia e della Transfobia». In F. Dicé, L. Ferraro, A. Postigliola, & P. Valerio (Eds.), *Pluralità Identitarie tra Bioetica e Biodiritto* (pp. 163–229). Mimesis Edizioni.

Giuffrida, A. (2021, June 22). Vatican Urges Italy to Stop Proposed Anti-Homophobia Law. *The Guardian*. Retrieved July 25, 2022, from https://www.theguardian.com/world/2021/jun/22/vatican-urges-italy-to-stop-anti-homophobia-law.

Godzisz, P., & Viggiani, G. (Eds.). (2018). *Running Through Hurdles: Obstacles in the Access to Justice for Victims of Anti-LGBTI Hate Crimes in Europe*. Lambda Warsaw.

Goisis, L. (2019). *Crimini d'odio: Discriminazioni e Giustizia Penale*. Jovene.

Goisis, L. (2020). *Crimini d'odio, Omotransfobia e Discriminazioni di Genere: Una Proposta de Lege Ferenda. Osservazioni alla Camera dei Deputati del 18.02.2020*. Osservazioni alla Camera dei Deputati, Retrieved July 25, 2022, from https://www.camera.it/application/xmanager/projects/leg18/attachments/upload_file_doc_acquisiti/pdfs/000/003/333/Osservazioni_Goisis.pdf.

Hardy, S., & Chakraborti, N. (2020). *Blood, Threats and Fears. The Hidden Worlds of Hate Crime Victims*. Palgrave Macmillan.

Il Post. (2022, May 5). Il PD Ha Ripresentato il DDL Zan, Identico, retrieved July 25, 2022, from https://www.ilpost.it/2022/05/05/pd-ddl-zan-seconda-volta/.

ISTAT (Istituto Italiano di Statistica). (2015). *Violence against Women in and Outside the Family. Year 2014*. Retrieved July 25, 2022, from https://www.istat.it/it/files//2019/11/Violence-against-women-_2014.pdf.

Licastro, A. (2019). L'Aggravante della Finalità di Discriminazione ovvero come Provare a Combattere i Pregiudizi Attraverso lo Strumento Penale. *Stato, Chiese e Pluralismo Confessionale, 28*, 95–128.

Lim, S. (2021, November 5). Italian Anti-LGBTQ Lawmakers Applaud the Defeat of Nondiscrimination Protections. *GLAAD*. https://www.glaad.org/blog/italian-anti-lgbtq-lawmakers-applaud-defeat-nondiscrimination-protections.

Lunaria. (2020). *Cronache di Ordinario Razzismo: Quinto Libro Bianco sul Razzismo in Italia*. Lunaria. Retrieved July 25, 2022, from http://www.cronachediordinariorazzismo.org/wp-content/uploads/quinto_libro_bianco_razzismo_def.pdf.

Mantovani, F. (2015). *Diritto Penale: Parte Generale*. Wolters Kluwer-CEDAM.

Marra, A. D. (2013). Le Persone con Disabilità. In P. Cendon & S. Rossi (Eds.), *I Nuovi Danni alla Persona: I Soggetti Deboli, Volume II* (pp. 467–518). Aracne.

Mason-Bish, H. (2013). Examining the Boundaries of Hate Crime Policy: Considering Age and Gender. *Criminal Justice Policy Review, 24*(3), 297–316.

McPhail, B. A. (2002). Gender-Bias Hate Crimes: A Review. *Trauma, Violence, & Abuse, 3*(2), 125–143. https://doi.org/10.1177/15248380020032003

Mellgren, C., Andersson, M., & Ivert, A. (2017). For Whom Does Hate Crime Hurt More? A Comparison of Consequences of Victimization Across Motives and Crime Types. *Journal of Interpersonal Violence*. https://doi.org/10.1177/0886260517746131

Micheletto, L. (2021). *Hate Crime Legislation and the Limits of Criminal Law. A Principled and Evidence-Based Assessment of Hate Crime Law and its Application to Italy*. PhD thesis, Ghent University. Retrieved July 25, 2022, from https://biblio.ugent.be/publication/8689579.

Miraglia, F. (2019). L'Aggravante Discriminatoria del Discorso d'Odio nella Giurisprudenza Italiana. In Amnesty International Italia (Ed.), *Barometro dell'Odio 2019* (45–50). Retrieved July 25, 2022, from https://d21zrvtkxtd6ae.cloudfront.net/public/uploads/2019/05/29202706/Amnesty-barometro-odio-2019.pdf.

Morassutto, L. (2013, August 24). Legge Contro l'Omofobia e la Transfobia: Il Coraggio Mancato e l'Occasione Perduta? *Articolo 29*. Retrieved July 25, 2022, from http://www.articolo29.it/2013/legge-contro-lomofobia-e-la-transfobia-il-coraggio-mancato-e-loccasione-perduta/.

ODHIR (Office for Democratic Institutions and Human Rights). (2014). *Hate Crime Data-Collection and Monitoring Mechanisms a Practical Guide*. Organization for Security and Co-operation in Europe.

ODHIR (Office for Democratic Institutions and Human Rights). (2020). *Hate Crime Victims in the Criminal Justice System*. Organization for Security and Co-operation in Europe.

Pagliarulo, G. (2014). La Tutela Penale contro Le Discriminazioni Razziali. *Archivio Penale, 3*, 1–30.

Paolini, E., & Paolini, M. C. (2022). *Mezze Persone. Riconoscere e Comprendere l'Abilismo*. Aut Aut Edizioni.

Pavich, G., & Bonomi, A. (2014). Reati in Tema di Discriminazione: Il Punto sull'evoluzione Normativa Recente, sui Principi e Valori in Gioco, sulle Prospettive Legislative e sulla Possibilità di Interpretare in Senso Conforme a Costituzione la Normativa Vigente. *Diritto Penale Contemporaneo*. Retrieved July 25, 2022, from https://archiviodpc.dirittopenaleuomo.org/d/3329-reati-in-tema-di-discriminazione-il-punto-sull-evoluzione-normativa-recente-sui-principi-e-valori-i.

Perry, J. (2019). *Facing All the Facts. Connecting on Hate Crime Data in Italy*. Facing all the Facts Project. Retrieved July 25, 2022 from https://www.facingfacts.eu/final-italy-country-report/.

Pezzella, F. S. (2017). *Hate Crime Statutes: A Public Policy and Law Enforcement Dilemma*. Springer International Publishing.

Pugiotto, A. (2015). Aporie, Paradossi ed Eterogenesi dei Fini nel Disegno di Legge in Materia di Contrasto all'omofobia e alla Transfobia. *GenIUS, 1*, 6–13.

Schweppe, J. (2012). Defining Characteristics and Politicising Victims: A Legal Perspective. *Journal of Hate Studies, 10*(1), 173–198.

Spena, A. (2017). La Parola(-)Odio. Sovraesposizione, Criminalizzazione e Interpretazione dello Hate Speech. *Criminalia 2016* (577–607). Retrieved July 25, 2022, from https://discrimen.it/wp-content/uploads/Criminalia-2016.pdf.

TGEU. (2017). *How to Win the Argument. Overcoming Myths in Legal Gender Recognition Discussions*, Retrieved July 25, 2022, from https://tgeu.org/wp-content/uploads/2017/02/Toolkit16_OvercomingMyths.pdf.

Toffanin, A. M. (2019). *La Ricerca sulla Violenza Maschile contro le Donne. Una Rassegna della Letteratura*. CNR (Consiglio Nazionale delle Ricerche) & IRPPS (Istituto di Ricerche sulla Popolazione e le Politiche Sociali). Retrieved July 25, 2022, from https://viva.cnr.it/wp4/.

Trapasso, M. T. (2010). Il Ruolo Fondamentale dei 'Coefficienti Soggettivi' nelle Fattispecie Penali in Materia di Discriminazione Razziale: Il Caso della Circostanza Aggravante delle Finalità di Discriminazione o di Odio Razziale. *Cassazione Penale, 11*, 3832–3844.

Viggiani, G. (2020). Il Femminicidio come Reato. Prassi Applicative e Prospettive de Iure Condendo. *GenIUS, 2019*(2), 130–145.

Vox (Osservatorio Italiano sui Diritti). (2022a). *La Nuova Mappa dell'Intolleranza 6*. Retrieved July 25, 2022, from http://www.voxdiritti.it/la-nuova-mappa-dellintolleranza-6/.

Vox (Osservatorio Italiano sui Diritti). (2022b). *La Mappa dell'Intolleranza 6. Misoginia*. Retrieved July 25, 2022, from http://www.voxdiritti.it/wp-content/uploads//2021/11/A3_Misoginia2021-01.jpg.

Weisburd, S., & Levin, B. (1994). On the Basis of Sex: Recognizing Gender-Based Bias Crimes. *Stanford Law & Policy Review, 5*, 21–47.

Winkler, M. M., & Strazio, G. (2011). *L'Abominevole Diritto: Gay e Lesbiche, Giudici e Legislatori*. Il Saggiatore.

Zanghellini, A. (2020). Philosophical Problems with the Gender-Critical Feminist Argument Against Trans Inclusion. *SAGE Open*. https://doi.org/10.1177/2158244020927029.

Zempi, I., & Smith, J. (Eds.). (2021). *Misogyny as Hate Crime*. Routledge.

5

Conclusions

1 Overview of the Research Results

This study offers a novel and innovative approach to assess the multiple aspects of hate crime laws and how they map onto the phenomenon of hate crime itself. The model developed in Chaps. 2 and 3 serves to create a multi-level framework which helps to understand the different dimensions of criminal laws addressing hate crime. By taking into consideration both Anglo-Saxon and European perspectives as well as empirical data on the phenomenon, this project examines the situation outside of the current Anglosphere-dominated silo of hate crime scholarship and at the same time moves away from the traditional descriptive legal analysis carried out by dominant continental European studies.

This work not only draws on a thorough review and analysis of the most relevant approaches to studying hate crime rooted in a number of disciplinary backgrounds, but it also takes existing scholarship forward by developing and expanding upon existing literature in the area. Moreover, it is the first work that examines Italian hate crime legislation from an interdisciplinary perspective. The analysis of Italian legislation

L. Micheletto, *Assessing Hate Crime Laws*, Palgrave Hate Studies,
https://doi.org/10.1007/978-3-031-19020-9_5

through the ILT can improve scholars' global understanding of how this multi-level test can be applied in practice and can potentially lead to policy discussions in other jurisdictions.

Crimes motivated by hate, bias, hostility or similar negative prejudice-based emotions against people or collectivities that are perceived as different from the dominant social groups are certainly not new in Europe and North America. In some cases, discrimination and oppression of minorities have constituted the backbone of entire political visions and social morals, and violence against the members of minority groups has been socially and often legally accepted.

Criminal law, on its part, constitutes one of the oldest and more violent expressions of the power that States (and similar entities) have on their citizens and other individuals that find themselves on their territory. Its justifications are deeply interwoven with the religious feelings and the morals of a given time and space. The identification, and more importantly, the acceptance, of boundaries to the State's power to criminalise and punish has not been, and is still not an easy task. Even within the limits of a constitutional democracy, deciding what, and how, to criminalise is ultimately a *moral* decision.

The increasing secularisation and evolution of Western democracies and the importance now accorded to human rights and freedoms in the law and as societal values have had a significant impact on how both hate crimes and the limits to the State's power to criminalise are understood and concretely addressed by the law. Actually, these two topics are strictly connected. On the one hand, the increasing awareness of the causes and impacts of hate crimes is usually followed and reflected by states' main or only recurrence to criminal law to tackle the problem. On the other hand, criminal law experts have been warning of the dangers of a disproportionate and indiscriminate use of criminal law.

Thus, hate crime law lies in the middle of a delicate balance between the need to foresee proportionate penalties for hate crime offenders, and that of limiting criminalisation only to a necessary minimum. In fact, what might seem justified from a victimology point of view may sometimes not be so from a legitimacy perspective.

These concerns have constituted the core of the present research. Chapter 1 introduced these themes, along with a more general presentation of hate crime and hate crime law in the international landscape and in Italy. Then, in Chap. 2, we tried to properly conceptualise hate crime and hate crime law through the elaboration of a four-tier framework. The framework pursues a double purpose: on the one hand, it can be used to both classify hate crime law and to normatively guide lawmakers to draft hate crime provisions according to the corresponding concept of hate crimes they consider appropriate for their jurisdiction and political aims. Thus, it constitutes a tool for a preliminary *descriptive* and *normative* analysis of these provisions. On the other hand, the models of hate crime law identified here constitute one of the objects of the legitimacy assessment along with Italian hate crime law.

The connection between interdisciplinary research on the causes, forms and impact of hate crimes with the different drafting methods suggests that the narrow (and more traditional) approaches often omit some key elements of the phenomenon. For example, many jurisdictions (including the European Union) have decided to include only a very small number of grounds in hate crime law (usually race, religion and ethnicity). Research shows however that also those crimes motivated by other features or group memberships of the victim present characteristics similar to the more traditional ones. On the same page, the requirement that hate be the only motive of these crimes would severely limit the scope of application of hate crime law, since there is a strong indication that these types of offences are more often committed by "ordinary" persons with a low bias motivation that can easily be compounded with other motives to commit the crime than by hate-fuelled extremists. Thus, those models that correspond to a wide hate crime concept appear to be better suited to address the phenomenon as they reflect its different aspects more accurately. Despite their relevance, these findings do not address the issue of which hate crime law models are *legitimate* from a criminalisation point of view. To cover this point, further steps are necessary.

In Chap. 3 we proposed an analytical and evidence-based instrument to examine hate crime law from a legitimacy viewpoint: the Integrated Legitimacy Test (ILT). The ILT embeds the key elements of the Anglo-American harm principle, the German *Rechtsgut* theory and the Italian *offensività* principle (Micheletto 2021). According to this approach, if the conduct causes serious harm to one or more dimensions of a standard victim's quality of life, and is sufficiently wrongful, we can consider that the State can legitimately criminalise it. The ILT has been applied to the different models of hate crime law previously identified by referring to multidisciplinary research on the added harmfulness and wrongfulness of hate crimes. Its application has allowed combining the different perspectives used in the continental European and Anglo-American contexts respectively to identify and address all the possible ways that hate crimes cause a negative impact to both direct and vicarious victims.

The first, general analysis of hate crime law *considered as a whole* (covering a limited number of grounds and in which hate/bias is the sole motive of the crime) has indicated that these kinds of provisions are legitimate. Bias crimes cause more psychological as well as normative harm to both direct and vicarious victims, and are more wrongful than parallel, non-bias motivated crimes. The separate analysis of the four tiers has shown that the models corresponding to a narrow and intermediate understanding of hate crimes are legitimate. The approaches reflecting a wide concept of hate crimes, however, have posed a number of legitimacy issues. Some of these problems can be nevertheless overcome by either interpreting a *prima facie* illegitimate provision in a narrow way that respects the ILT requirements, or, in some exceptional cases, by drafting the concrete legal provisions in a manner that reflects the actual situation of a given social group in a specific jurisdiction. Thus, it can be concluded that even if certain drafting methods may reflect a (wide) concept of hate crime closer to the reality of the phenomenon, they do not always fulfil the requirements of the ILT to be considered legitimate.

The analysis of the *grounds* that can be legitimately included in hate crime legislation—which is probably the most controversial point surrounding hate crime law—has given interesting results. An increasing number of studies have pointed to certain factors that render crimes motivated by bias more harmful than their parallel counterparts. What counts is that certain personal characteristics (whether immutable or not) are fundamental to one's identity *and* that the targeted group has suffered, or is currently suffering, discrimination, oppression, hostility, or is in a situation of social disadvantage linked to that personal characteristic. Hate crimes do not happen in a vacuum, but are usually surrounded by discriminatory acts and hate speech against the group at issue. Hate crime victims usually belong to groups that already suffer what is referred to as "minority pain" (Akhtar, 2014) or "minority stress" (see, e.g. Flentje et al., 2019) and have often already experienced incidents of discrimination and hostility. Thus, research has shown that not only do hate crime victims belonging to the traditional groups (defined by race, ethnic origins, religion, nationality) suffer more harm compared with victims of parallel crimes, but also those belonging to less traditional groups such as LGBTI people, women, people with disabilities, and probably individuals belonging to subcultures, the homeless and the elderly.

These conclusions have been particularly useful for the analysis of Italian hate crime law in Chap. 4. Overall considered, Italian law frames hate crimes *narrowly*. Only traditional grounds are taken into account, and hate must be the predominant motive (or, better, purpose)—of the offence. Italian lawmakers and doctrine chiefly focus on the instigator effect of bias offences, and much less on the actual harm caused to direct and vicarious victims. Thus, while the pivotal hate crime provision—art. 604-ter of the Penal Code—can be considered legitimate under the ILT, it still appears inadequate to properly reflect and thus tackle the phenomenon of hate crimes. On their part, the provisions that only implicitly can be considered bias crime law—covering disability and age—present some legitimacy problems due to their too wide scope: they apply whenever the victim presents a certain characteristic, regardless of any bias on the part of the offender, or of any direct causation relationship between the personal feature and the offence. From a more technical point of view, Italian hate crime law is poorly drafted and presents a number of inconsistency and lack of uniformity issues with respect to other criminal law provisions. As to the inclusion of the strands sex, gender, sexual orientation and gender identity (as well as disability and age) in hate crime law, the results are quite clear. Hate crimes committed because of one of these grounds do cause more harm and are more wrongful than parallel crimes. Thus, hate crime law covering these strands is *legitimate* under the ILT. It has also been noted that the arguments put forward by opponents to the inclusion of these grounds in hate crime legislation have been mostly based on non-scientific and explicitly or implicitly sexist, homophobic and transphobic assumptions. They thus fall foul of two of the most important premises of the ILT—empirical verifiability and respect for human rights and diversity.

2 Lessons from Italy

The great majority of OSCE participant States have passed criminal law provisions that foresee a sentence increase when a base offence is committed out of bias. Out of 57 participant States, 48 have passed hate crime laws that cover at least race and/or ethnic origins; religion is included in 45 States; sexual orientation is covered in 31 legislations; 22 include sex or gender; 21 cover gender identity; disability is included in 19 jurisdictions.[1] These numbers are quite impressive, and they reflect an actual commitment on the part of OSCE participating States to address and tackle hate crimes (Gião Hanek, 2017, 480–481). Some countries have a long tradition of tackling discriminatory-based violence and have managed to build a quite comprehensive legal framework to tackle hate crimes (e.g. the UK and the USA, see Gião Hanek, 2017, 468). However, in recent years, some countries with a relatively recent democratic history have managed to pass quite innovative and inclusive hate crime laws. For example, North Macedonia has taken several steps to progressively expand its hate crime legislation to less traditional grounds (see Mujoska Trpevska & Bitrakov, 2019). The same has happened in Albania, Bosnia and Herzegovina, Mongolia and Romania.[2] Foreseeing hate crime legislation does not mean that, in practice, bias-motivated crimes are actually investigated as such and that offenders are prosecuted and punished (Gião Hanek, 2017, 482). However, it certainly constitutes the first step in that direction.[3]

[1] This data has been collected by counting only those States that foresee hate crime provisions proper. It does not include those countries that provide general penalty enhancements without specifically identifying the strands included (e.g. Slovenia and Switzerland). For a comparative analysis of EU countries, see Van der Aa et al. (2021).

[2] See the OSCE/ODIHR database of legal reviews and legislation, where national laws are classified by topic (including hate crimes) and translated into English: https://legislationline.org/ (accessed 25 July 2022).

[3] Some countries that do not have a hate crime legislation proper manage however to investigate and prosecute hate crimes in their jurisdictions (e.g. Ireland, the Netherlands, Switzerland; see Gião Hanek, 2017, 475; 482).

What prevents other countries from following the same example? In Chap. 4, we have analysed Italian hate crime law, including the possible inclusion of sex, gender, sexual orientation, gender identity and disability along with the existing traditional grounds (race, ethnic origins, religion and belonging to a linguistic minority). It has been stressed how the numerous attempts to reform the existing law to include these grounds have all failed. The reluctance of the Italian Parliament to pass specific hate crime legislation against gender-based, homophobic, transphobic and disability hate crime can be more easily understood if analysed in light of the wider approach taken towards the rights of the groups concerned in Italy.

As regards gender-based violence, its conceptualisation as a form of hate crime is still underdeveloped. It is still often perceived as a form of interpersonal and domestic violence, a "private issue" where the social component is often overlooked. In a similar way, crimes against persons with disability are usually not recognised as hate crimes proper. The legislative proposals aiming at including new grounds in hate crime law have been chiefly focused on anti-LGBTI hate crime, and started including sex, gender and disability only in recent years, and somehow "incidentally". While the majority of the feminist movement has eventually started endorsing the inclusion of sex and gender in the law, only a small part of civil society organisations working with disability issues have actively participated in the debate (Belotti, 2021; Ability Channel, 2021). Therefore, the debate has been strongly shaped around the opportunity to include sexual orientation and gender identity in the law. It must be recalled that the proposed legal reforms had a wide scope that went beyond hate crime law proper. They included the amendment of non-discrimination and hate speech provisions, as well as a number of educational, policy and preventive measures, such as enhancing victim support and improving data collection. In fact, one of the key arguments that opponents used against the legal reform focused on the alleged violation of freedom of expression by the inclusion of sexual orientation and gender identity in hate speech and non-discrimination law. The scope of these provisions (which currently include only traditional grounds) is indeed quite wide and could certainly be improved to respect legitimacy parameters. However, it is quite revealing that the freedom of speech argument has been raised with particular virulence only with regard to the possibility to include anti-LGBTI hate speech.

More in general, the Italian Parliament suffers from a severe problem of immobilism when it comes to the enactment of laws protecting the rights of sexual minorities or that relate to the individual's self-determination. It suffices at have a look at Ilga Europe's rainbow map to see how poorly Italy scores when it comes to the legal protection of LGBTI rights in comparison to other EU countries (Ilga Europe, 2022). The few legal reforms in this regard have been strongly influenced either by the enactment of binding EU legislation[4] or by the judgments of the Constitutional Court, the Court of Cassation, and the European Court of Human Rights (ECtHR).[5] As one of the hate crime specialists interviewed by Perry (2019, 21) observes, "the journey towards recognising LGBTI people as a group targeted by hate crime is connected to broader civil rights struggles... It is difficult to say that a category of people is a target of offences if that very category is not even recognised from a legal point of view." This situation is not limited to the Italian context, but mirrors a wider problem that affects other European countries (see Godzisz & Viggiani, 2018). In Hungary and Poland, for example, the institutional and political hostility against LGBTI people has become so serious to induce the European Commission to take a legal action against these two member States in 2021 and 2022.[6]

[4] For example, the protection against homophobic discrimination in the workplace was introduced only after the transposition into Italian law of the Council Directive 2000/78/EC of 27 November 2000 establishing a general framework for equal treatment in employment and occupation; specific procedural guarantees for LGBTI victims of crimes has been granted by the implementation of the Directive 2012/29/EU of the European Parliament and of the Council of 25 October 2012 establishing minimum standards on the rights, support and protection of victims of crime, and replacing Council Framework Decision 2001/220/JHA, O.J. L 315, 14 November 2012.

[5] While marriage and adoption are still forbidden to same-sex couples, the judgments of the Constitutional Court (no. 138/2010), the Court of Cassation (no. 4184/2012), and of the ECtHR (*Oliari and Others* v. Italy, nos. 18766/11 and 36030/11, 21 July 2015) have eventually pushed the Parliament to introduce a form of registered partnership for homosexual couples. Act no. 76 of 20 May 2016 has granted to same-sex couples most, but not all, the rights warranted to heterosexual couples.

[6] See the press releases of the European Commission on 15 July 2021 https://ec.europa.eu/commission/presscorner/detail/en/ip_21_3668 and 15 July 2022 https://ec.europa.eu/commission/presscorner/detail/en/IP_22_2689 (both accessed 25 July 2022).

In this context, the role of international organisations is key to guarantee a sufficient level of protection to members of groups that are the target of hate crimes. This is especially so in those countries where the legislative protection of human rights encounters political and ideological hurdles. The OSCE's Office for Democratic Institutions and Human Rights and the Council of Europe have called on member States to extend their hate crime law to these grounds (see Chap. 1). Despite their significance, however, these documents are not binding. Nonetheless, the recent case law of the ECtHR and the increasing involvement of the EU in this field indicate that these two organisations are willing to play a greater role in the European region in the area of hate crime. In its recent ruling against Bulgaria, the ECtHR has finally taken an explicit position as regards the obligation on the part of member States to "ensure that violent attacks (in particular, those resulting in the victim's death) motivated by hostility towards the victim's actual or presumed sexual orientation are in some way treated as aggravated in criminal-law terms."[7] The EU, on its part, has started working on the inclusion of hate crime and hate speech among the "EU crimes" identified in art. 83 TFEU, on the grounds that these offences "violate the victims' fundamental right to dignity and equality."[8] This inclusion would provide the EU with the necessary legal basis to criminalise hate speech and hate crime at the EU level, and to cover also those grounds that are presently excluded by the 2008 Framework Decision. Obtaining the Council's unanimous agreement as required by art. 83 to pass this legal reform is not going to be easy, due to the well-known positions of certain Member States on LGBTI rights. So far, however, the Justice and Home Affairs Council has positively reacted to the Commission's initiative. In the press release of its March 2022 meeting, the Council in fact concluded that "[a] very broad majority was in favour of this initiative. Combating hate speech and hate crime is a major

[7] *Stoyanova v. Bulgaria*, no. 56070/18, 14 June 2022, § 79.

[8] Communication from the Commission to the European Parliament and the Council, A more inclusive and protective Europe: extending the list of EU crimes to hate speech and hate crimes, com(2021)777 final, p. 9. See also Buisman (2022).

priority for the European Union, and work on this proposal will continue with a view to reaching the required unanimous agreement as soon as possible."[9]

3 Policy Recommendations

The analysis carried out in the present research and the results obtained allow a formulation of a number of recommendations to lawmakers, both at international (including the EU) and national levels.

The legitimacy exercise performed of the four-tier framework in Chap. 3 has shown that the hate crime law models corresponding to a wide concept of hate crime present some legitimacy problems and should be used carefully. This remark aligns with the results of studies conducted on the practical feasibility and convenience of hate crime law models. Research suggests that a hybrid approach that combines different types of hate crime provisions would be best suited to address hate crimes. Gião Hanek (2017) has examined the emerging international legal framework on hate crimes, and the experience of those countries that have introduced hate crime legislation only recently. Based on this analysis, he suggests that States should address "the most frequent types of hate crimes by specific penalty enhancement type provisions (or a combination of SPEs and SOs), while covering the rest of possible hate crimes by a general penalty enhancement type provision" (Gião Hanek, 2017, 490). His suggestions seem reasonable. The OSCE and other international organisations have chiefly focused and promoted the use of general aggravating circumstances. However, as we have seen, these types of provisions can be problematic from a legitimacy viewpoint. Specific aggravating circumstances and substantive offences present fewer legitimacy problems, since they apply to a limited and specific set of base offences which can more easily correspond to the crimes that are commonly committed out of bias. Moreover, it has been pointed out that this model alone suffers from several practical shortcomings. For example, "[i]n countries transitioning

[9] See the press release of the Justice and Home Affairs Council, 3–4 March 2022, at https://www.consilium.europa.eu/en/meetings/jha/2022/03/03-04/ (accessed 25 July 2022).

to a hate crime model and which choose to introduce a GPE type law; this provision is rarely or never used" (Gião Hanek, 2017, 480). Furthermore, the use of specific aggravating circumstances or substantive offences gives more visibility to hate crime law. This, in turn better expresses the "symbolic or expressive dimension of criminal law" (Peršak, 2022, 119) since it conveys the message that the State is taking hate crimes seriously (see Gião Hanek, 2017, 490). More visibility would also facilitate data collection, which is pivotal to gauge the extent of the phenomenon.

Along with a combination of different drafting methods, hate crime legislation would certainly benefit from the inclusion of *definitions* of the most controversial aspects of the phenomenon. For example, the law could provide a definition of what is meant by hate crimes, thus distinguishing them from other discrimination-related incidents such as hate speech and discrimination. For instance, North Macedonia's recently amended hate crime legislation now defines hate crime as "a criminal act against a person or legal entity or property related to it, that is committed entirely or partially because of the actual or presumed characteristic of the person that refers to race, colour of skin, nationality, ethnic belonging, religion or religious belief, mental or physical disability, sex, gender identity, sexual orientation or political affiliation" (art. 112(41) of the Penal Code). Moreover, the law should explicitly include in the definition also hate crimes committed because of an erroneous perception of the victim's characteristics (like in the North Macedonia's case), and those committed by association (i.e. when someone is targeted because they are related to a person who belongs to a protected group) (e.g. art. 222A(4) of the Criminal Code of Malta). In those countries in which the terms used to identify the protected grounds may be perceived as not entirely clear (e.g. in Italy), lawmakers could provide a definition of these expressions. Defining what hate crimes are, and in what cases hate crime law applies, would be greatly beneficial for law enforcement and judicial authorities, as well as for data collection purposes.

As to the grounds to include in hate crime legislation, the time has come to extend the traditional set of protected characteristics (race, ethnic and national origins, religion) to other strands. These should include, at least, sex, gender, sexual orientation, gender identity and disability.

Evidence suggests that other characteristics, such as age and socio-economic status, are also good candidates for inclusion in hate crime law. On the other hand, an over-inclusive list of grounds does not seem to be desirable. In the OSCE region, few States foresee a long list of grounds that reflect, more in general, those covered by non-discrimination laws. For example, Belgian law includes marital status, birth, and fortune (arts. 377-bis, 405-quater, 422-quater, 438-bis, 453-bis, 514-bis, and 532-bis of the Penal Code; in a similar way, North Macedonia covers education, family or marital status, and property status (art. 39 of the Penal Code), and Romania includes wealth and social origin (art. 77 of the Penal Code). This choice may be preferred, and even advisable in the context of non-discrimination law and in general hate crime policies (e.g. data collection, educational activities and prevention measures). However, criminalisation principles demand that hate crime law proper include only those grounds for which there is evidence of the existence of crimes motivated or somehow related to these personal characteristics. Moreover, from a practical point of view an over-inclusive list of grounds may be detrimental for the protection of the social groups that are the actual target of bias-motivated offences. The expressive function of the criminal law in identifying which groups do, and which groups do not deserve specific protection, would be diluted. In this context, the negative criterion of innocence and desert plays an important role, because it allows distinguishing between deserving and undeserving characteristics (see Chap. 2, Sect. 3.2.2 and Chap. 4, Sect. 4.2).

Along with these more general considerations, the analysis carried out in Chapt. 4 has given some insights as to how Italian law-makers could improve Italian hate crime law. First, art. 604-ter could be amended as follows: (i) the application of the aggravating circumstance could be limited to certain crimes (or crime categories) that can be committed out of bias; (ii) the grounds sex, gender, sexual orientation, gender identity, disability and perhaps age, could be included among the protected grounds; (iii) the term "motive" could substitute the word "purpose". Second, if disability and age are included in art. 604-ter, the provisions currently covering these grounds (in particular, art. 36(1) of Act 104/1992 and art. 628(3)(3quinques) of the Penal Code) should be amended as follows: (i) the term "disability" should be updated and defined according to the standards adopted by the CRPD; (ii) since disability and age would be already covered by the amended art. 604-ter, these provisions should be redrafted following the model of art. 61(5)—i.e. requiring that the perpetrator has taken advantage of the disability or old age of the victim to commit the crime.

These suggestions have chiefly focused on hate crime law proper, in light of the narrow scope of the present study. However, properly tackling hate crimes requires a much broader approach that covers the enactment of non-discrimination and hate speech provisions, educational and preventive measures, and granting full equality to the social groups which are the target of these hideous kinds of offences.

4 Strengths and Limitations of the Study and Suggestions for Future Research

This research has pursued an ambitious aim: providing an analysis of hate crime law from a holistic perspective that integrates different legal research methods and interrelated disciplines. I believe that this purpose has been achieved, albeit not without difficulties. The adopted approach presents a number of strengths and weaknesses that will be discussed here.

First, the main strength of this study is also one of its limitations. The interdisciplinary approach adopted, while novel (especially in the Italian context) and key to address a criminal phenomenon from a holistic viewpoint, has made it not feasible to conduct an in-depth analysis of certain specific aspects of the issue.

Second, the reference to social research has been crucial both to describe the phenomenon under study and to feed the legitimacy assessment with empirical data. However, in accordance with my educational background this work has adopted a legal perspective in which social research has been relied on as an external tool, and not the other way round. Thus, it has not been possible to conduct specific socio-legal research on the matter or to directly assess empirical data. However, to overcome these problems reference has been made only to those studies that have been published in peer-reviewed journals or books.

Third, the application of the ILT has built chiefly on the results of empirical studies on this topic. However, no criminological or victimological studies of this kind have been found in Italy, and it has been necessary to rely on research conducted in other countries. Nonetheless, the examined studies have identified a number of strong trends and patterns. Thus, their results appear to be valid also for hate crimes committed in Italy, although there remains a need to conduct specific research in that geographical context.

Taking into account the remarks outlined here, a number of suggestions for further research can be identified. In the international as well as in the Italian context, legal research on hate crime should follow a holistic approach that takes interdisciplinary studies on the matter into account. This perspective seems to be quite common in certain contexts (e.g. in Anglo-Saxon countries), but it is still at a tentative phase in continental European countries. Psychological and victimological studies on the impact of hate crimes in Italy (and elsewhere), combined with an efficient data collection system, would be highly beneficial to get a better understanding of the phenomenon. In this regard, I believe that the role of international organisations such as the ODHIR and the EU (through the work of the FRA) is key in order to provide those States with little resources and capacity (and perhaps will) with the necessary tools to carry out independent research on hate crimes. Moreover, research concerning specific grounds (disability, age and socio-economic status) should be boosted.

References

Ability Channel. (2021, October 15). *Perché il Discusso DDL Zan Riguarda anche i Disabili?* Ability Channel. Retrieved July 25, 2022, from https://www.abilitychannel.tv/ddl-zan-disabili/.

Akhtar, S. (2014). The Mental Pain of Minorities. *British Journal of Psychotherapy, 30*(2), 136–153. https://doi.org/10.1111/bjp.12081

Belotti, A. (2021, May 18). Il DDL Zan È un'Occasione anche per le Persone Disabili. *Internazionale*. https://www.internazionale.it/opinione/adriana-belotti/2021/05/18/ddl-zan-disabili.

Buisman, S. S. (2022). The Future of EU Substantive Criminal Law. *European Journal of Crime, Criminal Law and Criminal Justice, 30*(2), 161–187. https://doi.org/10.1163/15718174-bja10032

Flentje, A., Heck, N. C., Brennan, J. M., & Meyer, I. H. (2019). The Relationship between Minority Stress and Biological Outcomes: A Systematic Review. *Journal of Behavioral Medicine*, December. https://doi.org/10.1007/s10865-019-00120-6.

Gião Hanek, A. (2017). International Legal Framework for Hate Crimes: Which Law for the 'New' Countries? In A. Haynes, J. Schweppe, & S. Taylor (Eds.), *Critical Perspectives on Hate Crime*. Palgrave Macmillan. https://doi.org/10.1057/978-1-137-52667-0_24

Godzisz, P., & Viggiani, G. (Eds.). (2018). *Running Through Hurdles: Obstacles in the Access to Justice for Victims of Anti-LGBTI Hate Crimes in Europe*. Lambda Warsaw.

Ilga Europe. (2022). *Rainbow Europe Map and Index 2022*, Retrieved July 25, 2022, from https://www.ilga-europe.org/report/rainbow-europe-2022/.

Mujoska Trpevska, E., & Bitrakov, K. (2019). *The New Concept of Hate Crime in Macedonian Criminal Legislation*. Project Come Forward: Empowering and Supporting Victims of Anti-LGBT Hate Crimes.

Perry, J. (2019). *Facing All the Facts. Connecting on Hate Crime Data in Italy*. Facing all the Facts Project. Retrieved July 25, 2022, from https://www.facingfacts.eu/final-italy-country-report/.

Peršak, N. (2022). Criminalising Hate Crime and Hate Speech at EU Level: Extending the List of Eurocrimes Under Article 83(1) TFEU. *Criminal Law Forum, 33*, 85–119. https://doi.org/10.1007/s10609-022-09440-w

Van der Aa, S., Hofmann, R., & Claessen, J. (2021). A Comparative Perspective on the Protection of Hate Crime Victims in the European Union. New Developments in Criminal Procedures in the EU Member States. *Erasmus Law Review, 3*, 170–180. https://doi.org/10.5553/ELR.000199

Index[1]

[1] Note: Page numbers followed by 'n' refer to notes.

L. Micheletto, *Assessing Hate Crime Laws*, Palgrave Hate Studies,
https://doi.org/10.1007/978-3-031-19020-9

Kolibri 360 GmbH
Ferdinand-Jühlke-Straße 7
99095 Erfurt, Deutschland
produktsicherheit@kolibri360.de